294783A6

D1551157

ATE DUE

The Ascent of Chiefs

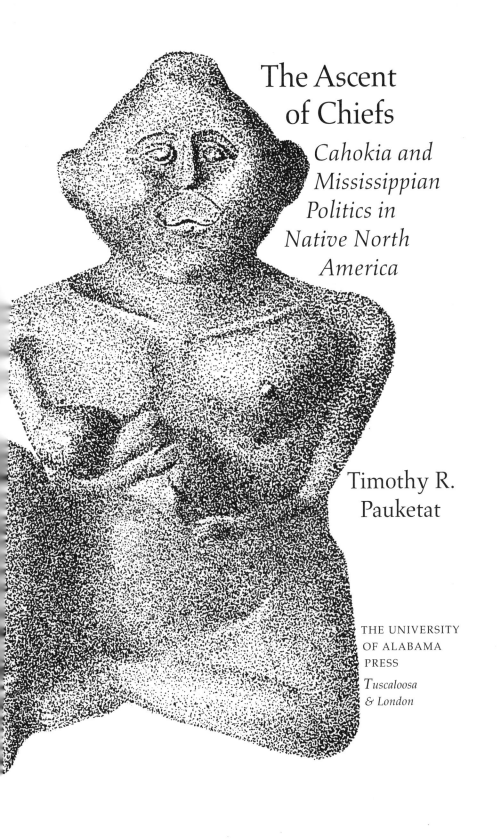

The Ascent of Chiefs

Cahokia and Mississippian Politics in Native North America

Timothy R.
Pauketat

THE UNIVERSITY
OF ALABAMA
PRESS

*Tuscaloosa
& London*

Library of Congress Cataloging-in Publication Data

Pauketat, Timothy R.
The ascent of chiefs : Cahokia and Mississippian politics in
Native North America / Timothy R. Pauketat.
   p.   cm.
Includes bibliographical references and index.
ISBN 0-8173-0728-1 (alk. paper)
1. Cahokia Site (East Saint Louis, Ill.) 2. Mississippian cul-
ture. 3. Chiefdoms. I. Title.
E78.I3P38   1994
977.3'89—dc20   93-42734

British Library Cataloguing-in-Publication Data available

For Stephanie, Regena, and Janet

Contents

Figures

Tables

Preface

Archaeological and ethnohistorical research in Southeastern North America is providing fresh insights into questions posed by social scientists about power, culture, inequality, ethnogenesis, and stratification. This study is intended to broach some of these same questions by focusing on the premier Mississippian polity in the Southeast. The theoretical direction of this study, while paralleling certain contemporary trends in American Anthropology, represents a break with previous archaeological efforts in the Southeast. As a result, I neither seek nor expect to satisfy all Mississippianists. However, I do hope to open new avenues of inquiry and to promote productive discussion about late-prehistoric North America.

These scholarly aspirations cannot be separated from my practical archaeological experiences in parts of the Mississippi Valley where modern urban expansion and agricultural land modification continue to obliterate much of the past. My experiences have defined to a large extent my own archaeological philosophy and methodology. The very data sets upon which this volume is based were salvaged prior to the building of a planned highway that was to bisect the Cahokia site. Until 1988 the boxes of sherds, lithic refuse, scattered bones, and charcoal from these excavations sat on shelves at the Illinois State Museum and the University of Illinois. John Kelly suggested to me that these data could provide the kind of diachronic information that I was then seeking relative to questions about Native American political centralization. I think he was correct.

My thoughts and ideas about Mississippian chiefdoms, prestate politics, and culture history have benefitted greatly from interaction with Richard Ford, John O'Shea, and Henry Wright at the University of Michigan and with other prominent Eastern Woodlands specialists like David Anderson, Alex Barker, Charles Cobb, Thomas Emerson, Gayle Fritz, James Griffin, John Kelly, V. James Knight, George Milner, Dan Morse, Jon Muller, Bruce Smith, and Paul Welch. The Illinois State Museum provided the lab space necessary for much of the artifact analysis, and for their courteous assistance I thank Terrance Martin and Michael Wiant. Likewise, I extend my gratitude to the excavators and directors of the Tract 15A and Dunham Tract projects, Warren Wittry (the 1961, 1977, and 1978 seasons), Robert Hall (the 1963, 1977, and 1978 seasons), William Iseminger (the 1985 season), and Charles Bareis (the 1966 Dunham Tract season).

The financial support for the research upon which this study is based was provided by the National Science Foundation (BNS-8815698), the Rackham School of Graduate Studies, and the Museum of Anthropology at the University of Michigan. The emotional support was provided by Stephanie L. Pauketat over the course of many years. My thanks go out to Judith Knight and the rest of the staff at the University of Alabama Press for bringing this volume to its present form. For all others who have helped in this endeavor, I extend my warmest gratitude. The opinions, views, and conclusions expressed herein are my own and do not necessarily reflect those of the institutions named above. I alone assume responsibility for the contents of this volume.

The Ascent of Chiefs

Chapter 1

Introduction
A Mississippian Leviathan

[A]mongst men, there are very many, that thinke themselves wiser, and abler to govern the Publique, better than the rest; and these strive to reforme and innovate, one this way, another that way; and thereby bring it into Distraction and Civill warre. . . . [I]t is no wonder if there be somewhat else required (besides Covenant) . . . which is a Common Power, to keep them in awe, and to direct their actions to the Common Benefit. . . . The only way to erect such a Common Power . . . is, to conferre all their power and strength upon one Man, or upon one Assembly of men, that may reduce all their Wills . . . unto one Will. . . . This is the Generation of that great LEVIATHAN . . . (Hobbes 1985 [1651]:226–227).

How was a "Common Power" erected among the ungoverned public? Why did people who lived free of ascribed hierarchy submit themselves to "that great Leviathan"? This problem lies at the heart of the social sciences. Indeed, understanding world-historical development demands tracing the history of authority and power and the origins of social stratification and political hegemonies. Archaeology is ideally situated to provide the empirical evidence needed to understand world-historical development and to comprehend the "Generation" of that great Leviathan.

Leviathans of the past remain buried in Greater Mesopotamia, Central Mexico, South and Central America, Europe, sub-Saharan Africa, the Far East, Southeast Asia, the islands of the Pacific, *and* southeastern North America. The generation of the Leviathan, that process of common surrender, is not necessarily synonymous with the coalescence of archaic states. It is, I submit, to be found in the centralization of political authority before or in the absence of the state. Social classes and the emergence of the sovereign had their beginnings in the prestate or nonstate transformations of simple ranked groups into regionally centralized polities.

Anthropologists most recently have called these elaborate regionally centralized polities "complex chiefdoms" (see Earle 1978; Steponaitis 1978; Wright 1984). In the past, similar formations also have been termed "ranked societies" (e.g., Peebles and Kus 1977; Renfrew 1982), "segmentary states" (Southall 1956:246–249), "sacral chiefships" (Southall 1956:245), "sacred" or "divine kingships" (Frazer 1947:83–106; see Sahlins 1985:34), "paramountcies" (Taylor 1975), "regal" and "aristocratic kingdoms" (Vansina 1962:332–333) or, simply, "chiefdoms" (Oberg 1955:484; Mitchell 1956:47ff.; Southall 1956:vii). Some of Friedman and Rowlands's (1978:216–222) "Asiatic states," a term derived from Marx's Asiatic mode of production (see Bailey 1981; Gledhill 1984; Wolf 1982:79–88), are similar chiefly political formations, as are cases of Morgan's (1974 [1877]:264) and Childe's (1954:69ff.) "Upper" or "Higher" stages of "Barbarism" and Weber's (1968:231ff.) "patrimonialism."

The common recognition of some form of nonstate polity based on sacral authority, a nonbureaucratized administrative hierarchy, and a tributary mode of production amidst disparate historical contexts provides a starting point for inquiry. This is not to say that the societal type—specifically "chiefdom"—should be conceptualized as a stage of evolution or that its utility lies anywhere except in the definition of a research problem (see Cordy 1981:25–29; Earle 1987a:280–281, 1991a; Feinman and Neitzel 1984; Flannery 1983:1; Kohl 1984; Muller 1987:10; Renfrew 1982:2; Steponaitis 1981:321; Wright 1977:381, 1984:43; cf. Spencer 1990:2–4). Only by focusing on the process of nonstate political centralization and not on typology will we be able to comprehend the Leviathan.

Nonstate political centralization entails concern with economy and society but not as abstractions that may be studied separate from polity. Of course, politics abstractly conceived are not amenable to ratiocination (see Jacobitti 1986:74). On the contrary, the order of politics is disorder. Politics are pragmatic in character, involving the actions of individuals in the reproduction of "power" relations, where power is defined as the ability of an actor to achieve or control an outcome regardless of the conflicting actions of others (Giddens 1979:88; Weber 1968:53; cf. Wolf 1990:586).

Politics are, however, rooted in cultural traditions (Rosenberg 1988:98). Understanding political actions within chiefly traditions, contexts alien to the modern world, requires recognizing that actors conducted themselves in accord with their own traditional values, beliefs, and meanings. It is equally significant to the present study that such cultural traditions be understood not as unitary phenomena but as disparate and malleable sets of ideologies or ethics, values, and ways of understanding experience defined at the level of the social group or subgroup.

As will be detailed in chapter 2, this study is founded upon a theory of practice and the political economy of chiefships. Members of groups or subgroups with specific interests in the maintenance of their traditionally defined social positions practice politics as a means to that end. The motives of these actors may be assumed to relate only to the reproduction of the interest group as they see themselves. The practices of different interest groups are not expected to intermesh in any sort of "organic solidarity" (*contra* Durkheim 1933; Service 1971: chapter 5). Their interests differ, their perspectives differ, and their actions may conflict with those of other groups or subgroups. These conflicting thoughts and actions comprise a dynamic that at once supersedes the intentional and the vitalistic. The net result of this dynamic may be dramatic and unforeseen consequences that alter the objective conditions under which the consciousness of individuals is continuously redefined. Collective consciousness can be transformed in this way, along with the political, economic, and social activities of actors.

Raised through just such a process, the Leviathan plants its feet on the ground, lifts its crown near the heavens, and casts its shadow across the land. Fried's (1967) enigmatic "stratified society" arises, and in its wake the transformation of social and economic relations: from the communities and local-authority structures of a kin-ordered mode of production arise the class-based regional-administrative-authority structures associated with a tributary mode of production (Wolf 1982:97). There exist few theoretical assessments of this process and fewer still empirical (which is to say archaeological) evaluations of theoretical constructs. An approach that slights neither the political dynamics involved in prestate centralization nor cultural history is needed. That is, the theoretical construct must be based in the processes of the cultural construction of consciousness and the actualization of such consciousness in the dynamic political arenas of nonstate social formations.

The empirical data, on the other hand, must be relatively fine grained so that we might gain insight into political actions and changing ideologies and thereby go beyond broad-brush statements about political-economic trends. The archaeological resolution that might permit the testing of such constructs rarely has been retrieved. This study provides a glimpse. The level of detail that is available permits discussion of change in terms of what appear to be significant community-wide events set in a context of a fine-scaled subphase chronology.

Late Prehistoric Cahokia

The shadow of the Leviathan once loomed large in the central Mississippi valley of the American midcontinent. In an expanse of Mississippi

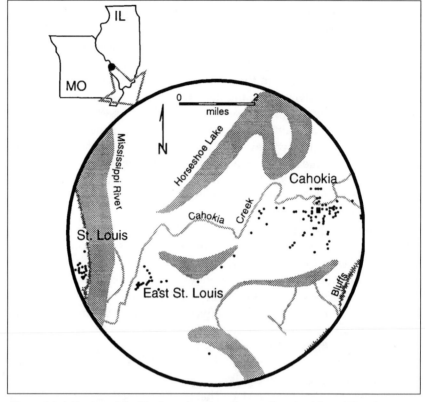

Figure 1.1. A Portion of the Northern American Bottom Showing Mound Distribution (adapted from Bushnell 1904; dots are mounds and mound clusters)

River floodplain called the "American Bottom"[1] opposite modern-day St. Louis and adjacent to the confluence of the Missouri and Mississippi rivers, the remains of this toppled and decayed giant are found in the form of Cahokia, part of the sprawling political-administrative complex[2] surrounded by smaller presumed administrative centers and scattered habitation sites dating to the eleventh through thirteenth centuries A.D. (figure 1.1).

This prehistoric American Bottom phenomenon and others like it

---

1. The colonial French population, upon ceding the Illinois territory to the British after the Seven Years War, preferred to live across the river in "Louisiana" (i.e., Missouri, by then ceded to Spain) and looked back upon Illinois with disdain, as it had then—thanks to George Rogers Clark—become the American floodplain or "bottom."

2. The locations or foci of political-hierarchical control and the residential base of elite decision-makers (cf. Wright and Johnson 1975:267).

throughout the southeastern United States are known to archaeologists as Mississippian. Mississippian archaeology in the American Bottom furnishes perhaps the best data set pertaining to nonstate political centralization because of not only the abundant prehistoric remains but also the large-scale archaeology that has taken place in the region since the 1960s, a consequence of the well-oiled machine of cooperating governmental and academic institutions fueled by the sweat of dedicated students and low-paid laborers.

The Mississippian phenomenon in the American Bottom had developed out of the local agricultural communities of the final two or three centuries of the first millennium A.D. There are hints that these pre-Mississippian or "Emergent Mississippian" communities were comprised of ranked groups, but it seems equally clear that such ranking was a local phenomenon, one that emphasized community, not class (see chapter 3). Yet out of this communal base a complex Mississippian polity appeared. Moreover, its appearance—the transformation of the social order in the region—was a sudden event, archaeologically speaking. Indeed, this phenomenon may well have occurred within the span of a "generation" (cf. Hobbes 1985:227). It would appear that somehow in the early eleventh century A.D. "the constraints were breached" (*sensu* Sahlins 1963:294).

Cahokia itself has been defined by some archaeologists to cover up to 14 square kilometers, part of what I will call the Central Political-Administrative Complex (see chapter 4). At Cahokia are found the remains of over 100 earthen mounds, most of which probably supported the temples, council houses, or residences of an elite population. The largest of the mounds, Monks Mound, towers some 30 meters above the surrounding floodplain. There is evidence of large-scale labor projects (involving land leveling and monument construction), rectangular plazas, a palisade, elite burials, and large residential areas—home to perhaps five to ten thousand people at one point. The archaeology of the floodplain hinterland and the surrounding dissected till plains has revealed the remains left by a rural population of farmers. The fruits of the labor of these households were harvests of local starchy seeds, maize, and cucurbits, supplemented with red meat, waterfowl, wild turkey, and aquatic resources. Given the internal complexity of the Cahokia site (see chapter 4), it would appear that the Mississippian elite relied upon both the fruits and the labor of these rural farmers.

While we know increasingly well the community and subsistence base of the outlying rural population, the integration (or lack thereof) of these rural food producers within the larger political economy of the region is less well known. The archaeological analysis of the political economy of the American Bottom has really only begun. What is becoming increasingly clear, however, is that the prehistoric American Bottom political entity was not simply an aggregation of rural households. Rural sites are not useful guides to what occurred in the Mississippian centers. The entire polity—indeed the interregional nexus of Mississippian polities—was a historically constituted whole.

The archaeological evidence upon which this study is based—residential architecture, domestic garbage, and elite monuments—provides a high level of diachronic resolution for the paramount administrative center of Cahokia (see chapters 5 and 6). The timing and effects of what seem to have been the consequences of elite political tactics and strategies of social reproduction are observable, archaeologically speaking. Cahokia burst upon the late-prehistoric landscape in the American midcontinent—a new order. This new order was powerful and expansionistic; it ushered in the historical development of distant Native American groups in the midcontinent (see Emerson and Lewis 1991; Stoltman 1991). This order was established as a political and cultural hegemony that strengthened its dominant position until that great Leviathan, after about a century and a half, stumbled and fell. That the Native Americans who lived in the area during initial contact with the immigrant Europeans knew nothing of Cahokia's prehistoric inhabitants is telling of the extent of Cahokia's ultimate demise. This demise, however, is of little concern for the problem at hand.

We are concerned at present with the processes of the formation of regionally consolidated chiefly authority and nonstate social classes. In the following pages, I propose that the regional consolidation of a Cahokia polity was based on the political actions of a restricted number of high-ranking people over a relatively brief period of time. I further propose that under the historical circumstances of consolidation, the political economy of the American Bottom was initially accompanied by expanded and transformed production-and-exchange activities supervised by the elite Cahokian patrons. Mississippian culture itself was a material expression of the enlarged interregional exchange of knowledge, materials, and people by which the elite perpetuated regional control in the midst of nonelite resistance. Within the span of half a century, these political-economic and cultural developments permitted the emergence of a "divine chiefship" and nonstate social classes—elite and nonelite, aristocracy and commoner (see chapter 7). Such elevated authority and stratified social conditions, I submit, gestate within nonstate regional hegemonies. In other regions around the world similar conditions may have been necessary precursors to the rise of early states.

The present study of the Cahokia-Mississippian phenomenon may, I hope, shed light on other past Leviathans around the world. It most certainly will contribute toward revising perceptions of the relationship of Cahokia to other midcontinental Native American cultures in late prehistory. It also provides considerable resolution into the long-standing problem of the origins of regional hegemonies and social stratification and into the relationship between ideology, politics, and cultural tradition of interest to all concerned with how the competing interests and identities of human organizations structure both history and tradition.

Chapter 2

Chiefdoms in Theory and Practice

The so-called neoevolutionary and functional-ecological anthropology of the 1950s and 1960s searched for "functionally interrelated constellations" at the societal level (Oberg 1955:472). To Service (1971 [1962]:134), chiefdoms were redistributional societies "with a permanent central agency of coordination" that comprised an intermediary stage of social evolution between the tribe and the state (see Welch 1991:9–11). Defined thus, and with "no formal, legal apparatus of forceful repression" (Service 1975:16), chiefdoms were seen to have evolved from their non-hierarchical predecessors as managerial adaptations to regional imbalances in the natural distribution of necessary subsistence goods. Archaeologists often projected unmitigated population growth as the causal factor leading to the need for an ascribed managerial leadership (e.g., Sanders and Price 1968).

Empirical evidence to counter the notion that managerial redistribution (*sensu* Service 1971) was the organizational basis of chiefdoms has been forthcoming from Africa, Mexico, Polynesia, and the southeastern United States (Earle 1977, 1978; Feinman and Neitzel 1984; Feinman and Nicholas 1987; Finney 1966; Muller 1978; Peebles and Kus 1977; Smith 1978:488–491; Steponaitis 1978; Taylor 1975:35; Welch 1991). Likewise, it has been demonstrated that, in regions where political centralization occurred, the population had not reached levels thought necessary for it to constitute the driving force of social evolution (Barker 1992; Blanton et al. 1981:222–225; Drennan 1987; Earle 1978:163–165; Feinman 1991:242; Feinman et al. 1985:361–362; Wright and Johnson 1975:274–276; but contrast Kirch 1984).

Service's manager-chief, along with other "management" or "integration" approaches (Earle 1987a:292–293), has been contrasted with the "political" or "control" perspective (Brumfiel and Earle 1987a; Earle 1987a:292–293; Haas 1982; Tainter 1988:32–37). The results of these comparisons point in the direction of an emerging consensus in favor of the latter (Brumfiel and Earle 1987a; Earle 1989). Strictly speaking, given that each perspective is linked historically to distinct axiomatic systems, it is at best awkward to compare which best fits the empirical record (*contra* Haas 1982). The theoretical underpinnings of the political approach lie in large measure in Marxian political economy and Weberian action-based social theory, incorporating elements of idealism and historical materialism (cf. Vincent 1990). Neither are founded upon the notion of a "universal human tendency toward ambition and self-aggrandizement" as misconstrued by Tainter (1988:35). The roots of the managerial thesis lie in functionalism and Spencerian "organic" evolutionism (see Stocking 1982:122; cf. Dunnell 1980), untenable within most present-day theoretical frameworks (e.g., Sahlins 1976:chapter 4, 1985:52; but see Tainter 1988:37).

The Political Approach to Chiefdoms

From the political or control perspective, the essence of a chiefdom is its (centralized) political structure, not its economic system. "Simple" chiefly administrations may consist of a single tier of local officials who retain close ties with their local communities (Earle 1978, 1991a:3; Steponaitis 1978; Wright 1984). These simple hierarchies may be distinguished from structurally elaborate chiefly hierarchies. A "complex" hierarchy of chiefly control may be defined as consisting of an apical administrative tier superordinate to structurally analogous secondary administrative controls (Earle 1978:11, 1991a:3; Steponaitis 1978:420; Wright 1977:381; cf. Sahlins 1985:33–35). That is, a chiefly hierarchy is "not internally specialized in terms of different aspects of the control process (e.g., observing, deciding, coercing)" (Wright 1984:42). The difference between hierarchical levels is a matter of the degree of legitimized power. Internal-structural differentiation characterizes the state control hierarchy (Wright 1977). Chiefly administrations in which warring, speaking, or religious duties are performed by someone other than the paramount do not signal the bureaucratization of the control hierarchy as much as they do "ambiguities" of chiefly administration (*sensu* Sahlins 1985:91; see also Earle 1978:18–19).

As further considered by Wright (1984:42–43), it is important to recognize that control within complex chiefdoms may be exercised by individuals drawn from a "class" of people "which cross-cuts many local subgroups" (Wright 1984:42; e.g., Earle 1978:12–16). Class here is defined as a "ranked group whose members compete with each other for access to controlling positions and stand together in opposition to other people" (Wright 1984:42–43). Where class strata crosscut social relations, the elite are appropriators of the productive output of a nonelite population of "primary producers" (*sensu* Peebles and Kus 1977). An aristocratic class "utilizes and exhibits kin-ordered ties as a mark of its distinctiveness and separateness" from a commoner class (Wolf 1982:98). The former recognizes itself as "a genealogically separate group, more closely related to each other than to the members of the local commoner populations" (Earle 1978:12–13). A nonelite class need not be seen as completely cut off genealogically from the elite group. The nonelite occupy the lower tiers of a ranked-hierarchical or conical-clan structure in which aristocrat-commoner kin linkages are retained. In practice, however, this structure or genealogical charter (e.g., Knight 1990) fails to adequately model the low frequency of commoners so linked with higher ranks. That is, a genealogical rift in a quantitative sense is a component of nonstate class relations, the structure of elite-nonelite kin ties serving to define social distances as much as anything else.

As currently conceptualized, the chiefly personages of both simple and complex hierarchies engage in political negotiations and struggles in order to perpetuate their authoritative positions and preserve their perceptions of the social order as a whole. While such social reproduction similarly constrains the form of social and economic relations, the latter are unnecessary defining attributes of chiefdoms. Thus attention actually has been focused away from a societal type—chiefdom—and onto political process (Earle 1987a:279, 1989:87; see papers in Earle 1991b). Without a doubt, the chiefdom concept has become "something different" from what it used to be (Spencer 1987:369). It is from this political vantage point that a recent seminar on chiefdoms produced a "new synthesis" that focused on "the dynamics of chiefdoms" (Earle 1989, 1991b).

We should recognize, however, that despite the overt concern with diachrony and political dynamics, synthesis is not theory (Spriggs 1988:65–67). Synthesis certainly is an important step in a larger research program, but without further theoretical construction, it risks tautology in that the "theory" used to explain chiefdoms is to an extent a montage of comparative information about chiefdoms. The challenge is not only to think of chiefdoms in different terms, albeit political ones, but to employ theory in a manner with which to explain long-term change. This challenge can be bridged to an extent by an anthropological critique of political economy. The results build on and extend the political approach to chiefdoms. This critique provides a jumping-off point for the exposition of a theory of practice and a political economy of chiefships that form the theoretical core of the present study.

Political Hegemony and the Anthropological Critique
of Political Economy

The process of political centralization by definition results in a (political) core or center and a dispersed periphery (Ekholm and Friedman 1979:43). The relational characteristics of such an arrangement provide something of a "core-periphery" logic with which archaeological constructs have been concerned in recent years (Champion 1989; Rowlands 1987). There are recurrent qualities associated with cores and peripheries from various historical epochs, but the scale and structure of core-periphery relations is not analogous between epochs (Kohl 1987:16). This point has been overlooked in recent speculative constructs dealing with Cahokia and its role in eastern North America (Dincauze and Hasenstab 1989; Little 1987; Peregrine 1991, 1992); the proponents may be accused of propogating an entirely inappropriate neo–Adam Smithian view of Native American cultural developments (Brenner 1977). These speculative constructs have assumed a continent-wide economic hegemony where only a region-wide political hegemony is demonstrable (see Milner 1990:26–27).

Stripped of inappropriate assumptions regarding scale or structure, what remain of a World Systems approach are the definitional characteristics of hegemony. In the terms of nonstate political hegemonies, three such characteristics apply. First, core groups may be said to "dominate" relations with peripheral groups *within a region* since the peripheral groups have fewer political-alliance options, making peripheral-group social reproduction more "dependent" upon a small set of core-group allies (see Rowlands 1987:5). Second, nonstate core groups marginalize peripheral groups to variable extent through the process of accumulating and transforming resources extracted from the periphery (which might be construed as the core exploiting the periphery) in order to reproduce the political hegemony (Ekholm and Friedman 1985:110; Kohl 1987:16). That is, to the degree that the productive activity of the peripheral groups is limited by the process of the core reproducing itself, the periphery cannot achieve political-economic parity with the core. The peripheral groups in a sense are alienated from their own social reproduction because their reproduction is articulated with that of the core (Gledhill and Rowlands 1982:146–147).

Last, the reproduction of the local political hegemony is dependent in part upon the reproduction of the interregional social formation involving a "prestige-goods economy" (Friedman and Rowlands 1978). For instance, recent studies of late-prehistoric exchange in southeastern North America have stressed the pan-regional circulation of finished valuables as a means by which high-ranking personages perpetuated the ranked hierarchy (Brown et al. 1990:263–265; Cobb 1989:80–81; Muller 1987:18–19; Peregrine 1992). The legitimation of authority in chiefly polities was inextricably tied to the ability of authorities to demonstrate knowledge of and control over geographically or temporally distant phenomena (Helms 1979, 1988, 1992). Physical objects were an important tangible materialization of such linkages with or control over the extrasocial or cosmic realm (Helms 1979:109) and were used "to attract clients and allies to compete for political leadership and to cement horizontal alliances that enhance existing power" (Brumfiel and Earle 1987:3). Insufficient access to such prestige goods could have threatened the position of a particular officeholder by inhibiting the formation and maintenance of alliances (Wright 1984). Thus nonstate core groups themselves of necessity were (loosely) articulated. The reproduction of one was at the same time the reproduction of the network of reciprocating "peer polities" (Renfrew 1987; Spencer 1982: 51–56).

This articulation of core groups, especially as it involved each group's attempts to demonstrate control over the extra-social, begins to address the deficiencies of a core-periphery analysis that focuses on only economic domination, dependency, and peripheralization. Economic domination, dependency, and peripheralization may be components of nonstate political centralization, but in and of themselves, they do not constitute a sufficient processual explanation of this centralization. In fact, I submit that the core-periphery constructs are sterile in the absence of a political-ideological element—a component of an anthropological critique of political economy—that transcends the problems of scale and structure.

As exemplified in the work of Helms, political ideology is central to the production and reproduction of social order at regional and interregional scales. Carrying this analysis a step further, Marcus and Fischer (1986:85) state that "the production of cultural meaning and symbols, as a central practice or process in social action, deserves more emphasis. . . . [T]he use of the specific Marxist keyword of production . . . signals an effort [by anthropologists] to meet materialist and political-economy perspectives on their own terms. Not only is the cultural construction of meaning and symbols inherently a matter of political and economic interests, but the reverse also holds—the concerns of political economy are inherently about conflicts over meanings and symbols. . . . [A]ny materialist-idealist distinction between political-economy and interpretive approaches is simply not supportable."

Political-economic analysis and interpretations of cultural meanings and symbols are to be articulated within a dialectical understanding of the internal-structural or cultural logic and the core-periphery or socio-historical context (Comaroff 1982; Godelier 1977, 1978; Sahlins 1981, 1985). Emphasis is placed on understanding the social and political negotiation of cultural meanings as these affect and are affected by social actions in given contexts. The history of what individual human agents or actors think and do is of principal concern.

Such an actor-centered approach—one elevating the role of human agency in historical developments—is elaborated in the following pages as a theory of practice. Practice theory provides the framework for the interplay between human consciousness, culture, and social action. It bypasses the theoretical problems of utilitarian logic or goal-seeking actors—the teleological rationale that accompanied the functional-ecological and evolutionist paradigms—by analyzing the motivations of actors and the historical consequences of social action. A practice-theory framework, incorporating Antonio Gramsci's (1971) notion of hegemony, is adapted here to produce a modified political approach to chiefdoms. This construct draws upon ethnohistorical and ethnographic cases to highlight particular points but has an abstract logic rooted in practice theory and the sociopolitical structures of nonstate hierarchy.

A Theory of Practice

In order to engage a theory of practice and construct a political economy of chiefships, we need to comprehend human consciousness. It has been said that, to some degree, consciousness is a social product. Consciousness, however, is also a product that, by way of its cultural construction, mediates the actions of individuals within particular sociohistorical contexts (see Durkheim 1933:279; Marx 1968:118–119; Marx and Engels 1989:47, 51–52; Weber 1958:23–31). Thus we must understand not only society; we must understand also the mechanism that mediates social relations and the cultural meanings and symbols embodied in the consciousness of individual human agents. This mechanism is the practice (*praxis*) of human agents. Practice—productive and communicative actions of people (*sensu* Ball 1983:86–91)—reproduces the cultural meanings and symbols of a particular cultural tradition (cf. Bourdieu 1977; Giddens 1979, 1982; Ortner 1984; Sahlins 1985). People, as active agents of their cultural tradition, conduct themselves according to prescribed beliefs, values, and conceptualizations that filter their perceptions of the social and physical environment (Rappaport 1979:97). That is, what people do or aspire to do is constrained by the "objective conditions" or cultural tradition of which their actions or aspirations are also a product (Bourdieu 1977:166).

The interconnectedness of practice and tradition does not mean that change is inhibited. Rather, the practice of individuals and the concomitant reproduction of the cultural tradition are also alterations of tradition "insofar as in action, the categories by which a present world is orchestrated pick up some novel empirical content" (Sahlins 1985:144). In other words, the use of traditional or "conventional concepts in empirical contexts subjects the cultural meanings to practical revaluations" (Sahlins 1985:145). The reproduction of tradition is at the same time and to variable extent departure from tradition due to the incongruities between individual and collective knowledge or power and the dynamic articulation of internal structures with external conditions (Comaroff 1982:145). Simply put, actors aspire to perpetuate the status quo as they understand it, but unintended outcomes of actions can alter the status quo.

Ideology and Hegemony

It is an error, however, to characterize the cultural-tradition status quo as a unitary entity in terms of either a Durkheimian "collective consciousness" or a Weberian weltanschauung, as incorporated into a contemporary definition of culture as "integrated ethos and worldview" (Ortner 1984:131). We may speak of ideologies within traditions as the mode of articulation between tradition and the consciousness of individuals. More precisely, ideologies are the means by which "interest groups" or "subcollectivities" (from this point on simply to be called "subgroups") acquire consciousness of themselves, as these subgroups constitute nodes of social interaction within the larger social formation (Gramsci 1971:324, 327; Pearce 1989:27; Sumner 1979:12–14).

Ideology is an "intellectual" system[1] of beliefs that explain—in the terms of the traditional metaphysics—the social order for a subgroup (Shils 1972:29; Sumner 1979:16). In Rappaport's (1979) terms, it is a "cognized model" of the world; it legitimizes the social status quo through an appropriation of traditional or cosmological referents. Ideologies from this perspective are not mere epiphenomena or false consciousness as they are for materialists of various persuasions. Ideologies shape the actors' interpretation and understanding of events and "create the terrain on

---

1. Distinguishing system—"derivative and organizational"—from structure—"basic and generative" (Rosenberg 1988:11).

which men move . . . [and] acquire consciousness of their position" (Gramsci 1971:377). These are dynamic entities, expressing or projecting values and beliefs that themselves are open to various interpretations within a larger sphere of social negotiation.

To the extent that subgroups either acquiesce to or share the ideas of a dominant social group, we may speak of a "dominant ideology" relative to subordinate ideologies. However, it is an error to assume that a dominant ideology erases the subordinate ideologies within the social formation and subverts the contradictions between the cultural tradition and social order as legitimized in ideology (Comaroff 1982:159–160; Giddens 1979:72; McGuire 1992:140–142; Patterson 1986; Silverblatt 1988). Writing in the 1920s and 1930s, Antonio Gramsci provided a means by which to conceptualize the dynamic interrelationship between consciousness and ideology by using a notion of "hegemony" (see also Abercrombie et al. 1980:11–15; Comaroff and Comaroff 1991:19ff.; Laitin 1986:19).

> [T]he independence and autonomy of the subaltern group which it [the ruling class] claims to represent are in fact sacrificed to the *intellectual hegemony* of the ruling class . . . (Gramsci 1971:160 [emphasis added]).
>
> [T]he fact of hegemony presupposes that account be taken of the interests and the tendencies of the groups over which hegemony is to be exercised, and that a certain *compromise equilibrium* should be formed—in other words, that the leading group should make sacrifices of an economic-corporate kind. But there is also no doubt that such sacrifices and such a compromise cannot touch the essential; for though *hegemony is ethical-political*, it must also be economic, must necessarily be based on the decisive function exercised by the leading group in the decisive nucleus of economic activity (Gramsci 1971:161 [emphasis added]).

A dominant ideology appropriates the consciousness of individuals not by coercion, but rather by consensus, a process of the interpenetration of the dominant ideas or the reconciliation between this ideology and subordinate ideologies. Such appropriation is believed to occur in the context of ritual or other communicative media (see Barth 1989:29; Bloch 1989:124–133; Rappaport 1979:175–217; Roseberry 1989:45). The sponsor or interest group in control of the communicative medium will effect such appropriation or reconciliation of ideas.

Core subgroups for instance will "seek to establish a universal diffusion of the acceptance and observance of the values and beliefs of which they are the custodians" (Shils 1975:9). The appropriation of the cultural tradition vis-à-vis a dominant ideology is tantamount to the alienation of individuals from their common values, ideas, and meanings—the peripheralization of subaltern ideologies and the transformation of consciousness (see Marx 1978:77, 111). Alienation leads to the internalized contradictions at the level of individual consciousness. Individuals may hold contradictory attitudes, beliefs, or values rooted either in their "common sense" or in their "theoretical consciousness" (Gramsci 1971). Common sense or practical knowledge is unreflective spontaneous thought rooted in cultural tradition that guides practical activity (Giddens 1979, 1982; Gramsci 1971:419–422; Jacobitti 1983:369, 1986:80; Pompa 1975:27–36; Sahlins 1985:51; Sumner 1979:16).[2] Theoretical consciousness or discursive knowledge is that which may be reflected upon and explicated by actors (Sumner 1979:16). It includes the adopted ideas, values, and beliefs of the dominant group and may not be in accord with their practical knowledge or common sense of the cultural tradition as incorporated in ideologies.

The prospect of a contradictory consciousness is that subordinate resistance to dominant ideologies is always present and the source of conflicting thoughts and actions. The divergent, opposed, or conflicting thoughts and actions of human agents, in turn, can lead to the departure from tradition or cultural transformations mentioned earlier. Such a cultural-historical process would have mediated change in nonstate chiefly formations. Understanding in a diachronic sense what motivated human agents within chiefly formations and, ultimately, comprehending the generation of the Leviathan will not emerge from a synthesis of chiefly politics. Instead, understanding is to be brought about by implementing a theoretical argument linking the structural principles of chiefly hierarchies and nonstate cultural hegemonies with practice theory. By doing this, we may develop a "theory of motivation" (Ortner 1984), what I for present purposes call a political economy of chiefships, which will inform an analysis of the Cahokian Leviathan.

A Political Economy of Chiefships

The nonstate consolidation of political power in the form of legitimate authority and the reproduction of these authority structures can best be understood as a process through which tradition and ideology are negotiated. In such a historical development, the degree to which the ideas of the dominant subgroup became the dominant ideas was a process of alienation from tradition or common sense. The core-periphery logic applies here, but in cultural, not economic, terms.

2. It is, like Bourdieu's (1977:72) *habitus*, culture internalized by the individual (Bidet 1979:203; Ortner 1984:148).

The extent of subgroup alienation defined the bounds of social action—both theirs and that of other subgroups that comprised the hegemony. Chiefly officeholders, for example, may not have been able to exert much authority where a common ethic of equality and reciprocity existed. On the other hand, where a cultural hegemony involved the alienation of commoners from this ethic and an incorporation of dominant-group ideas in the theoretical consciousness of the masses, an officeholder may have been able to exert considerable control over the productive activities of commoners. Subsequent transformations of political office or social relations and the continued appropriation of the traditional forms of consciousness of the masses permitted—indeed necessitated—paramount actions of a different scale than those of his or her chiefly predecessors. The historical transformations of chiefly authority are very much components of a long-term process (cf. Anderson 1990:193–194; Steward and Faron 1959; Thomson 1908:60). Practice is not a simple correlate of political structure. The development of sacral chiefly authority—a divine chiefship—cannot be understood simply in terms of the aggregate qualities of chiefly political strategies. The Hobbesian *generation* of that great Leviathan was structured in terms of the hegemony of the pre-Leviathanic era.

A hegemony of local ranked relations and the politics of subgroup social reproduction is a starting configuration from which to project the long-term transformations of consciousness and practice. Such a rank hegemony and the expansionistic tendencies and structural weaknesses of chiefly organization as they converge in the form of the regional consolidation of chiefly authority, nonstate class relations, and the development of a divine chiefship comprise the central focus of a political economy of chiefships. We shall not be concerned at present with the origins of social ranking and hereditary chiefly office. Suffice it to say that the emergence of ranked hierarchies was necessarily a regional process involving a nexus of interacting groups (see Halstead and O'Shea 1982; Sahlins 1972; Webster 1990). Ranking by definition is a social order involving the intergroup negotiation of social inequalities, and unless we assume large, well-bounded, autonomous and endogamous aggregates of subgroups (e.g., Carneiro 1981:64), we perforce speak of regional interaction.

A Rank Hegemony

In a regional setting in which the relations between corporate (descent) entities were ascriptively ranked and authority was located within the community, social reproduction would have meant legitimizing subgroup positions relative to the known other (subgroups and groups) and to the unknown supernatural. This reproduction of rank in terms of the known (via social experience) and unknown (beyond social experience) would have been at once the reproduction of a traditional egalitarianism and the usurpation of this tradition by the ideas, values, and beliefs of a dominant group. Affirmation of ranked relations might have taken the form of successful feast giving or material distributions in ritual contexts. Through ritualized affirmation, the diffuse cosmological order would have been transformed into a centralized hierarchy of cosmological precepts (see Sahlins 1968:chapter 6).

The relations between high- and low-ranking subgroups within locally centralized polities would have been as reciprocal bonds between kin (Wolf 1982:99, 389–391). "Leadership is here a higher form of kinship, hence a higher form of reciprocity and liberality" (Sahlins 1972:132). The "ethic of chiefly generosity blesses the inequality; . . . the ideal of reciprocity denies that it [inequality] makes any difference" (Sahlins 1972:134–135). Relatives and affines they would have been, and as a community they would have acted. Low-ranking subgroups would have conceded to the high-ranking subgroup(s) not immediately but through the ritual appropriation of their traditional (common-sense) ideologies over the long run (cf. Leach 1965:106).

Clearly, high-ranking subgroups within a rank hegemony would not have constituted an appropriating class, as earlier defined, nor need they be seen as "ambitious" or "self-aggrandizing" in the sense of Tainter (1988:35). Like the low-ranking subgroups, the practice of chiefly individuals simply would have reproduced the ranked relations as they had come to be, not as the chiefly individuals desired them to be in any teleological sense (see Sahlins 1972:134). Given this cultural hegemony, we might expect that low- and high-ranking individuals alike would have viewed the chiefship as the élan vital of the land. A people "cannot live without lands and without a chief," said the Tikopians (Firth 1983:333); "the mind of the people is concerned for the chiefs" (Firth 1979:159). Chiefly sanctity would have required reciprocation for the material and religious benefits that chiefship bestowed upon the community including the intercession between the known social order and the unknown supernatural, the management of ritual activities, the banking of resources in case of community shortage, and the hosting of visitors and ceremonies.

At the same time, the political power of the high-ranking subgroups would have been greatly inhibited by the traditional values and beliefs of the masses. The chief could "exact no truckling homage where every member of the tribe is a blood relation" (Thomson 1908:59). The generosity and not the avarice of the politically wise officeholder would have served as a means of retaining his or her following. Loss of power and ultimately position would be a very real consequence of high-ranking officeholders who awoke the contradictory consciousness of the masses by demanding too much or returning too little to the low-ranking subgroups. In a political arena where, by virtue of the importance and ease of manipulation of kin ties, subgroups could realign themselves with other high-ranking subgroups (who except in unusual cases [e.g., Rousseau 1977:232] would have sought to attract additional followers), loss of chiefly power would have been a simple matter of followers walking out on their chiefs (Fried 1967:133).

To the extent that a chiefly ideology had appropriated a traditional ethic of reciprocal relations, we can expect that low-ranking subgroups would have contributed food, wealth objects, and labor to chiefly personages as expected of them. They would have made the contributions only insofar as to reproduce the perceived balance of the universe and hence their own social positions and then only because of the perceptions that certain benefits did derive from the institutionalized inequality. The chiefly subgroup, to the extent that it ensured the loyalty of low-ranking subgroups, would have reciprocated through the redistribution of subsistence goods and the distribution of valuables or prestige items (see Earle 1977; Peebles and Kus 1977; Steponaitis 1978). Redistribution, in this light, was a high-ranking-subgroup strategy of social reproduction (Wolf 1982:97).

The Factional Politics of Simple Chiefdoms

Besides the realm of relations between high- and low-ranking subgroups—mediated through the idiom of kinship—there would have existed a political arena of power relations between high-ranking factions (Brumfiel 1989:127–128; Comaroff 1982:151–152; Eisenstadt 1959:210; Goldman 1967; Lloyd 1965:79; Nicholas 1965, 1966:53–55; Powell 1967:179). Although a leader from a high-ranking subgroup may have relied upon low-ranking subgroups for support, it is between high-ranking factions that prestige and power were gained or lost. Low-ranking subgroups presumably could not have presented a direct or immediate threat to the political interests of the chiefly subgroups.

High-ranking subgroups would have vied for the same resources, the loyalty of the same followers, and the favor of the same deities. In fact, the individuals within an officeholder's own subgroup, potential heirs to office, would have constituted the officeholder's principal rivals. Because of the ambiguities of kinship and inheritance, multiple high-ranking claimants would have existed for any given office. Ostensibly for this reason, high-ranking relatives of an officeholder might not have been advisors to that officeholder. In one ethnographic case, low-ranking individuals (but respected elders) were advisors because they enforced the officeholder's orders and executed "his exactions to a degree that his fellow aristocrats would not" (Lehman 1963:147). Potential competitors to chiefly officeholders who emerged within the subgroup might have left voluntarily or by force to found new domains (e.g., Mitchell 1956:68; Powell 1967:186). A side effect of this process might have been the extension of the geographical limits of the original subgroup's alliance network.

Rivalry between high-ranking subgroups could have taken two related forms, competitive exchange and violence (Brown 1979:726; Hall 1977:503–505; Rey 1975:49). Through either of these, prestige could have been gained or lost. Competitive exchange, including feasting and conspicuous displays of wealth, would have been a means of demeaning and indebting other subgroups. Such competitive feasting itself could have resulted from or led to subgroup warfare. Success in warfare, which amounted to feuds between or within high-ranking subgroups, also would have been a means of accruing prestige while denigrating opponents, hence restoring balance by ensuring the social reproduction of the victorious.

To ensure success and reproduce the status quo in either competitive exchange or warfare, chiefly subgroups would have sought to enlarge their alliance network among other high-ranking subgroups. Marriage alliances would have constituted a principal means of establishing concrete links between high-ranking subgroups. The establishment of affinal linkages would have been a means of negating to an extent the affine as rival, providing instead a source of warriors and material support. Polygamy would have been a practical means of broadening an affinal alliance network, the larger networks also benefiting indirectly the subordinate affines of the chiefly subgroup (Wolf 1982:97; Wright 1984:50). Marriages between a local high-ranking subgroup and a distant subgroup would have furthered the reproduction of high rank by extending the local subgroup's access to or control over extra-social knowledge and exotic sumptuary articles (see Helms 1979).

The exchange of precious objects would have been an integral component of high-ranking alliances. The nonlocal objects themselves or the locally transformed nonlocal raw materials would have been "items of wealth and symbols of authority" (Earle 1978:185). Within the local domain, these "prestige goods" would have served as coupons for transactions in all spheres of social life (see Brumfiel and Earle 1987; Friedman and Rowlands 1978; Helms 1979).

Prestige goods would have been given away by high-ranking office-holders to political underlings—potential usurpers of political office—as a means of solidifying support (by indebting followers) and minimizing rivalry within the chief's domain (Helms 1988:118; Wright 1984:45). At the same time, the products of skilled craftspersons could have been (controlled and) used by officeholders for long-distance exchanges with political allies (Brumfiel and Earle 1987; Friedman and Rowlands 1978). Thus, the circulation of prestige goods could have been controlled to an extent by sponsoring craftspersons and thereby controlling the quantities or qualities of the prestige goods.[3]

Political Oscillation and the Patron-Client Transformation

Successfully competing in the factional political field of ranked social formations meant high-ranking subgroups would have aspired to outcompete rivals by *expanding* alliances, exchanges, craft subsidization, or warfare (Earle 1978:172, 183–184). The factionalism and inter-subgroup competition within simple chiefdoms would have produced unstable political landscapes and power asymmetries. Such asymmetrical configurations were the chance outcomes of the disorder of politics, warfare, demographic shifts, environmental setting, and chance food-production fluctuations (see Friedman and Rowlands 1978:203). Fairly minor politically mediated crises could have caused the fragile structure of alliances and community consensus to break apart. Yet, in practice, a decentralized formation would swing back to a centralized one because subgroups in such circumstances would have reestablished relations of power. Long-term political developments thus might have consisted of "cycles" of centralization and decentralization (see Anderson 1990). However, it is important to recognize that, in the long run, historical trajectories would have been more than sequences of comparable rise-and-fall episodes. A cultural tradition is by definition not susceptible to this sort of short-term political oscillation. Thus, where centralization reemerged from the ashes

3. The configuration of craft production-and-exchange relations within or between polities is a matter better resolved on a case-by-case basis, since these relations are affected by the political tactics of high-ranking subgroups. The patterns of craft production and exchange, that is, will depend much on political-historical factors. Craft production or task specialization should not be viewed as a correlate of some level of social evolution (Costin 1991; Feinman and Neitzel 1984).

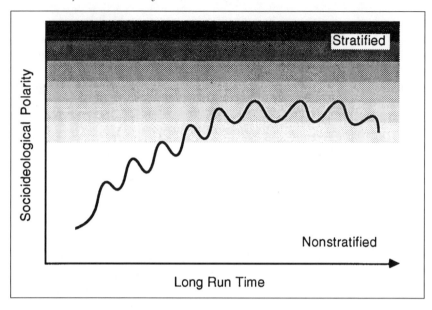

Figure 2.1. The Development of Incipient Stratification

of hierarchy, the estrangement of people from their former values, beliefs, and meanings could have progressed with little interruption (Figure 2.1; cf. Friedman 1982:179–180).

Of course, increased alienation of the low–ranking subgroups from their traditional ethic of equality and reciprocity is not a necessary concomitant of the centralization, decentralization, and recentralization trajectories of simple chiefly polities. In fact, increasing equalitarianism— estrangement from a chiefly tradition—rather than increased socio-ideological polarization could have occurred under certain social and physical environmental conditions over the long run. The historical trajectory of any particular social formation would have depended very much on the history of chiefly politics in the context of the local food-production system and long- and short-term environmental change. The important point here is that the appropriation of tradition via a dominant ideology was an ongoing process related to but apart from the arenas of chiefly politics. In other words, politics and culture may be separated for the purpose of analyzing these processes.

It is useful for the present discussion to note that putative aristocratic or commoner "classes" have been recognized among certain simple and unstable ranked political formations of Southeast Asia and the South

Pacific (Buck 1949:337; Firth 1983:89; Hickey 1982:37; Kirsch 1973; Leach 1965:163; Lehman 1963:108; Powell 1967:168; Rousseau 1979; cf. Needham in Izikowitz 1979). It may be that these classes were the historical results of their being peripheral to the state-level cores in China, Southeast Asia, or Indonesia. It also may be the case that some culturally unique social divisions are not well translated as "classes" in the sense earlier defined as ranked groups whose members stand together and who act as a political-economic entity in opposition to other people (cf. Bargatzky 1988). On the other hand, if these are social classes in the aforementioned sense, their significance is not necessarily lessened by their mode of origin (even if derived from their interaction with a state-dominated core). That class strata might exist where the common sense of the masses demarcated clear limits upon the authority of elite officeholders is important to note (e.g., Leach 1965).

From a practice-theory perspective, it is arguable that similar status-group distinctions, what we might think of as incipient class relations, were necessary preconditions of the regional consolidation of political authority. The consolidation of chiefly power at a regional level presupposes considerable social distance between high- and low-ranking subgroups given the limits of political-economic expansion in the context of a rank hegemony as discussed above. The problem at hand hence becomes one of social stratification over the long run and its relationship to regional political consolidation and the legitimation of an elevated chiefship.

Incipient-class status-group distinctions could have developed within locally centralized simple chiefdoms through the continual extension and readjustment of political alliances along with the long-term fission and fusion of both high- and low-ranking subgroups. Wright (1984:49) notes that "with time, intermarriages and disputes among the ranking families will disperse claimants to office." The net effect of dispersal, marriage alliances, and the engagement by high-ranking subgroups in prestige-related warfare would have been the emergence of a shared interregional elite identity. A shared identity ultimately could have engendered elite endogamy, although this may have been denied as a rule within the cultural tradition (e.g., Firth 1983:339; Hickey 1982:38). Even where exogamous relations and kin ties with the local community were immutable rules, the net result of high-ranking marriage networks, especially where polygamy existed, could have been endogamous tendencies within elite groupings at regional or interregional levels (cf. Bargatzby 1988). Moreover, given the interregional networks of high-ranking subgroups, the expansion of one high-ranking core would have entailed the expansion of the other core groups with which it interacted. Such mutually beneficial expansion of articulated cores would have occurred even where power imbalances also were reproduced (Spencer 1982:53–56; e.g., Southall 1956:227). The regional development of the cores, however, would have amounted to the increased peripheralization of low-ranking subgroups.

Intermarriage among low-ranking subgroups would have removed many from the "prospects of exercising chieftainship" (Buck 1949:338). The prestige of, the protection offered by, or the benefits of being attached to a particular high-ranking subgroup would have served as a basis for the realignment of low-ranking subgroup alliances and the physical reposi-tioning of these subgroups across the landscape (e.g., Leach 1965:98, 163, 168). This process of subgroup dispersal could have redefined the graded rank distinctions into relations between patrons and clients by loosing the subgroups from their traditional kin-ethic of reciprocity in lieu of more advantageous political-kin alliances and a patron-client ethic (cf. Brumfiel and Earle 1987; Webster 1990). That is, the function of kinship—albeit not the form—may have been transformed under these conditions (see Wolf 1966:2–3). These conditions, as socially reproduced, would have set the stage for the consolidation of chiefly authority on a regional level, al-though they need not be seen as necessarily resulting in regionally central-ized polities.

Wolf (1982:97) proposes that the transformation of kin-ordered to tributary modes of production occurred as follows:

> [T]he form and idiom of kinship may be maintained even as a dominant group transforms divisions of rank into divisions of class. . . . The pursuit of affinal strategies requires that the chiefly lineage concentrate wealth from marriage exchanges in its own hands. This implies . . . widen[ing] elite control over affinal exchanges [and] . . . inheritance. . . . [T]erritorial proliferation of high-ranking personnel may create a plurality of power centers. . . . Members of the chiefly lineage can become contenders for the chiefship, or create new domains of their own by separating from the parent body. Competition for power feeds back, in turn, upon the processes of accumulation and redistribution. Contenders for power must accumu-late adequate "funds of power" and redistribute them selectively to gain followers, rather than open resources to general redistribution.

Wright (1984:49–50) sums up the process of the emergence of complex chiefdoms as follows:

> Whatever the explanation of the development of a chiefly class, each family within it will have far-flung marriage alliances, very different from the local networks of commoners. Claims of geographically distant prestigious links or temporally distant divine links will be emphasized in the competition for offices. Once office is achieved, one's ritual prerogatives will be bol-

stered with claims to cosmic powers resulting from these links. As such claims to power become grander, the need to materially reciprocate commoners for their gifts becomes less, and "reciprocity" or "redistribution" can be transformed into tribute mobilization. . . . The centripetal flow of tribute must aggrandize the center, simultaneously giving the paramount the possibility of becoming more than a first among equals and making the other office holders permanent political and ritual subsidiaries.

Both constructs leave the question of rate open (Gledhill 1988:12–13). Both also leave the problem of the areal extent of control unaddressed. Such a transformation might have occurred in a relatively confined space, the subjugation of the larger region and the transformation of society and economy occurring at a gradual pace. Conversely, an avaricious officeholder might have subjugated a wide area in an abrupt manner. Greater or lesser strategic emphasis by a high-ranking subgroup on a certain political strategy, such as those resulting in or entailed by warfare, would have variable impact on both the rate and scale at which such a transformation occurred.

Modes of Regional Political Consolidation

As described above, power asymmetries among the factions within a political arena were an unavoidable component of simple chiefly formations. The consolidation of authority by a high-ranking subgroup was motivated by nothing more than the intent to reproduce these asymmetries as they had come to be. Yet the regional consolidation of chiefly authority or the formation of a complex chiefdom may have occurred slowly or rapidly, may have incorporated a small or large portion of a region, and may have been accomplished with or without significant bloodshed.

In practice, officeholders or potential consolidators may have acted based to varying degree on a *concern-for-self* or a *concern-for-others*—by which is meant their low-ranking kin (figure 2.2; cf. Kuper 1965:69). Their accommodating, collaborating, arrogant, or avoidant political stance and thus the rate and scale of consolidation would have depended in part on the historical configuration of the cultural hegemony (within which their own consciousness would have formed) at the point of regional consolidation (figure 2.3). Of these stances, political avoidance probably would not have led to regional consolidation; certainly there are ethnohistoric accounts of officeholders who avoided territorial expansion while others sought it (e.g., Powell 1967:190; Southall 1956:227). Under these and other historical conditions, regional consolidation may never have occurred.

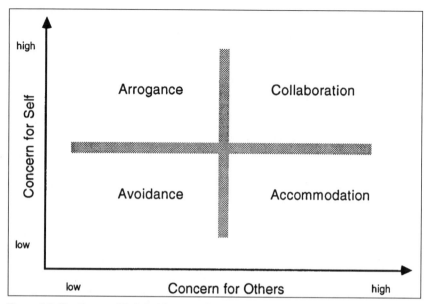

Figure 2.2. The Range of Political Stances of Actors

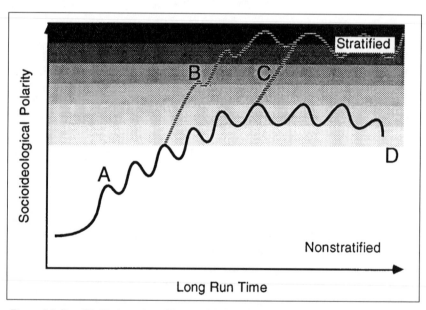

Figure 2.3. Possible Trajectories of Regional Political Consolidation: (a) Consolidation Unlikely; (b) Consolidation Possible (aggressive, collaborative strategies required to maintain it); (c) Consolidation Possible (arrogant strategies may maintain it); (d) Consolidation Never Occurs

A gradual consolidation of power, perhaps on the order of decades, is consistent with accommodative tactics or a historical situation in which the political actions of high-ranking subgroups (interregional elite-group formation, warfare, and exchange) were equally weighted. Where class had not interpenetrated tradition, it is doubtful that accommodative tactics could have led to regional consolidation. Through accommodative tactics, the asymmetries of the political arena gradually would have been reproduced as the incremental increases of tribute flowing toward a powerful center. That is, increasing centralization of certain ritual, productive, and distributive controls, which increasingly would have included the neighboring centers as subordinates, would have been made possible through the increased funds-of-power via an expanding resource base. This may have been facilitated by high-ranking subgroup fissioning (e.g., Mair 1964:119; Mitchell 1956:68; Sahlins 1985:44; Southall 1956:230; Terray 1978:289–290). Members of the incipient paramount subgroup would have acted to reproduce this changed set of relations, leading perhaps to the aggrandizement of the paramount center and the peripheralization of the subordinate or subsidiary centers (figure 2.4).

The increasing funds-of-power would have been used in an accommodative-consolidation trajectory to extend the interregional alliances and control over exotic sumptuary items or raw materials and claims to distant or supernatural sources of power by controlling the local production of craft goods for use in long-distance exchanges or local distribution. Control would have been facilitated by subsidizing skilled craftspersons at the center(s) of chiefly administration, contributing to the social and demographic transformation of the center (Brumfiel and Earle 1987; Earle 1987b; Welch 1991:176–178). The craft itself, or the artisan even, might have assumed a sacral quality in local arenas (Helms 1992:188). Warfare may have been an additional means of accruing prestige in accommodating traditional limitations on authority but—given a rank hegemony—would have been less an alternative for controlling land or permanently subjugating rivals. Among the ethnographic and ethnohistoric cases of chiefly formations, warfare was an immediate political strategy that often did not involve the acquisition of territory, slaves, or booty or result in decisive outcomes or large numbers of casualties.[4]

The accommodative-consolidation process could be expected only

4. For examples of chiefly warfare, see Buck 1949:346; Earle 1987a:297; Gibson 1974; Hadfield 1920:170; Kirch 1984:197ff.; Kuper 1965:126; Leach 1965:91–92; Little 1967:242ff.; Hann 1988:chapter 8; Oberg 1955:484; Oliver 1974:chapter 12; Peebles and Kus 1977:444; Roosevelt 1987:154; Rountree 1989:85–87; Wilson 1990.

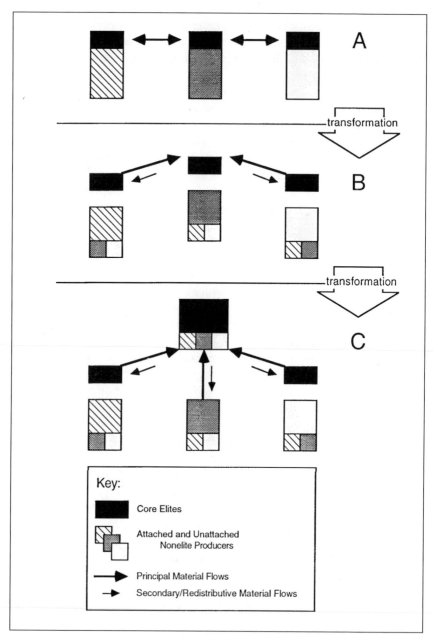

Figure 2.4. The Transformation of Local Chiefly Polities into a Regionally Centralized Polity (highlighting the detachment and relocation of subgroups)

where incipient class distinctions had crosscut the ranked hierarchy and would have resulted in a region being enveloped in an incremental fashion, perhaps involving chiefdoms in the process of being subordinated by more than one dominant group (e.g., Little 1967:247). However, the regional consolidation may have assumed a less incremental appearance if, at some point, an elite faction(s) was able to place its members or allies in the offices of a number of formerly quasi-autonomous neighboring chiefdoms at the same time (*sensu* Sahlins 1972:144). Comaroff's (1982) account of the twentieth-century Tshidi of southern Africa lays out a concrete example: "[W]here some measure of hierarchization was present, it became possible for the officeholder to build a power base by creating material and political alliances, often expressed in affinity, with influential individuals, and by contriving segmentary relations within the ruling descent group so as to reduce some agnates to subordinate status. If successful, this permitted the placing of supporters in important positions and encouraged the consolidation of a faction of 'chief's men,' for whom centralization . . . became a shared interest (Comaroff 1982:158)."

The placing of supporters in chiefships beyond the local office would have linked the two or more (formerly competing) chiefly centers in a dominant-subordinate relationship (e.g., Beinart 1982:13; Kuper 1965:57; Lambert 1971:155; Little 1967:247; Mair 1964:141; Richards 1940:84, 90; Riesenberg 1968:61; Southall 1956:57, 77, 187–188). Where such relationships had not previously existed, this extension of the chiefly domain would have constituted the first phase of regional political consolidation that might have proceeded rapidly afterwards (Service 1971:141–143). Since subsidiary officials and members of the paramount's own court would have been potential usurpers of the paramount office (Webster 1975:466), it would have behooved the paramount to restrict the number of officials and the complexity of the political hierarchy (Wright 1984:43). The pragmatic officeholder would have eliminated the threat of potential rivals. Likewise, while the paramount would have exerted control over the subsidiary officials, these officials would have retained considerable authority over their own local districts.

This sort of consolidation conforms more to a collaborative political strategy and may have involved violent upheaval (warfare, assassination, and so on) and group subjugation. In fact, it is arguable that warfare necessarily would have been a prominent component of achieving regional dominance under some sociohistorical circumstances: "Chiefs who want to break through the limitations of the kin order must lay hold of mechanisms that can guarantee them independent power over resources. Such chiefs must either allocate some of the labor under their control to another mode, or enter into the relations of that mode directly, be it as tributary overlords or as participants in capitalist production. To effect such change requires new political instruments of domination . . . (Wolf 1982:99)."

Warfare is one such instrument of domination that takes on added significance in terms of the rate and scale of the regional consolidation of political authority. It could have provided the means of circumventing the brakes of a traditional rank hegemony. Speaking of precolonial Fiji, Thomson (1908:59) declares, "Had there been no war . . . the power of the aristocracy would have been limited." He continues: "The chief of a conquering tribe rose to be head of a complicated social body; the members of his tribe an aristocracy supported by the industry of an alien plebs composed of tribes they had conquered and fugitives from other conquerors" (Thomson 1908:59). Pervasive warfare in certain historical settings may have been a significant factor in the restructuring of chiefly rules of succession and the disarticulation of traditional community kin ties (e.g., Buck 1934; Linares 1977:65–70; Oliver 1974:777–782). Terray (1975:114) provides an account of the expansion of the Abron kingdom in Africa whose elite practiced "quiet infiltration as well as violent warfare in order to enslave the country." They knew "well how to profit from the heterogeneity and divisions among the resident populations" (Terray 1975:114).

On the other hand, the consolidation of regional power in the absence of incipient class relations might have been unlikely if too wide a rift were created between tradition and the political world of core elites, as in the arrogant overlord scenario advocated by Carneiro (1981). The political economy in an arrogant trajectory would have included the violent acquisition of territory, material goods, and slaves or captives along with the subjugation of populations (Carneiro 1981:65–67). This is a different kind of warfare by virtue of its intensity (Rey 1975:49–50). An illustration is found in the Vietnamese central highlands where from time to time a leader in one village would "gain ascendancy over several other villages, forcing them to supply him with warriors" (Hickey 1982:37). In one instance, allied chiefly families under Kdam Yi defeated rival chiefs in war. He "took not only their belongings but also their serfs and all the inhabitants of the villages they ruled" (Hickey 1982:38). This sort of overlordship, however, normally ended with the death of the chief (Hickey 1982:38), perhaps—if we can take this account at face value—a sign of the incongruity between the high-ranking political aspirations and subordinate ideologies (cf. Leach 1965:89). Indeed, the disjunction between the collective consciousness of commoners and the political tactics of the overlord would have severely limited the legitimation of superordinate authority.

While there is no reason to accept the specific argument by which Carneiro (1981) derives both social ranking and stratification, it is useful to consider warfare as it pertains to his assertion that it permitted a "threshold" to be crossed (Carneiro 1981:38), or that it served as the means by which, to borrow Sahlins's phrase again, the constraints—the kin-reciprocity ethic—could be breached. Without such an instrument of domination, the factional disputes within the emerging superordinate stratum and the resistance of subordinates in the context of a rank hegemony may have greatly inhibited regional consolidation.

Even where warfare was the means by which a high-ranking subgroup established regional dominance, continued aggression in itself could not have sustained the new paramountcy since the consensual integration of primary producers would have been necessary in an expanding political economy (given the stipulations of practice theory as articulated with the Gramscian notion of hegemony). Conquest and capture is not a reliable means of reproducing authority in the long term; an arrogant strategy is viable only in the short term or in relations with nonlocal rivals. Instead, the superordinate stratum would have had to promote a sense of organic solidarity between ranked subgroups or a kind of "kinship coalition" with the subordinate clientele (Wolf 1966). The appearance and dissolution of regional consolidation within a span of a generation thus might signal an arrogant overlord rather than a collaborative chief.

In a collaborative political development, the generosity of the high-ranking subgroup(s) and the sanctity of chiefly office could have increased uniformly with the expansion of the domain. A dramatic increase in chiefly power brought about by the subjugation of other high-ranking subgroups might have been acceptable even in the context of a rank hegemony due to the nominal sharing of benefits with a large corpus of followers—the collaboration of patron and client (Webster 1975:468). In other words, a chiefly ideology—itself fettered by the ranked, kin-based organizations—could have provided the basis for the actions of high-ranking individuals which transformed a kin-based altruistic ethic simply by reproducing (or promoting) the local bonds of solidarity but not the more distant (competitive) relations.

Chiefship Transformed

The problem of how regional consolidation occurred has been related to the political actions of high-ranking individuals in political arenas, the resistance and alienation of low-ranking clients, and the long-term cultural-hegemonic process. The regional consolidation of political authority entailed the establishment of a paramount officeholder over lesser chiefly officeholders—a complex chiefly hierarchy. The paramountcy and the regionally consolidated polity, however, need not have corresponded with divine chiefship or consolidated sacral authority, respectively. Transformations of chiefship could have occurred in a number of ways related to the rate and scale of political consolidation.

Under incremental-consolidation conditions, the gradual development of the divine chiefship and a chiefly ideology legitimizing class relations would have paralleled increasing consolidation. The transformation of the social and physical landscape and the incremental centralization of ritual activities at a paramount administrative center would have occurred at the same pace, the center itself gaining a sort of inertia by appropriating the sacred (cf. Steponaitis 1978:449).

Where dramatic, large-scale political realignment occurred—as under arrogant or collaborative strategies—the center of the overlordship or new paramountcy would have been abruptly altered as a mark of the deposition of the old order and the imposition of the new, perhaps a signifier in a larger discourse between the paramount and the paramount's followers. Where the overlord or paramount collaborated with loyal followers in a kind of kinship coalition, the consolidation or materialization of sacral authority would have appeared *subsequent* to a period of dramatically increased elite-controlled distribution of valuables, elite-subsidized production of material objects, demographic restructuring, and the intensification and control over production of comestibles. In other words, given sociohistorical circumstances in which some degree of a rank hegemony influenced the actions of individuals, the post-consolidation collaboration could have been a means by which the increased claims to authority could have been legitimized.

Whereas the political consolidation of a region in an incremental manner (e.g., via accommodative tactics) might have provided less opportunity for structural failure given the progressive alienation of subgroups, there may have been a high potential for structural disintegration where consolidation was abrupt and large scale. The political instabilities of such a newly imposed order would have corresponded to the difficulties of grooming an heir for an orderly succession given the factionalism and political instability of complex chiefly hierarchies (see Abrahams 1966; Comaroff 1978; Helms 1980:727; Marcus 1977; Wright 1984). The political tactics of the paramount, given the structural weaknesses of such an arrangement consolidated (in a rapid manner) under a rank hegemony, might have included some element of "populism" (Marcus 1989:178) perhaps not unlike that which characterized the Powhatan of seventeenth-century Virginia (Barker 1992). Populism as a political ploy might not have been necessary in a situation where the mode of consolidation involved smaller-scale expansions of the chiefly domain over a longer period of time or where elite-commoner divisions already had become the common-sense understanding of the world.

Counteracting the fissioning tendencies and structural weaknesses of the large-scale consolidated political hierarchy meant establishing regional control over the means of legitimation. Increased sanctity would have provided an effective means of legitimation. The successful paramount would have sought to increase production of prestige goods to be passed out to followers or to enlarge and intensify interregional exchange relations. In a related vein, the successful paramount could have sought to control the symbols and meanings of local domains to benefit the new political structure. Rapid social and cultural change could have accompanied such a political-religious movement. Paramount political tactics also might have included extending claims into the realm of the supernatural, creating a political-religious milieu in some ways like that associated with western missionization (cf. Comaroff and Comaroff 1986; Morrison 1985; Simmons 1983).

With time, the popularity or religiosity of the paramount could have translated into the assimilation of traditional forms of consciousness or subordinate ideologies with elite ideas of social order, thereby permitting class to interpenetrate common sense. Given subordinate resistence rooted in extant nonelite ideologies, however, such interpenetration or diffusion might have required a generation to occur. A new generation of subordinates whose consciousness had been molded in part under the conditions of regional consolidation may have been less resistant to elite ethics and worldviews.

As the establishment of a regional control hierarchy was based to greater or lesser extent on an already established sanctity of chiefly office, increased sanctity would have been a component of the continued expansion of the political economy. Ultimately, consolidation of sacral authority would have been the promotion of the paramountcy in which the officeholder became the lord of time and space. Cosmogony and cosmography would have been co-opted by a chiefly ideology in which aristocratic and commoner subgroups would have defined themselves less in terms of horizontal kin ties and more as they related to the paramount. The commoners "united" with the aristocracy in a sort of "hierarchical solidarity" would in fact have been alienated from their own social reproduction (Sahlins 1985:45, 51). They would have had no history without the elite.

The divine chiefship would have been at the temporal and spatial center of the universe. Commoners would have become the subjects of appropriation in a hierarchy in which authority was exercised for the benefit of the elite rather than common interests.

The appropriation of products and labor would have been a legitimate right of the elite within what would have been becoming a "tributary mode of production" (Wolf 1982). In these contexts, the mobilization of support for the elite stratum may have taken the form of direct or indirect collections of food, valuables, or labor. Labor may have been supplied, and tribute may have been carried to administrative centers during ritual events. Tribute may have been collected by a visiting paramount chief and the chief's entourage. In addition, it may have been funneled to the paramount from the primary producers through local elite officials.[5]

The elite could have reciprocated in a token manner to commoners through sponsoring ritual events and feasts or by providing food from elite storehouses in times of shortage. More important (from a practice-theory perspective), the elite would have been able to demonstrate the legitimacy of their claims to the sacred by virtue of their control over ritual events. This control would have provided the context for the reconciliation of disparate ideas, beliefs, and values or the appropriation of commoner consciousness by an elite ideology (Kus 1983). Elites reproducing their worldviews, ethos, and cultural values would have done so by ritually projecting a set of elite ideas about their place in the world and their relationship to the forces beyond that world (see Pauketat and Emerson 1991). Successful projection or diffusion of these ideas would have amounted to successful social reproduction. The diffusion of such elite ideas or the appropriation of subaltern ideologies by this dominant ideology would have happened over decades or even centuries. The ultimate alienation of the nonelite from their former ideologies or the appropriation of their traditional consciousness would have amounted to Sahlins's (1985) "hierarchical solidarity" in which a nonelite class was cut off from its own social reproduction.

The increasing identification of the elite with the temporally and

---

5. For examples of support mobilization, see Chilver and Kaberry 1967:142; Earle 1978:183–92; Ekholm 1972; Goldman 1970:505–11; Goody 1982:63; Hadfield 1920:33; Hann 1988:105; Knight 1990:11; Lambert 1966:162–63, 1971:154; Lehman 1963:141, 149; Mair 1964:161–62; Malinowski 1961:153ff.; Oberg 1955:485; Peebles and Kus 1977:425–26; Read 1970:67; Richard 1961:252ff.; Riesenberg 1968:77–83; Roosevelt 1987:154; Rountree 1989; Sahlins 1958:4–5; Salomon 1986:130; Schapera 1940:68; Smith and Hally 1992; Southall 1956:79ff.; Steponaitis 1978:422–26; Taylor 1975:38; Vansina 1962:326.

spatially distant unknowns as a component of a nonstate class hegemony ultimately could have led to a situation in which the commoners would have been shielded from the potent and dangerous supernatural powers of elite officeholders (Sahlins 1985:97). As near-sacred beings, the person and activities of elite officeholders would have assumed an aura of sacrality, a divine presence in this world. As in Polynesia, Africa, or southeastern North America, the paramount might have been elevated to the status of a local god, with the nonreligious, aggressive, or warrior functions becoming the task of young elite individuals or junior lines of descent (Scarry 1990:243; Sahlins 1985:90–99). The days of populism or of a collaborative chiefship would have been long gone.

It is important to situate this divine chiefship not in the political arena per se but in the cultural hegemony. The chiefly ideology as it had come to guide the practice of elite individuals would not have been a ruse or a screen to dupe nonelite subjects knowingly and intentionally. The elite ideology would have promulgated the central values and beliefs, including that paramount office embodied order and sanctity. In a loose sense, elite perceptions of their responsibilities to underlings would have been altered to the point that we may identify a chiefly theocracy of sorts, a divine chiefship based on a nonstate class hegemony.

Elite actions in a chiefly theocracy would have been tantamount to an arrogant strategy since the rift between aristocrat and commoner would have been perceived as great. The elite would have acted in opposition to commoners, not in collaboration with them. Accommodative or collaborative political strategies on the part of paramount lords would not necessarily have been a component of the reproduction of sacral authority. Maintaining the divine chiefship status quo may not have involved expanding or intensifying the political economy at the same pace as had been the case prior to the consolidation of sacral authority. Witness, for example, the modern-day sanctity of Polynesian chiefly heirs in the absence of any action on their part to reproduce that sanctity (Firth 1979:159; Marcus 1977:298, 1989:196). However, the falling rate of expansion may have reduced the ability of lesser elites to acquire the prestige goods (via the paramount) that they needed to maintain their own following (Pauketat 1992).

It is questionable whether such a high level of elite sanctity and concomitant arrogant tactics would have been compatible with the structural weaknesses of a chiefly political hierarchy. The internal dissention and external competition that wracked elite subgroups could have placed an upper limit to political expansion. The increasing tributary demands placed upon primary producers could have been met with considerable nonelite resistance, itself rooted in preclass subordinate ideologies. The contradictions between the stratified social order and the common-sense components of traditional ideologies may have found expression in the growth of factional opposition to the paramount and the rebellious actions of lesser elites. The growth of factionalism could well have initiated a decentralizing process irreversible in the short term (Pauketat 1992). Given one or more secular crises under these sociohistorical conditions of "administrative stress" (Scarry 1990), structural collapse might have ensued (cf. Comaroff 1982:158).

Yet structural collapse need not have been total. The usurpation of power by lesser elites could have served as a means of reinstating collaborative and accommodative tactics. However, because a dominant ideology of class had become a component of the cultural hegemony, recentralization on a regional level would have taken on a much different character than the initial consolidation of regional control.

Summary and Theoretical Propositions

Sociopolitical development rests on the historical processes involving the consciousness of human beings (Jacobitti 1983:382). Actors conduct themselves relative to this consciousness—as it was socially defined by ideologies within a dynamic cultural hegemony—reproducing and transforming the cultural tradition. Social classes and the emergence of the sovereign have their beginnings in the nonstate transformations of simple ranked groups into regionally centralized polities. In order to comprehend these Leviathanic transformations, it is necessary to measure how change occurred.

Where social ranking and institutionalized chiefly office existed, it can be expected that interelite competition would have provided the basis for the initial disconnection of both high- and low-ranking subgroups from the traditional community. The degree of such disconnection or the rate at which it might have occurred is very much a matter of the sociohistorical specificities of individual cases as these involved chance political outcomes, warfare, or interannual variability in food production within and between polities. Ultimately, the disarticulation of traditional reciprocal bonds between and among high- and low-ranking subgroups may have resulted in patron-client social relations.

Sometime during this long-term development of simple chiefly hierarchies, the political strategies of elite individuals—by reproducing the configuration of power relations as they had come to be—may have included the firming up of regional alliances by subordinating or otherwise gaining control over the territory and chiefships of rivals. This regional consolidation would have taken different forms depending upon when and how it was accomplished. Where this occurred as a large-scale event, we should find archaeological evidence of a qualitative shift in all aspects of social life and in the residues derived from elite-controlled exchange networks (due to the dramatically expanded economic base of the consolidated polity). Where this occurred as a series of small-scale events, no short-term qualitative changes should be visible. Rather, continuous increase in the kinds of exotic goods, the signs of craft-goods production subsidization, and the tribute mobilized toward the regional capital should be in evidence.

The configuration of the post-consolidation cultural hegemony will be archaeologically visible as the kinds of centralized and subsidized production activities and as the material symbols of the newly elevated chiefship. Indication of the rate and scale of nonstate regional consolidation will be reflected in archaeological artifact assemblages (of disposed household possessions and production debris), architectural remains, and community organization. Where a large-scale integrative event occurred in the context of a rank hegemony or in the early stages of a class hegemony (where chiefship was not yet the political-religious high office that it was in certain New and Old World divine chiefships), the successful reproduction of the new paramountcy would have left behind signatures of a collaborative chiefship. These signatures, relative to earlier and later phases of political-economic development, would include evidence for dramatically increased levels of craft production, labor mobilization, material redistribution, and centralized administration of interregional exchange. Such signatures also would include contextual evidence of the increased prominence or altered meanings of political-religious symbols.

These qualitatively distinct signatures of a collaborative chiefship would contrast markedly with the archaeological traces of incremental change associated with an accommodative chiefship based on a gradual regional consolidation and nonelite acceptance of a class hegemony. Where a small area was initially included in the consolidation, where the process was drawn out, or where the success of the regional integration floundered over a lengthy period of time, temporal coincidence of changes in the social and physical environments will be lacking. The density of exotic goods and craft-goods residues, for instance, will appear to increase gradually through time without dramatic qualitative increases.

In short, the larger the region encompassed by political consolidation, the greater the rift between the material assemblages, architectural form, and community organization that precede consolidation and all subsequent traces. The length of time that it took for substantial alterations of the demographic structure of a region would have paralleled the extent of consolidated political control. Likewise, the subsequent form and developmental trajectory of paramount authority would have depended to some extent upon the configuration of the cultural hegemony at the point of consolidation. Ultimately, the efflorescence of sacral authority as the full expression of nonstate stratification is linked to the mode of consolidation and the strategic stance of elite officeholders. The crystallization of nonstate class relations where the chiefship was elevated to the divine represents the fullest expression of nonstate hierarchization. The contradictions within such a class hegemony, however, would have included decentralization as a component of centralization (Pauketat 1992). Barring reintegration of the hierarchy into a state, the collapse of the paramountcy was likely (see Wright 1977, 1986). The expansion of paramount authority, a definitional characteristic of chiefly political economy (Service 1971; Spencer 1982), would not have been possible beyond a certain threshold given the structural limitations of chiefly hierarchies.

From the theoretical perspective developed in this study, it is important to understand the dissolution of a regionally integrated polity in the context of long-term cultural change. Minor political upheavals, succession disputes, or food-production failures were probably all sources of political-economic contraction and perhaps sources of secular change, which is to say "change in the specific persons or groups occupying specific structural positions" (Welch 1991:191). Oscillation of the political economy may have materialized as fluctuations of exotic-material or craft-production refuse. However, from the cultural-hegemonic perspective advocated in this study, it is not anticipated that these minor political-economic fluctuations or secular changes alone would have resulted in large-scale structural disintegration of the elite-nonelite social relations.

Given a divine chiefship, however, structural change or political-economic dissolution could have resulted from increasing factionalism in the face of nonelite resistance to the expanding demands of an elite stratum. Socioideological contradictions may not have been alleviated through secular change. The signs of collapse of the regional power base— a "structural change" by virtue of its being a change in social relations (Welch 1991:191)—should be apparent in the form of a reduction of exotic-goods circulation, a decrease of centralized and subsidized production activities, and a loss of access to the large labor pools that characterized earlier phases of regional integration. Potentially, collapse could be followed by reconsolidation, as occurred in various parts of the world in prehistory (see Friedman and Rowlands 1978; Wright 1984). However, the main point remains that secular change would not have resolved the contradictions within the formation, necessarily grasped in terms of the historical development of a cultural hegemony. The limits of chiefly control and expansion would have been reached.

Chapter 3

The Sociohistorical Context of the American Bottom Region

Nonstratified and stratified native polities integrated local areas or entire regions in the North American Southeast and midcontinent during the late-prehistoric and early-historic periods (see Barker and Pauketat 1992). The "Mississippi period" is dated from about A.D. 1000 to the time of European contact, depending on the specific local historical setting (Smith 1986; Steponaitis 1986). In the American Bottom, there is little evidence of Mississippian inhabitants after A.D. 1400 (Jackson, Fortier, and Williams 1992).

Mississippian, then, is a term used by archaeologists to identify a late-prehistoric temporal period but also to identify an organizational "adaptation" and a configuration of cultural elements in the Southeast (see Brown 1985; Dye and Cox 1990; Ford 1974; Griffin 1985, 1990; Knight 1986; Morse and Morse 1983; Muller 1986:170–178; Peebles 1990:26–29; Smith 1978a, 1978b, 1984, 1990b; Williams and Shapiro 1990). As an "adaptation," Mississippian is said to be a maize-field agricultural system featuring a hereditary manager-chief (see Muller 1986; Smith 1978a). As a configuration of cultural elements, it has been seen as a set of disparate traits (i.e., rectangular wall-trench houses, substructure platform mounds, and shell-tempered pottery) and a Native American socioreligious organization, ritual pattern, or worldview as it involved social hierarchy and agricultural fertility (see Brown 1985; Griffin 1967, 1985, 1990; Hudson 1984:6–11; Knight 1986).

Given the polysemy that underlies the present-day usage of Mississippian, judicious application of the term seems wise. If we discuss Mississippian economy, Mississippian society, Mississippian worldview, and a Mississippi(an) period all in the same breath, how can we hope to explain "its" emergence? The formalization of the "Emergent Mississippian" concept is but a recognition of this lack of isomorphism between the various material, social, and ideational realms (e.g., Kelly 1990a). "There is no single, simple, all encompassing and comforting theoretical explanation for the Mississippian emergence" (Smith 1990a:2) because there is no single, all-encompassing monolith called Mississippian. In a similar vein, it is necessary to recognize the temporal and spatial fluidity of the ideas, beliefs, and values between and *within* late-prehistoric Southeastern groups. Particular sociohistorical formations should be the focus of our efforts, from there establishing the spheres of elements shared between subgroups and groups as these elements found meaning at local and supralocal levels (Smith 1984:30, 1990a:1–3).

No matter how the term is applied, most Southeastern archaeologists regard Mississippian as an archaeological "culture" (e.g., Knight 1986:677; cf. Peebles 1990:25). Differences in points of view seem to stem from the extent to which Mississippian is seen in "anthropocentric" or "geocentric" terms, to use Hall's distinction (1977). Those who favor a geocentric or adaptationist definition see Mississippian as an adaptive *cultural system*. Those who favor an anthropocentric perspective integrate notions of worldview, cosmology, and socioreligious institutions into discussions of the Mississippian *cultural tradition*.

A vice of the former includes the analytical separation of Mississippian from socioreligious phenomena—like the "Southeastern Ceremonial Complex"—engendering the relegation of the socioreligious to epiphenomenon (see Waring and Holder 1945; papers in Galloway 1989). This is partially a consequence of the connotations of uniformity evoked by a single concept (like Mississippian) and the vestiges of an early twentieth-century archaeological tradition that viewed Mississippians as distinct migrating populations who carried Culture and a socioeconomic pattern around the Southeast (Smith 1984).

The modern anthropocentric perspective represents something of a continuation of a pre-1960s culture-historical paradigm but only as it now treats political and sociological processes. Interestingly, even most of the anthropocentrically inclined researchers remain within a cultural-materialist paradigm where change originates not within the cultural, political, or socioreligious but from material contingencies (e.g., Knight 1986:682). Like the anthropocentric versus geocentric definitions of Mississippian, approaches to the explanation of the Mississippian emergence include those that focus on the independence of each regional development versus those that incorporate some element of dependency between regional formations (Smith 1990a:2). This "analogy-homology dilemma" is but an ongoing discourse in Eastern United States archaeology. Archaeologists writing in different decades or those drawing upon a particular anthropological school of thought weight differently the explanatory power of various ideational or material factors.

For instance, demography and domestic production are integral aspects of a social formation from any theoretical vantage point. However, if increasing population or the adoption of maize agriculture is seen as fundamentally generative—if they are used to explain the social and the ideological—then accounting for the Mississippian emergence becomes a simple question of techno-environmental determinism. Culture as ideational structure becomes secondary to the driving force of evolution, a mere overlay upon social relations as these reflect subsistence contingencies. This particular perspective, made most forcefully in recent years by Muller (1986; Muller and Stephens 1991), would appear to exclude social groups like "Upper Mississippian" entities outside the floodplains of the Southeast from the realm of explanation in Mississippian terms (cf. Conrad 1989:100; Emerson 1991:222).

From this strict ecological perspective, the unit of analysis is the biologically reproducing population. Intragroup social tensions, contradictory interests, and competing factions are not elements of importance in explanation (see Muller 1986:37–43). The Mississippi-period economy becomes a static, monolithic entity; variations in chiefly political structure are not recognized to be related to culture change (compare Muller 1978:288 with Anderson 1990 or Steponaitis 1978). Hence reference is made to "chiefdom-level" societies in general rather than attending to the dynamic political-structural variation, sociopolitical boundaries, or prestige-goods economies of individual polities as these relate to larger interregional formations (Cobb 1988:chapter 2; Muller 1986:38–43; see also Webster 1990).

Another theoretical point of view holds that ecology or economy cannot fully account for late-prehistoric dynamics (Marquardt 1985, 1986). The legitimation of institutionalized authority has been seen as related to the benefits of centralized buffering redistribution and chiefly protection of communal storehouses from outside raiders (e.g., Kelly 1990a; Morse and Morse 1990; Scarry 1990; Welch 1990). A "single level of hierarchical offices could have mitigated subsistence risks and carried out alliances" (Steponaitis 1983:173). Institutionalized authority may have emerged before or after the adoption of maize (Lynott et al. 1986; Welch 1990:220). In either case, simplification of the human ecosystem accompanied the transition to maize agriculture, increasing the risk of productive failure (see Ford 1974, 1977, 1979; Peebles and Kus 1977:443; Scarry 1986; Smith 1978a; Steponaitis 1983:173, 1986; Welch 1990:218).

However, Ford (1979:238) also has stated that agriculture itself was a consequence of sociocultural development. This perspective is similar to that advocated by Bender (1978:210–214) in that change is possible only as politically or socially mediated and hence we must explain change in social terms, not technoenvironmental ones. Viewing Mississippian as cultural system ignores this and conflates tradition and ecology. Emphasizing this analytical separation between tradition and ecology is Steponaitis's (1983:173) statement that the ecological argument is insufficient to explain a number of complex Native American polities in the Southeast. I suspect, as does he, that "the answer will not be found in any purely functional explanations that involve 'stresses' in the environment. Rather, it is conceivable that the development resulted from an interaction of social and ideational processes that, in large part, progressed with a momentum that was generated internally" (Steponaitis 1983:173).

Indeed, in the American Bottom the emergence of a single level of hierarchical offices does not correspond to the archaeologically recognized Mississippian tradition, but rather loosely correlates with the Emergent Mississippi Period. The efflorescence of the Mississippian tradition in the American Bottom appears coeval to the enlargement and elaboration of the Cahokia site. Given our current level of understanding, discussed in forthcoming pages, only with considerable pain can a physical-environmental explanation be fitted onto the Cahokia-Mississippian case.

The Physical-Environmental Setting

The American midcontinent is a land of considerable physiographic diversity. To the west of the Appalachian Highlands, south of the Great Lakes, and east of the Missouri River and the Great Plains lie the weakly to moderately dissected glaciated surfaces of the Central Lowlands (Thornbury 1965). To the south and bordering the Central Lowlands are the unglaciated Interior Low Plateau of southern Illinois, southern Indiana, and Kentucky and the rugged terrain of the unglaciated Ozark dome to the southwest in Missouri and Arkansas. The mid-South is dominated by the Mississippi alluvial plain, part of the Coastal Plain province that extends up through the Ozarks and the Interior Low Plateau (figure 3.1).

Just below the confluence of the Missouri, Illinois, and Mississippi rivers in the northern end of the American Bottom, the run-off from over 700,000 square miles of the American midcontinent passes through the channel of the Mississippi (Kelly 1980:8). From this point, the Mississippi River and its floodplain cut a path through till plains of the Central Lowland, the Ozarks, and the Shawnee Hills (of the Interior Low Plateau) southward to Thebes Gap where the ancient Ohio and Mississippi rivers met the Coastal Plain. The floodplain of the Mississippi River from this northern point south to the confluence of the Kaskaskia River, some 160

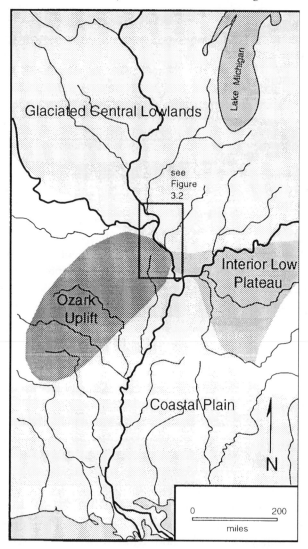

Figure 3.1. The Physiographic Regions of the North American
Midcontinent

kilometers in length, ranges from roughly 5 to 18 kilometers in width
(White et al. 1984:17). The floodplain in this 160-kilometer stretch—the
American Bottom—consists of Holocene fluvial and lacustrine deposits:
point bar ridges, natural levees, swales, sloughs, meander scars, and
terraces. These features are reminders of the dynamic degrading and
aggrading processes of the meandering Mississippi River during the

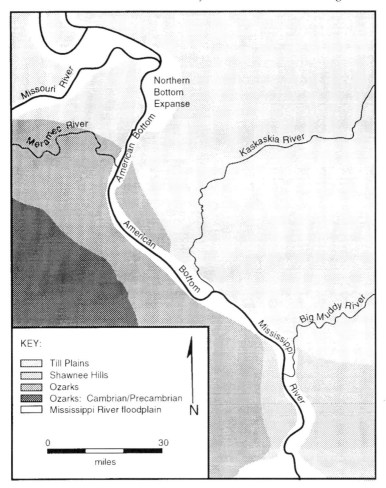

Figure 3.2. American Bottom Region Physiography

Pleistocene and Holocene epochs. The widest point is found in the north where the thinly bedded strata of Pennsylvanian-age sedimentary deposits permitted the waters of the ancient Mississippi and Missouri rivers to scour out a broad pocket of floodplain hereafter called the Northern Bottom Expanse (figure 3.2).

The American Bottom is bordered on both sides by bluff escarpments—the truncated beds of limestone and sandstone representing the edges of a broad geological syncline called the Illinois Basin to the east and the Ozark Uplift to the west (White et al. 1984:16; Willman et al. 1975). These bluffs, with the exception of the Northern Bottom Expanse, are vertical cliffs jutting up nearly 100 meters in some places. The subtle slopes of the northern bluffs consist of soft, thinly bedded coals, sandstones, shales, and limestones capped with thick deposits of löess. At the base of the bluffs is piled talus and colluvium. Upland streams unload reworked aeolian and glacial sediments upon entering the bottom from the east, resulting in the accretion of alluvial fans along its eastern margins. The Mississippi River runs along the western side of the bottom and appears to have done so for more than a thousand years, a result of the isostatic rebound of the formerly glaciated eastern uplands (Munson 1974; Yarbrough 1974).

For the last few millennia, the uplands to either side of the American Bottom were covered by hardwood forest, with scattered natural prairies in the well-drained interfluves of the northern glaciated portion of the region. Oaks and hickories dominated the wooded uplands; red cedars and hill prairies topped the bluff crests. Throughout the Holocene, the floodplain probably supported lush plant growth and animal life (cf. Smith 1978a:496). Writing in the early nineteenth century, Brackenridge (1814:186) described the American Bottom as "a tract of rich alluvial land, extending on the Mississippi, from the Kaskaskia to the Cahokia river, about eighty miles in length, and five in breadth; several handsome streams meander through it; the soil of the richest kind, and but little subject to the effects of the Mississippi floods. A number of lakes are interspersed through it, with high and fine banks; these abound in fish, and in the autumn are visited by millions of wild fowl."

Bottomland forest, grassland, and aquatic zones formed a patchwork of microhabitats on the floodplain (see Chmurny 1973; Fowler 1978:457–460; Gregg 1975; Hus 1908; Kelly 1980:chapter 2, 1990a:113–115; Milner 1990:5; Norris 1974:1–15; Welch 1975). Given the multiple finds of bald cypress wood recovered in archaeological contexts, it is possible that now-extinct cypress-lined rivers or oxbow lakes existed in the region or in nearby regions during late prehistory. A vast prairie noted by early Euro-American travelers covered portions of the Northern Bottom Expanse, notably in the vicinity of Cahokia, probably in part an anthropogenic effect of the late-prehistoric human occupation (see Brackenridge 1814:187; Fowler 1977:6–9, 1978:459, 1989:15–21; Hall 1980:452; Kelly 1990a:115).

The Pre-Mississippian Community

The late-prehistoric occupation of the American Bottom region preceding the expansion of Cahokia and the appearance of cultural elements identified as Mississippian includes terminal portions of the Late Woodland period and the subsequent Emergent Mississippi period. A summary of the archaeological chronology used to trace the diachronic social and economic trends of American Bottom late prehistory is followed by a survey of Late Woodland and Emergent Mississippian sociohistory.

Archaeological Chronology

The conventional archaeological chronology of the American Bottom region is based largely on ceramic seriations and uncalibrated radiocarbon assays. In the Northern Bottom Expanse, the end of the last phase of the Late Woodland period, called Patrick, has been dated to A.D. 750 (Fortier, Maher, and Williams 1991; Kelly 1990a, 1990b). A transitional Late Woodland to Emergent Mississippi "Sponemann" phase has been recognized in this northern area, although not in the central American Bottom. In fact, the remainder of the Emergent Mississippi period has been divided into parallel (but perhaps clinal) phase schemes for the northern and central portions of the American Bottom (figure 3.3). In the Northern Bottom Expanse around the Cahokia site, the Emergent Mississippi period has been broken down into four phases: Collinsville, Loyd, Merrell, and Edelhardt (Kelly et al. 1984; Kelly 1990a; Fortier et al. 1991). While A.D. 750 or 800 to 1000 is the conventional chronological span for the Emergent Mississippi period, Hall (1991) has presented a calibrated chronology that adjusts this frame to A.D. 925–1050.

In like manner, Hall's (1991) calibrated Mississippian chronology for the Northern Bottom Expanse represents a compression of the conventional uncalibrated chronology (Kelly 1990a; Milner et al. 1984). While his calibrated scheme represents a first approximation and questions exist about the uncritical use of certain FAI–270 assays, Hall's scheme does represent a step toward refining the existing chronology and will be adopted here. Using Hall's calibrated scheme, the Lohmann phase dates to A.D. 1050–1100, having as a loosely defined counterpart the Lindhorst phase to the south (Kelly 1990a). The subsequent Stirling phase occupies a 100-year span (A.D. 1100–1200). The Moorehead and Sand Prairie phases date to A.D. 1200–1275 and A.D. 1275–1350, respectively (figure 3.3). The Sand Prairie phase apparently witnessed the intrusion of a Bold Counselor Oneota occupation into the bottom around A.D. 1300 (Jackson et al. 1992).

My own seriation of Tract 15A and Dunham Tract (15A-DT) pottery[1]

1. Using K-Means clustering algorithms and multidimensional scaling. The temporally sensitive variables used in the formation of Emergent Mississippian and Lohmann

has produced a series of subphases that may be used to subdivide further the 15A-DT remains (Pauketat 1991b). There are three Emergent Mississippian subphases (EM-1, EM-2, EM-3), three Lohmann subphases (L-1, L-2, L-3), two Stirling subphases (S-1, S-2), and two Moorehead subphases (M-1, M-2). The first Emergent Mississippian subphase is poorly represented in the 15A-DT remains but corresponds to a portion of the Loyd phase. The subsequent Merrell phase also seems underrepresented among the 15A-DT remains, although the EM-2 subphase includes some late Merrell-phase remains among what otherwise corresponds to the early portions of the Edelhardt phase in the conventional chronology. The EM-3 subphase is the 15A-DT equivalent of the late Edelhardt phase. Presumably, the three Emergent Mississippian subphases each represent about two to three decades. The EM-2 to EM-3 subphases appear to constitute a continuous occupation between roughly A.D. 1000 to 1050, using the calibrated chronology.

The Edelhardt-to-Lohmann phase remains on Tract 15A seem to represent an unbroken occupational continuum. Since the Lohmann phase has been assigned to a fifty-year slot, the three Lohmann subphases may each represent two to three decades of occupation (like the EM-2 and EM-3 subphases). The two Stirling subphases probably encapsulate longer portions of time given the 100-year duration of the Stirling phase. Likewise, the two Moorehead subphases may each represent three to four decades within the calibrated seventy-five-year span.

Late Woodland Period

The Native American populations of the American midcontinent and Southeast had tended plants and cultivated gardens for millennia (Ford 1985), relying more heavily upon plants as staple crops down through the centuries: first cucurbits, then starchy and oily seed plants, and, last, Mesoamerican cultigens (Ford 1985; Johannessen 1984a; Smith 1992b). At around A.D. 600 in the American Bottom region, occupants of the hills and floodplain grew squash, gourd, tobacco, marsh elder, sunflower, and a variety of starchy seed plants like maygrass, goosefoot, little barley, and knotweed. Berries, fruits, wild beans, and nuts also were harvested along

---

subphases include percent of sherd temper and surface treatment attributes. The Stirling and Moorehead subphases were based on temporally sensitive jar rim ratio-scale attributes including lip-protrusion and rim-curvature indices (see Pauketat 1991b:chapter 4).

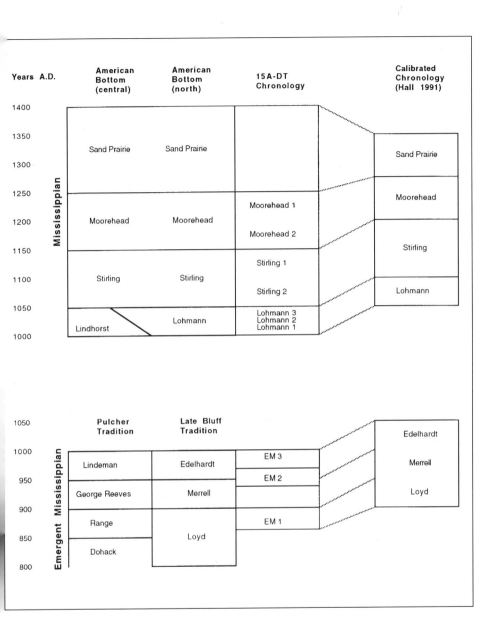

Figure 3.3. The Late-Prehistoric American Bottom Chronology

with other plant-food supplements (Johannessen 1984a:202–203, 1987; Johannessen and Whalley 1988). Maize was at best insignificant and perhaps entirely absent in the diets of most scattered Late Woodland social groups.

Depending on their immediate surroundings, animals taken for food included fish, white-tailed deer, fowl, and other small mammals, birds, and reptiles (Kelly and Cross 1984:226, 1988; L. Kelly 1987; cf. Kuttruff 1974:125–151; Styles 1981). The bow and arrow were probably adopted shortly after A.D. 600 (Kelly et al. 1984b:124) and may have affected hunting patterns, although it is conceivable that they had an equal if not greater impact on the efficacy of intergroup violence (Ford 1974:402–403; Hall 1980:436). In any case, reliance upon locally available aquatic and terrestrial fauna along with the gardening of the plant foods mentioned above continued a subsistence pattern that had developed in the midcontinent and Southeast over centuries.

The Patrick phase included aggregates of households in the Mississippi floodplain proper and in primary tributary valleys (see Kelly et al. 1984b; e.g., Binford et al. 1970; Kuttruff 1974). Small and perhaps short-term settlements were probably characteristic of some upland areas removed from major drainages (Bentz et al. 1988). The remains of communities that have been excavated in the American Bottom include small semi-subterranean and often-rebuilt keyhole-shaped huts arranged around small courtyards or in a linear fashion (Kelly 1990b:78–87; Kelly et al. 1987; Fortier et al. 1984). Also included in the village remains are large rectangular buildings that have been interpreted as functionally distinct dwellings (Kelly 1990a:119, 1990b:84–85; Kelly et al. 1987:176–178; Fortier et al. 1984:38–43, 217). Settlements varied from single-building homesteads to multiple-building hamlets or villages. The excavations at the Range site uncovered the remains of one community that had consisted of over thirty-five buildings (Kelly 1990b:79; Kelly et al. 1987:421–430).

There is no evidence of lasting intersubgroup social inequality within the community. Rather, the Patrick-phase remains have been used to argue for shifting, horticulturally based, segmentary social organizations (Kelly 1990b:86). Kelly (1990b:86) states that Patrick-phase "village-level communities are distinguished by the presence of multiple structure clusters" representing "larger social units composed of a number of households." These structures cluster rather loosely around courtyards, suggesting to Kelly (1990b:87) that control of village space by a segment of the community may have been sporadic at best.

This communal and horticultural social formation of the Patrick phase, however, is the antecedent of later Emergent Mississippian communities in which intersubgroup social inequality may have become institutional-ized. Already during the Patrick phase there exist signatures of horticul-tural intensification including large deep pits presumably "used for the storage of both wild and cultivated plants" and large thick-walled bowls presumably "used to parch seeds" (Kelly 1990a:122). Moreover, the den-sity of population as indicated by the number of sites and the areal extent and density of occupational debris at sites in the floodplain appears to have been increasing during the Patrick phase relative to earlier Late Woodland phases (Kelly 1990a:118). The material culture of the American Bottom at this time displayed a considerable homogeneity. For instance, pottery used throughout the region included grog-tempered and cordmarked conoidal jars and hemispherical bowls (Kelly et al. 1984b:plates 19–20). Decorative embellishment of pots typically consisted of notches or dowel impressions on the interior edges of vessel mouths.

Emergent Mississippi Period

Community organization, intercommunity interaction, food produc-tion, and material culture underwent marked shifts beginning in the ninth century A.D., using the calibrated chronology. Whereas maize is virtually absent from Late Woodland sites, 34 percent of the archaeological features at the transitional Late Woodland–Emergent Mississippi Sponemann site in the Northern Bottom Expanse produced carbonized maize (Parker 1991:416). Bits of maize are found in over half of the features associated with the Emergent Mississippian Dohack and Loyd phases (Kelly 1990a:126). By the late Emergent Mississippi period, maize was typically deposited in 70 percent of the features at any given site (Johannessen 1984a:203). The apparent addition or increased usage of certain vessel forms like stumpware and bowls as domestic utensils probably was related to this increased production of maize (Kelly 1980:145, 1990b:108).

Documented Emergent Mississippian habitation-site plans illustrate the increased significance of the central courtyard as a stable organiza-tional feature (Kelly 1990a; Kelly et al. 1990). A series of communities at the Range site featured small rectangular and semi-subterranean buildings of variable size—some with interior hearths and some rebuilt—arranged around courtyards. Already by the Dohack phase at the Range site, these courtyards contained a central post, four distinct central pits in a quadripartite arrangement and large rectangular buildings. The consis-tent emphasis on the courtyard and its central post or pit features has been interpreted to indicate that certain Native American notions of cosmologi-cal order were incorporated into the basal social fabric of Emergent

Mississippian life (Kelly 1990a:129–130). Although the evidence remains equivocal, here may be indication of the shift from a diffuse socio-ideological base to a centralized one in which a changing social order found legitimation in cosmological referents.

The diversity of building form and the complexity of the community configuration increased through the ninth and tenth centuries A.D. By the George Reeves phase at the Range site, community order appears to have consisted of a central courtyard group that included a large building (42 square meters) flanked by a series of other courtyard groups (Kelly 1990b:98).

> This community pattern marks a dramatic break with earlier occupational episodes at the Range site in that it represents the amalgamation of a number of different kinship groups at a single location. . . . This central plaza is . . . symmetrically flanked by a series of additional courtyards, each with its associated houses. . . . [T]his community pattern reflects the spatial distribution of a series of ranked social groups and represents the best evidence currently available for the initial emergence . . . of a ranked form of sociopolitical organization in the American Bottom region. Although no mound construction is present, the large rectangular structure at the one end of the central courtyard is perhaps the chief's house (Kelly 1990b:99).

There may have been around 100 structures within the bounds of a subsequent (Lindeman-phase) Range-site community. The spatial arrangement of buildings and pits in this largest of villages, however, was more compressed and contained fewer storage pits relative to earlier phases (Kelly 1990b:108). In fact, this compression and storage-pit reduction appear to have continued a Late Woodland–to–Emergent Mississippian trend at the Range site. This archaeological trend might reflect the increasing integration of households within the community, the increasing use of the landscape for crops rather than residences, and the changing methods or locations of household and communal storage (see Kelly 1990a, 1990b).

By the end of the Emergent Mississippi period at the Range site, the number of households within the community had been drastically reduced. This shrinking of community size may have been a consequence of the centralization of populations at local administrative centers (Kelly 1990b:105), perhaps even corresponding to the rise of Cahokia. No excavated confirmation is yet available from possible Emergent Mississippian centers nearby like the Lunsford-Pulcher site. Clearly, however, the Range site and most former large community aggregates in the Northern Bottom Expanse were reduced by the Mississippi period to small homesteads seldom supporting more than one household (Emerson 1991, 1992; Kelly 1990b; Mehrer and Collins 1989).

Possible Emergent Mississippian Administrative Centers

Kelly (1990a:135) anticipates that the same sort of Emergent Mississippian community plan as seen at the Range site, with principal courtyard groups featuring a prominent domicile flanked by other courtyards, may account for the distribution of mounds and artifactual debris at the nearby Lunsford-Pulcher site. Like the large structures at Range, the mounds at Lunsford-Pulcher may have been surmounted by community buildings or the houses of chiefly officeholders. Three large mounds are strung out along the east bank of Fish Lake with associated Emergent Mississippian artifactual debris spread out to the east of the mounds.

A series of such large archaeological sites featuring mounds is stretched out in a linear pattern, and sites are spaced 16 to 23 kilometers apart along the length of the American Bottom (figure 3.4). These may date to the Emergent Mississippi period (Kelly 1990a:142; Kelly 1980:193–197; Milner 1990:9; Porter 1974:23–24). In the Northern Bottom Expanse beyond Lunsford-Pulcher, the Lohmann and Cahokia sites have Emergent Mississippian components and may have been the administrative centers of Emergent Mississippian political entities. An extensive Emergent Mississippian occupation of the Cahokia locality is illustrated by the habitation remains on Tracts 15A and 15B, the Powell Tract, the Merrell Tract, and the Ramey Tract. A minimal average population figure for the later portions of the period may be guessed at around 1,000 people. Grassy Lake, some 19 kilometers to the north of the Cahokia site, appears to have a substantial Emergent Mississippian occupation as well, although a row of prehistoric mounds there may date to earlier Middle and Late Woodland occupations (Griffin 1951; Moorehead 1929:62–64).

Emergent Mississippian Ceramic Traditions

Most significantly, archaeologists working in the American Bottom have recognized distinct local ceramic traditions associated with the Emergent Mississippi period (Friemuth 1974; Griffin 1977; Hall 1966, 1975; Harn 1980; Kelly 1980, 1990a; Milner 1990:9–10; Porter 1963a:17–18, 1963b:9–10, 1963c:10–11; Vogel 1975).[2] These ceramic traditions have served as the basis for the delineation of separate phases for the Northern Bottom Expanse and the central American Bottom (Kelly et al. 1984a). Emergent Mississippian pottery from the immediate vicinity of the Cahokia site and

2. An extensive body of comparative data on the factors surrounding the procurement of pottery-making materials may be used to infer that pots with distinctive pastes were made in isolated localities (Arnold 1985:35–60).

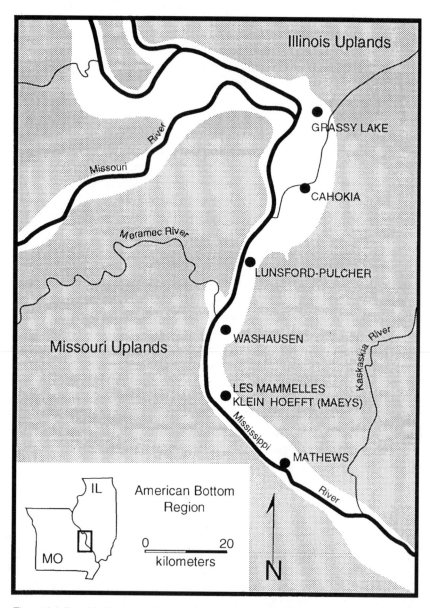

Figure 3.4. Possible Emergent Mississippian Centers in the American Botton Region

most of the Northern Bottom Expanse has been identified as the "Late Bluff" tradition by Kelly (1980:78, 1990a:figure 53). As a local ceramic tradition, it is characterized by grit- and grog-tempered jars, bowls, and stumpware. Distinctive pastes characterize the vessels produced from various upland-shale muds and bottomland-lacustrine muds (see Porter 1963a–c). The use of crushed cobbles from upland glacial tills and grog from recycled potsherds is telling of the locally available tempering materials. In the late Emergent Mississippian and earliest Mississippian ceramic assemblages, crushed shell begins to offset grog as the dominant form of temper in the local tradition.

In the central American Bottom, "Pulcher tradition" pottery typifies Emergent Mississippian ceramic assemblages (Kelly 1990a). These are almost always limestone tempered, the limestone being locally available from the nearby bluffs. There are subtle differences of vessel morphology and surface treatment between these Pulcher-tradition pots and Late Bluff ware (see Kelly et al. 1984a). These are stylistic differences not in the strict sense of iconic or emblemic content but in terms of tradition and interaction. Style in this sense may transmit a kind of social information but also may be seen to change through passive intergenerational and interactional means (cf. Sackett 1985; Weissner 1985).

Equally significant in characterizing these traditions is what could be the lack of a clinal distribution of the wares across the American Bottom. Rather than a gradual falloff of grog- and shell-tempered wares with distance away from Cahokia and nearer to Lunsford-Pulcher, there may be a sharp distributional boundary (figure 3.5).[3] This distributional boundary may be the result of an actively maintained sociopolitical rift that appeared during the Emergent Mississippi period. Such group identities might have formed in the context of a high degree of intergroup interaction and dynamic group membership (cf. Braun and Plog 1982; Hodder 1977). In such a dynamic social milieu, the low-ranking subgroups could have become ever more defined relative to the high-ranking subgroups while at the same time alienated from the traditional (Late Woodland) kin ethics.

On the other hand, the distribution of a series of red-slipped Pulcher-tradition bowls and seed jars seems to vary independent of the distributional limitations of limestone-tempered jars and cordmarked bowls, suggesting that they were sought and acquired through exchange. These "Monks Mound Red" bowls and seed jars are tempered with finely crushed limestone and have thinned vessel walls and thick, well-

3. Data sources: Berres 1984; Emerson and Jackson 1984, 1987; Esarey and Pauketat 1992; Finney 1985, 1987; Hanenberger 1990b; Holley 1989; Kelly 1980.

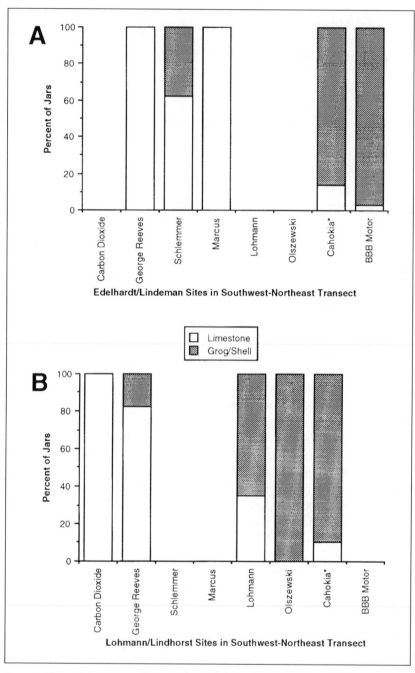

Figure 3.5 The Distribution of Late Bluff and Pulcher Tradition Wares (Cahokia samples: a, Merrell Tract; b, ICT-II)

smoothed, and orangish-red slips on smooth surfaces (Griffin 1949:52).[4] These attributes may be indicative of labor inputs greater than those of other utilitarian vessels (figure 3.6). They exhibit little in the way of fire-related residues or wear as do utilitarian jars and cordmarked bowls. Thus these classic Monks Mound Red forms were likely manufactured especially for public or high-ranking uses or exchange (*sensu* Kelly 1980:147–148).

The frequency of Monks Mound Red containers in domestic garbage through time does not correspond to that of other limestone-tempered pots at American Bottom sites. At the Lohmann site, midway between the Cahokia and Lunsford-Pulcher centers, there is a "trend towards *more* limestone-tempered seed jars relative to shell-tempered examples" (Esarey and Pauketat 1992:111, emphasis added). This trend contrasts with the general limestone-to-shell-temper trends observed among other vessel forms. There appears to be a regional technological trend away from limestone temper, a trend that might also indicate "the decreased importance or amalgamation" of central American Bottom potters or pottery technologies within the Northern Bottom Expanse communities. This occurred at the same time that decorated limestone-tempered Monks Mound Red pots found increased usage (Esarey and Pauketat 1992:158).

If Monks Mound Red ceramics were centrally produced and distributed, then the appearance of the finely crafted red-slipped bowls and (decorated) seed jars during the late Emergent Mississippi period may be a sign of the development of social ranking and institutionalized political offices in the American Bottom.[5] Unfortunately, definitive evidence of simple chiefly hierarchies either from the possible Emergent Mississippian centers or from mortuary remains is not available. Consequently, our understanding of the regional development of the American Bottom region remains incomplete.

4. Kelly (1980:67; Kelly et al. 1984a:142) has dated the earliest occurrence of red slips on limestone-tempered containers to the Merrell and George Reeves phases. These are not, however, the classic well-smoothed and slipped Monks Mound Red bowls and seed jars of the terminal Emergent Mississippian and early Mississippian complexes.

5. The overall design configuration on Monks Mound Red seed jars (and their shell-tempered counterparts) takes the form of simple circumferential circles or rectanguloidal or quadripartite arrangements of punctates on the upper vessel surface (figure 3.6). The focal element of the vessel orifice along with the quadripartition of decoration thus recapitulates the community patterns identified by Kelly (1990a, 1990b) to have appeared shortly before the first Monks Mound Red seed jars (cf. Pauketat and Emerson 1991).

The Mobilization of Comestibles in Pots

The Monks Mound Red vessels are an example, albeit perhaps one produced under extra-domestic conditions, of a container involved in exchange networks. Many other local vessels whose production probably was not subsidized by chiefly officials were also involved in such exchanges. Late Bluff and Pulcher-tradition jars made from the distinct upland and bottomland pastes appear to have been moved about extensively in the American Bottom region. Highly visible jars made from the upland-shale muds found to the north of the Northern Bottom Expanse commonly appear at Cahokia, Lunsford-Pulcher, and surrounding sites (e.g., Emerson and Jackson 1984; Kelly 1980, Kelly et al. 1984a; Milner 1984b:77; Ozuk 1990; Pauketat 1990; Porter 1963c:11, 1984:167–168; Vogel 1975). Likewise, the grog-tempered and limestone-tempered wares probably produced in floodplain settings in the vicinity of Cahokia and

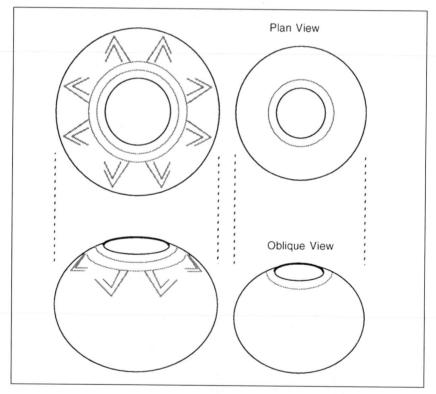

Figure 3.6. Monks Mound Red Seed Jars (adapted from Kelly 1980:figure 5)

Lunsford-Pulcher, respectively, are also widely distributed in the region. In fact, given the intensity of exchanges involving pots, it is perhaps not an exaggeration to suggest that the use lives of few jars would have expired in the same place as they began.

At the Range site, jars having northern upland-shale pastes are most common early in the Emergent Mississippi period (Kelly 1990a:145). Throughout the American Bottom, jar techno-morphological diversity increased through the Emergent Mississippi period, perhaps representing both intensified exchange and the centralization of potters from diverse ceramic-tradition backgrounds (Emerson and Jackson 1984; Finney 1987:279; Kelly 1980:58–75; Pauketat 1990:74). This intercourse of disparate manufacturing technologies and local stylistic traditions (and no doubt people) appears to be the principal factor that guided ceramic change during this dynamic period and, as an aside, the reason why the Emergent Mississippi period is so amenable to division by archaeologists into relatively short phases. For instance, once notched-lip appliques appeared in one part of the bottom, they appeared in the others. Once red slips showed up in one locale, they became an attribute of local vessels everywhere (see Kelly 1980).

Added to this factor is the increasing numbers through the Emergent Mississippi period of nonlocal vessels and lithic artifacts from southern Illinois, southeast Missouri, and the central and lower Mississippi River alluvial plain. The exotic vessels include jars, bowls, beakers, and bottles of the Dillinger Cordmarked, Yankeetown Incised, Kersey Incised, Varney Red Filmed, and Coles Creek Incised types. The identification of some exotic types remains problematic and a matter of some contention (cf. Emerson and Jackson 1984; Kelly 1980; Holley 1989). However, the identification of other pots (though by no means all) as exotic in origin is beyond quibbling (see examples in Bareis 1976; Kelly 1980; Pauketat 1984, 1990). Likewise, certain foreign, lithic raw materials (e.g., Fort Payne and Mill Creek chert) and tools (e.g., projectile points and chert hoe blades) not present in Late Woodland refuse have been identified among Emergent Mississippian remains (Kelly 1984a).

It is reasonable to suspect that the movement of local vessels (perhaps unlike small, decorated, nonlocal bowls, beakers, and bottles) was actually secondary to the movement of the goods that they contained. For example, given their morphology, use-related wear, and fire-related surficial deposits, jars were likely utilitarian containers used occasionally as simple vehicles of comestible mobilization. It is difficult to envision such ordinary containers as the principal exchange items themselves. No studies have yet delved in detail into the relationship between quantity of vessels, size of vessels, and distance of their final location of discard from their putative manufacturing origin, but we may tentatively infer that the distribution of distinctive jar varieties or Monks Mound Red pots indicates a high rate of intercommunity interaction or managed distribution of comestibles. Certainly, exchange or redistribution of comestibles would be expected where the (competitive) negotiation of social ranking or mobilization of comestibles for festivals or communal ceremonies (sponsored by high-ranking subgroups) was a component of the regional formation.

The Mobilization of Deer Meat

Lucretia Kelly (1979, 1990a, 1990b) has been instrumental in documenting the evidence for changing patterns of faunal utilization during the Emergent Mississippi period. Of concern here are her observations concerning the mobilization of animal resources during the Late Woodland-to-Emergent Mississippian continuum. To begin, Patrick-phase domestic refuse includes a diversity of mammal, bird, and fish taxa. However, during the earliest subsequent Emergent Mississippian phase, there is evidence in the form of reduced quantities of deer and projectile points in refuse that hunting of large mammals may have decreased. At the same time, the quantities of "passerines, small marshbirds, small mammals, and fish increase" in Range-site domestic refuse (L. Kelly 1990b:511). This diachronic pattern may have been a result of redirecting domestic efforts away from "the procurement of larger animals" and "toward the newly acquired maize agriculture" (L. Kelly 1990b:511).

However, the decreased usage of deer evident in the early Emergent Mississippian remains from the Range site is reversed in the later Emergent Mississippian remains from Cahokia. Based on the Edelhardt-phase faunal remains from Cahokia's Merrell Tract, L. Kelly (1979:16) concludes that "only the most desirable cuts of [deer] meat (upper forelimb and hindlimb) were being returned" to the Cahokia site. From the features beneath the East Palisade at Cahokia, L. Kelly (1990a) observed a greater minimum number of individual deer in Merrell-phase features compared to the preceding Loyd phase (L. Kelly 1990a:110, 118). The Merrell-phase quantity, in turn, was exceeded by that associated with the subsequent Edelhardt phase that "yielded by far the largest mammal assemblage" of which more than 90 percent of the identified elements derived from "the main meat-bearing portion of the deer" (L. Kelly 1990a:122).

The faunal data are suggestive of an increasing reliance by Emergent Mississippian Cahokia inhabitants upon an increasingly nonlocal meat source, while the precise mechanisms involved remain uncertain. While these mechanisms may have included Cahokia residents themselves going on hunting trips, the trend toward more and more such hunting trips or the increasing importation of deer meat during the Emergent Mississippi period in and of itself remains significant (see also Kelly 1980:118–120). In short, deer meat was being mobilized to support some segment of the population of Cahokia during the later phases of the Emergent Mississippi period. The other faunal data, involving smaller animals less amenable to an analysis of differential butchering practices, are of reduced value for delineating patterns of staple-goods mobilization. Similarly, while there may be hints of the mobilization of maize during the Mississippi period (Esarey and Pauketat 1992:159), the evolving plant-food habits of the Emergent Mississippian groups in the American Bottom complicate the recognition of plant-food mobilization patterns (Lopinot 1992).

Discussion

The specific beliefs and values of the Patrick-phase horticulturalists are unknown. However, given the relative weakness of community centrality, it may be projected that centrifugal tendencies of horticultural sociopolitics had not been overcome (see Ford 1979:237). At the same time, the evidence for increasing population density and the Patrick-phase intensification of horticultural production anticipate the subsequent Emergent Mississippian developments. Thus these archaeologically visible changes have been given causal significance in archaeological explanations.

Rather than assume, however, that absolute population growth was occurring region-wide during the Late Woodland period, thereby causing socioeconomic change, it is useful to recognize the implications of the regional reproduction of interconnected horticultural groups (with or without absolute population growth). The biological and social reproduction of such horticultural groups like the Late Woodlanders of the American midcontinent would have been possible, for instance, via intraregional (e.g., matrimonial) networks (see Bender 1978:210–214). We might expect that these social alliances would have provided the context for the ritual negotiation of regional productive asymmetries over the long run much like what Blanton et al. (1981) have proposed for the early Formative period of the Valley of Oaxaca in Mexico.

In the American Bottom region, the dispersed Late Woodland groups in the smaller upland stream drainages to the north, east, and west of the Mississippi floodplain most likely would have experienced fewer annual productive overruns compared to bottomland groups, given the optimum "net energy subsidy" of the bottom (Smith 1978a:496). That is, in a regional setting, the horticulturalists with access to the broad Mississippi flood-plain would have been less dependent upon upland production. Matrimo-nial alliances of upland subgroups with bottomland subgroups would have provided the means by which upland entities perpetuated their own social positions while insuring against the occasional bad year (*sensu* O'Shea and Halstead 1989). Yet over the long run, such alliances would have prompted increasingly close links to the bottomland subgroups and would have permitted these bottomland people to establish themselves in apical power positions in such connubial networks.

Thus, in a regional setting—although not necessarily visible in local archaeological contexts—the communities of the American Bottom proper in effect might have established a kind of social dominance over periph-eral upland groups during the Late Woodland period. Some upland households could have been drawn into the Mississippi River floodplain itself because of the advantages and subsistence security of floodplain society. Relative population growth, if not also absolute population growth, for the American Bottom proper would have resulted.

The appearance of social ranking in the Emergent Mississippian com-munity would have been the formalization of a Late Woodland process. Moreover, the intensification of maize production initially might have been aimed at producing a reliable surplus so that the increasing require-ments of emerging high-ranking subgroups could be met. The data remain equivocal on this point, but the potential exists for resolving the issue of agricultural intensification relative to social change. Resolution, however, lies not in the remains from most communities, but from the regional configuration of sites. Future research must address itself to this key question.

The enlargement of the Range-site community through accretion and the establishment of a highly structured community plan (which included large buildings prominently located *vis-à-vis* the courtyard) correspond to the advent of highly visible and well-made Monks Mound Red serving and storage dishes, the appearance of exotic ceramic vessels and lithic items, and the intraregional exchange of (comestibles in) pots. Socio-political divisions may find expression in the archaeologically identified Late Bluff and Pulcher ceramic traditions. The community, perhaps for reasons of economizing friable soils or perhaps as a result of a changing organizational ethic, became compressed at the same time it was enlarged. On the other hand, community storage in pits, as represented at the Range site, was reduced. No data exist to resolve the matter of where the goods formerly stored in pits were later stored. Excavations of the possible Emergent Mississippian centers may resolve this problem.

If the distribution of exotic pots and lithic artifacts is any clue, then by the final Emergent Mississippian phase, high-ranking subgroups in the American Bottom may have engaged in extensive long-distance exchanges. It is plausible that these high-ranking subgroups had established long-distance marriage alliances that resulted in the relocation of spouses and affines (and hence potters) from distant groups to the American Bottom. With them would have arrived their own local traditions, ceramic and otherwise. Such extensification of matrimonial connections over time could well have resulted in the appearance of distinct pottery-manufacturing enclaves, representing disparate traditions, at the administrative centers. Shell-tempered pottery, for instance, an anomaly in early Emergent Mississippian feature fills and probably nonlocal in origin, is relatively common in late Emergent Mississippian garbage, perhaps being locally produced (by nonlocal potters?).

There may well have been considerable numbers of individuals relocating to the American Bottom region during the tenth and eleventh centuries A.D. because of the enlargement of high-ranking marital networks and because of low-ranking subgroup perceptions that living in close proximity to high-ranking families was beneficial to their own social reproduction. We should not, however, equate this Emergent Mississippian coalescence itself with Mississippian culture. To be sure, the antecedents of Cahokia-Mississippian are the local Emergent Mississippian entities; equally clear is the significance of the American Bottom in an interregional setting (Hall 1966, 1975; Kelly 1980, 1990a, 1991a). Yet as an explanation of Mississippian, the sum total of these details is insufficient. They do not tell us how or why the Mississippi period is characterized by a regionally centralized polity that featured artifacts, architecture, and community arrangements that have no local antecedents.

Previous Perspectives in the Development of Cahokia-Mississippian

Kelly (1990a:139–143) and Hall (1991:14–18) have summarized most of the previous discussions of the development of Cahokia-Mississippian in terms of the emphasis placed on (1) the migration of intrusive Mississippians into the American Bottom or the contact that local Late Woodland populations had with southern (e.g., Caddoan) cultures, or (2) the local evolution or adaptation of Late Woodland populations as Mississippian maize agriculturalists. The migration thesis was propounded by Porter (1974, 1977, 1984), Friemuth (1974), and Perino (1971:141). They believed that a small group of Mississippians from outside the region was "instrumental in effecting the acculturation" of Emergent Mississippian groups (Perino 1971:141). Long-term regional interaction, acculturation, and local evolution rather than migration were envisioned by Vogel (1975:70) and Hall (1966, 1975). According to Hall (1966:6), the "evidence suggests that Woodland peoples were being drawn into the Mississippian orbit at Cahokia over a period of perhaps three or four centuries and that the face of Mississippian culture itself was also changing in response to this interaction and that between Cahokians and other Mississippians."[6]

Without a doubt, the particular migrationist or interactionist slant favored in these explanations is rooted in distinct schools of thought. However, it is instructive that the adherents of both scenarios were equally well acquainted with the extensive salvage data from the American Bottom yet managed to reconcile those data with these seemingly disparate viewpoints. Neither side is entirely wrong. Rather, each side emphasized different aspects of the same phenomenon. The migration/contact proponents emphasized the archaeological traces of political change, while the local evolution/interaction proponents emphasized the traces of cultural or ideational change. Both viewpoints can be integrated within a modified political approach to chiefdoms (see chapter 2), and there has been some movement in that direction.

Emerson (1991:234) has stated that by the late Emergent Mississippi period "the American Bottom may have been the setting for a minimum of a half-dozen civic-ceremonial centers supporting simple chiefdoms" and that some "of these centers (Pulcher, Cahokia, or East St. Louis) may have already incorporated some of their smaller neighbors to form small-scale complex chiefdoms." He further perceives an elite group's dominance in the increased "homogeneity of the cultural assemblages during the Lohmann phase" that was fully consolidated at Cahokia during the Stirling phase. Milner (1990:27) has described "an extended period of population growth" leading to an "ever-escalating rate" of political centralization "as once roughly equivalent polities became dwarfed by the manpower mobilization potential of a Cahokia-dominated system" (Milner 1990:29). Milner (1990:28) also notes the possibility that relatively "autonomous" elite subgroups in the Northern Bottom Expanse were displaced by "individuals from Cahokia" at some point in the sequence, resulting in a "qualitative shift in organizational complexity" (Milner

6. The evidence for Robert Hall included Tract 15A, also analyzed here.

1990:28). Mehrer and Collins (1989) have noted the significance of the establishment of a Cahokia site plan during the initial Mississippian phase (*sensu* Fowler 1974), along with the "public statement" the elites appear to have been making with the establishment of other "temple towns." Kelly (1990a:146) has suggested that the "multiple mound complexes at Cahokia" were the result of a series of "high-level lineages from elsewhere in the American Bottom and beyond coalescing at Cahokia" during the incipient Mississippi period.

It is fair to conclude that the above Cahokia researchers see a gradual or escalating process of political centralization, punctuated perhaps by some political changes or symbolic statements, although the relationship and timing of the latter relative to regional consolidation is unclear. As Emerson (1991) points out, no analyses of Cahokia data have addressed this critical question. The rate and scale of political consolidation, along with the mechanisms by which such consolidation would have been accomplished and legitimized, have been poorly understood.

As outlined above, we can be relatively certain that traditional Late Woodland community life was giving way to a more dynamic Emergent Mississippian social landscape given the evidence for intraregional and interregional exchange; the attendant high rate of ceramic techno-morphological change and advent of local ceramic traditions; hints of centralized production, distribution, and mobilization of foods; and the growth of communities and their internal courtyard-group organization. We also may suspect that regional asymmetries in production, warfare, and alliances existed between and among high- and low-ranking Emergent Mississippian subgroups. It remains plausible, although undemonstrated, that an emerging high-ranking ideology found expression in the items like Monks Mound Red pots produced under the aegis of high-ranking subgroups or in the long-distance ties evident in artifact assemblages from Cahokia.

While there remain deficiencies in our archaeological controls over the Emergent Mississippian data, it is possible to reach an understanding of how and why a Cahokian Leviathan arose in the American midcontinent. How and why knowledge may be developed through the application of the theoretical approach detailed in chapter 2. The evaluation of a construct of the regional consolidation of political authority and the emergence of divine chiefship requires diachronic information of a high resolution. Such data are available in the form of certain areally extensive excavations at Cahokia. These data are described in the following chapter.

Chapter 4
Central and Rural Mississippian Patterns

The great number of mounds, and the astonishing quantity of human bones, every where dug up, or found on the surface of the ground, with a thousand other appearances, announce that this valley was at one period, filled with habitations and villages. The whole face of the bluff, or hill which bounds it to the east, appears to have been a continued burial ground (Brackenridge 1814:186).

It is difficult now to comprehend, but at the time of the founding in A.D. 1699 of the first French mission amongst the Cahokia[1] and Tamaroa Indians, the floodplain and surrounding blufftops of the Northern Bottom Expanse—an area of less than 1,200 square kilometers—contained over 200 earthen mounds dating to the late prehistoric period. Perhaps as many as 180 of these earthworks, including the largest mounds in North America, were concentrated within what I have loosely called the Central Political-Administrative Complex, an area no greater than 30 square kilometers (figure 1.1). These were arranged at what were among the three largest late prehistoric administrative centers in North America—Cahokia, East St. Louis and St. Louis. Unfortunately, since 1699, the mounds and the surrounding landscape have been systematically destroyed by Euro-American civilization. The contemporary archaeological projection of the past thus is most assuredly a pale reconstruction.

Yet American Bottom archaeologists are poised to address the sorts of research problems not even conceivable in many parts of the world because of the maturity of research in the American Bottom region. American Bottom archaeologists have a firm grasp of late-prehistoric regional settlement patterns, the spatial organization of communities, and

---

1. From which the names of the Cahokia site, the town of Cahokia, and Cahokia Creek derive, but no ethnic relation to the prehistoric Mississippians.

interhousehold subsistence variation in both a synchronic and diachronic sense. This advanced state of American Bottom archaeological research no doubt is related to its shared history with the urban center of St. Louis, from its heyday as a gateway city on the American frontier of the early nineteenth century to its present status as an expanding metropolitan complex. The last three decades especially, witness to the federally funded construction of interstate highways, have propelled American Bottom archaeology to its current level.

The Background of Archaeological Research

Earthen mounds or "Indian ancient tombs" were recognized in the bottom by the colonial French of the 1700s (Fowler 1989:15). However, the first Euro-American to call attention to the presence of the numerous earthworks at the Cahokia site proper was Henry Brackenridge in 1811 (1814; see Fowler 1989:101–102). By the middle of that same century, the growth of the city of St. Louis and its lesser neighbor, East St. Louis, had wreaked considerable havoc on the archaeological remains of the American Bottom region. By 1869, the massive Mississippian mounds in the city of St. Louis had been leveled (Bushnell 1904:11–13; Chapman 1980:166–170; Peale 1862; Williams and Goggin 1956). The St. Louis mound group, after which St. Louis had acquired the nickname "Mound City," had consisted of some twenty-six or more mounds occupying the sloping blufftops of the western bank of the Mississippi River (figure 4.1).

Just across the Mississippi on the low-lying floodplain were around forty-five or more late-prehistoric mounds. These earthen monuments, occupying the East St. Louis site, likewise were destroyed between 1830 and 1880. What the plough did not level, the expanding city of East St. Louis (then Illinoistown) flattened and erased or covered over (Fowler 1978:470; Kelly and Gums 1987). Brackenridge (1814:187) described the East St. Louis site as he saw it in 1811: "I crossed the Mississippi at St. Louis, and after passing through the wood which borders the river, about half a mile in width, entered an extensive open plain. In 15 minutes, I found myself in the midst of a group of mounds . . . resembling enormous haystacks scattered through a meadow. . . . Around me, I counted forty-five mounds, or pyramids, besides a great number of small artificial elevations; these mounds form something more than a semicircle, about a mile in extent, the open space on the river."

As described by Brackenridge, the East St. Louis site would have been the second or third largest late-prehistoric center in North America in

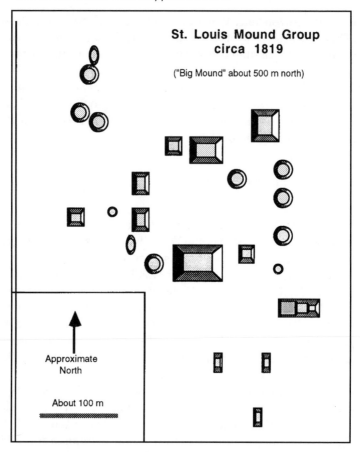

Figure 4.1. The St. Louis Mound Group (adapted from Chapman 1980)

Figure 4.2 (facing page). The Northern Bottom Expanse Mississippian Centers or Other Sites with Mounds (solid dots are Mississippian site with mounds; open dots are other mound sites)

number of mounds (the largest being Cahokia).[2] Actually, the Cahokia and East St. Louis sites seem to have been eastern and western clusters connected by a continuous distribution of mounds along the south and east bank of the Cahokia Creek (figure 4.2). Other mounds may have lined the western bluffs of the Mississippi River (e.g., Wiegers 1982).

2. For comparison, Moundville in Alabama had twenty-two mounds in an area covering about 100 hectares (Steponaitis 1983b). The Lake George site in Mississippi included thirty mounds in an area covering 22 hectares (Williams and Brain 1983:1). The Rich Woods site in southeastern Missouri contained more than thirty-five mounds (Chapman 1980:217, 221; Thomas 1985:175–183). The Hoecake site in the Cairo Lowlands of Missouri may have included fifty-four mounds (Williams 1974:55).

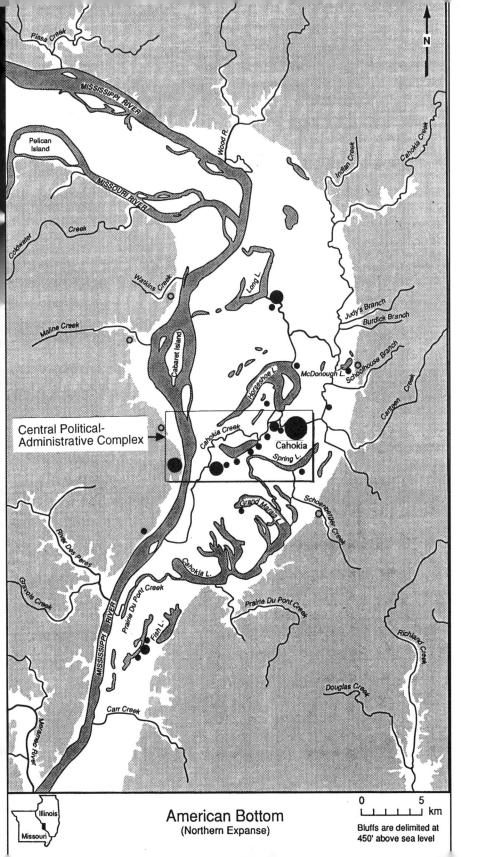

N

Plaza Creek

MISSISSIPPI RIVER

Pelican
Island

MISSOURI RIVER

Wood R.

Indian Creek

Cahokia Creek

Coldwater

Creek

Watkins Creek

Long L.

Judy's Branch

Burdick Branch

Maline Creek

Cabaret Island

Horseshoe L.

McDonough L.

Schoolhouse Branch

Canteen Creek

Central Political-
Administrative Complex

Cahokia Creek

Cahokia

Spring L.

Grand Marais L.

Schoenberger Creek

River Des Peres

Cahokia L.

Gravois Creek

MISSISSIPPI RIVER

Prairie Du Pont Creek

Prairie Du Pont Creek

Richland Creek

Fish L.

Carr Creek

Meramec River

Douglas Creek

Illinois

Missouri

American Bottom
(Northern Expanse)

0   5
|__|__|__|__|__| km

Bluffs are delimited at
450' above sea level

The Cahokia site itself escaped complete destruction because of its distance from the primary channel of the Mississippi River and the urbanization that was occurring there. Interest in the antiquities and archaeology of the area was developing during the late nineteenth and early twentieth centuries (e.g., Bushnell 1904; Fowke 1913; Howland 1877; Throop 1928). The documentation from this period provides some of the only details we will ever know about certain features of the Cahokia, East St. Louis, St. Louis, and Mitchell site complexes (see Fowler 1989:20–24). By the early twentieth century, the expanding urban character of the region had begun to envelop the Euro-American farms of the Cahokia-site locale itself.

It was at this point that archaeology really entered the American Bottom region (Fowler 1974:10, 1977:12). The first order of business consisted of dispelling the contention that the mounds were natural terraces, an idea that received support even from a most prominent geologist of the day, N. M. Fenneman (Fowler 1977:12, 1989:101–105). This documentation justified the purchase and preservation of the central cluster of mounds at the Cahokia site in the form of the Cahokia Mounds State Park. Warren K. Moorehead was instrumental in securing the park purchase and conducted large-scale excavations of a number of the Cahokia tumuli (Moorehead 1922, 1923, 1929). For instance, he removed an entire side of the Kunnemann Mound using a crew of some eight to twelve workmen in a two-to-three-week period during 1921 (Pauketat 1993).

Other mound salvage operations took place during the 1930s and 1940s as the Cahokia site continued to be engulfed by a growing urban area. The second-largest earthen monument at the site, the Powell Mound, was razed in 1930 by its owners in order to increase the farm's cultivable area (Ahler and DePuydt 1987). The construction of residential subdivisions at and around Cahokia led to further destruction during the 1940s and early 1950s, along with some noteworthy salvage archaeology (see Holder 1958; Perino 1971:120; H. Smith 1977). During 1954, Preston Holder of Washington University in St. Louis excavated the Wilson or Junkyard Mound, one of the artificial elevations between the Cahokia and East St. Louis sites doomed to be replaced by a "hot sheets" motel (Leonard Blake, personal communication, 1990). Excavations at the Kunnemann Mound by Holder followed in 1955 and 1956 (Pauketat 1993). Other excavations took place at Mound 31 and 34 during the 1950s by the Illinois State Museum, the University of Michigan, and the Gilcrease Institute (Fowler 1989:84–85, 88–89). This period was also the one in which Dr. James B. Griffin of the University of Michigan launched his "Central Mississippi Valley Archaeological Survey," which focused some effort on Cahokia (Griffin and

Spaulding 1951), as did Gregory Perino and the Gilcrease Institute of Tulsa, Oklahoma (Perino 1971).

The coming years witnessed the rapid expansion of archaeological research (and urban growth) in the American Bottom region. The watershed was the Federal-Aid Highway Act of 1956, which, besides establishing a federally funded interstate highway system, provided for the salvage of archaeological sites to be destroyed in its path (Fowler 1977:14–15). "By 1958 it was clear that there was to be a massive highway building program for the East St. Louis area, much of it going through the north side of the Cahokia Site west of Collinsville, and another satellite community to the north along Long Lake at Mitchell, Illinois" (Porter 1974:208). Highway interchanges were planned to cut through the heart of the Cahokia site area at tracts of land designated 15A and 15B, Dunham and Powell (figure 4.3). The Powell tract was excavated in 1960 by the University of Illinois under the direction of Donald W. Lathrap and Charles J. Bareis (Bareis and Lathrap 1962; see O'Brien 1972). Large-scale excavations were conducted at 15A and 15B by the Illinois State Museum under the leadership in 1960 and 1961 of Warren Wittry and in 1963 of Robert L. Hall (Hall 1964; Wittry 1960a, 1960b, 1961; Wittry and Vogel 1962). Charles J. Bareis conducted block excavations of the Dunham Tract in 1966. James W. Porter at Southern Illinois University was responsible for salvage operations at the Mitchell site in 1960–62 (Porter 1974).

A number of smaller excavations at Cahokia and other late prehistoric sites in the American Bottom region were conducted during the 1960s and early 1970s (e.g., Anderson 1977; Bareis 1967, 1972, 1976; Melbye 1963; papers in Fowler 1975b). These included highway salvage and research projects investigating features of the Cahokia site. The Cahokia research during the late 1960s and early 1970s, dominated by Melvin Fowler and the University of Wisconsin at Milwaukee, included such notable projects as delineation of a section of the central palisade wall, excavation of the elite mortuary at Mound 72, and the topographic mapping of the entire site (see Fowler 1974, 1975a, 1977, 1978). Portions of Monks Mound, the central platform at the site, were excavated by the University of Wisconsin at Milwaukee, the University of Illinois, and Washington University (Benchley 1975; Bareis 1975a–b; Reed 1977:33–34; Reed, Bennett, and Porter 1968).

By the middle of the 1970s and through the 1980s, however, the focus of regional archaeology shifted to Cahokia's hinterland. The FAI-270 Highway Mitigation Project focused on the excavation of dozens of sites, most in their entirety, along a stretch of planned interstate highway through the American Bottom (Bareis and Porter 1984). The samples of community

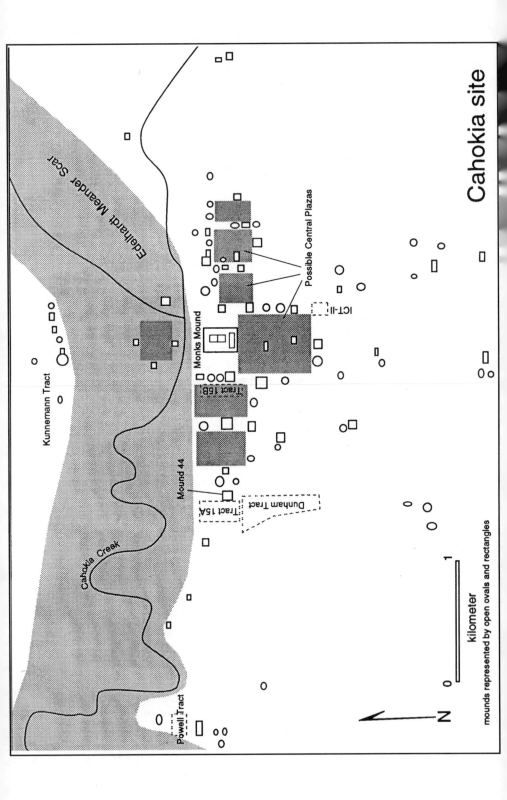

Cahokia site

Edelhardt Meander Scar

Kunnemann Tract

Cahokia Creek

Powell Tract

Mound 44

Tract 15A

Tract 15B

Monks Mound

Dunham Tract

ICT-II

Possible Central Plazas

N

kilometer

mounds represented by open ovals and rectangles

0   1

plans, domestic refuse, and mortuary remains now available in published form are unparalleled anywhere in the United States. There have been additional large-scale excavations at Cahokia (Collins 1990; Holley 1989), and these are contributing to the understanding of the diachronic patterns of Mississippian development. However, much of what was excavated in the 1960s and early 1970s remains unanalyzed and unpublished. These data sets hold promise for enlarging our perceptions of the Cahokia-Mississippian phenomenon especially now that the FAI–270 project has better defined its temporal and spatial parameters (see Kelly 1990a; Kelly et al. 1984a; Milner 1990; Milner et al. 1984).

Rural Settlement Patterns and Secondary Mississippian Centers

The settlement models of Fowler (1974, 1975a, 1978) and Porter (1974) notwithstanding, the most parsimonious interpretation of the American Bottom settlement patterns of the late eleventh and twelfth centuries A.D. consists in the recognition of a dynamic three-tiered settlement hierarchy (Milner 1990:20–23; Esarey and Pauketat 1992; Pauketat 1989:290). Milner (1990:21) points out that, given current evidence, it "is unlikely that the settlement system was as strictly hierarchical" as implicit in the four-tiered site hierarchy presented by Fowler (1978). The number of mounds at sites is not a reliable means of inferring hierarchical relationships but may "serve as better barometers of site longevity and the volatile nature of social relations featuring competing chiefly lineages with varied histories" (Milner 1990:21). A particular elite subgroup might have "dominated a particular territory for a variable length of time. These areas presumably differed somewhat in overall size and encompassed multiple outlying dispersed communities consisting primarily of farmsteads" (Milner 1990:21). From Milner's (1990:22–23) point of view, the Mississippian elite of Cahokia "dominated the region" although "the strength of ties among the elite strata of the mound complexes undoubtedly varied over time and with distance from the principal center."

It is important to recognize Cahokian domination of the region since it would have enabled the transformation of the social and physical land-scapes of American Bottom late prehistory. Cahokia was a paramount center, a qualitatively different place. Yet the apical position of the Cahokian lords would not have imparted great political stability or economic integration to the polity (or polities). Neither would have Cahokian dominance meant that the rural community or the outlying Mississippian centers were economically dependent upon Cahokia. In fact, as has been demonstrated by recent archaeobotanical and archaeozoological analyses, the population outside the Central Political-Administrative Complex seems to have been self-sufficient in subsistence production (see Johannessen 1984a; Kelly and Cross 1984; see also Smith 1978a).

The Dispersed Population of Primary Producers

One of the principal products of the FAI-270 Highway Mitigation Project has been the revelation of the composition of rural settlement outside the Central Political-Administrative Complex. Approximately fifteen habitation sites that date to the eleventh or twelfth centuries A.D. have been excavated by the FAI-270 project (Emerson and Jackson 1987; Finney 1985; Fortier 1985; Jackson and Hanenberger 1990; Kelly 1990a; McElrath and Finney 1987; Mehrer 1982; Milner 1982, 1983, 1984a; Milner et al. 1984; Yerkes 1987). A handful of rural sites had been excavated prior to the initiation of the FAI-270 project (Bareis 1972, 1976; Blake 1955; Norris 1974, 1975). Other rural sites in the immediate American Bottom hinterland have been excavated since the late 1970s (Hargrave 1982; Jackson 1984; Koldehoff 1990a:55–57; Prentice and Mehrer 1981).

Based on this sample, Emerson (1991) and Mehrer (1988) have observed a series of significant community-organizational and domestic-architectural and storage changes over the duration of the Emergent Mississippi to Mississippi periods. These consist of (1) the dissolution of large Emergent Mississippian aggregates and the dispersion of Mississippian households across the landscape, (2) the diversification of rural Mississippian homestead form, (3) the increased reliance upon subterranean storage inside domestic dwellings, and (4) the demographic shifts in rural settings.

The dissolution of the large community at the Range site occurred at the end of the Emergent Mississippi period (see Kelly 1990b). Elsewhere in the Northern Bottom Expanse, large nucleated communities probably dissolved at this time except for those established as political-administrative centers (featuring one or more platform mounds). There is no clear evidence in the American Bottom proper of Mississippi-period social aggregates outside these secondary centers on the scale of the Emergent Mississippian communities at the Range site (Kelly 1990a; Mehrer 1988; Mehrer and Collins 1989; Milner 1990).[3] In their place were numerous

3. Community dissolution may not have characterized late Emergent Mississippian rural settlements marginal to the bottom (e.g., Bareis 1976).

scattered rural homesteads, each consisting of one or at most several households (Pauketat 1989:295).

All indications are that these small settlements were capable of satisfying their own subsistence requirements without regular intervention from centralized authorities (Emerson and Milner 1981; Johannessen 1984; Kelly and Cross 1984; Mehrer 1982; Yerkes 1987:196). Indicative of a diverse diet of large and small mammals, terrestrial birds, waterfowl, aquatic reptiles, and fish, the bones of many different animal taxa are found on sites. The homestead occupants grew maize, cucurbits, starchy seed plants, and a range of other plant foods and medicines. As depicted in figure 4.4, the diachronic patterns of carbonized maize deposition in homestead refuse appear to involve decreasing amounts of kernels relative to the number of cobs until this index (as represented in the sample from the Radic site) rebounds in the Moorehead phase (Johannessen 1984b, 1985a–c; Parker 1992, personal communication 1988; Whalley 1983, 1984). While other depositional processes deserve consideration (Lopinot 1992), the paucity of shelled maize at Lohmann- and Stirling-phase homesteads may be a direct reflection of its appropriation by elites at centers.

Of the rural changes during the Mississippi period, Mehrer (1988:138) notes that there "was an architectural trend from relatively little variation

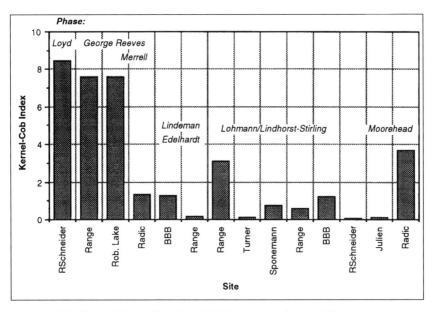

Figure 4.4. The Ratio of Maize Kernels to Cob Fragments at Selected Sites

and lack of interior bulk storage in the earlier phases to more variation with abundant interior storage in Stirling times and then to considerable variety but less interior storage in later times." The trend toward interior storage pits, like a parallel trend witnessed at Cahokia, may be the archaeological signatures of the attempts on the part of households to hide their staple stores, presumably from the eyes of appropriating social forces (DeBoer 1988:10; Mehrer 1988:152–153). Stirling-phase homesteads included some larger or more stable settlements that have been referred to as "nodal hamlets" (Emerson 1992). These sites typically contain three to four rectangular structures and a circular sweat house.

The larger-than-average Stirling-phase homesteads (i.e., in terms of the number of structures) and their longer-than-average occupation spans would seem to indicate that stable residential groups occupied the rural location for a lengthy period of time. Perhaps the social position of the households that left behind these "nodal" remains were more important in the local rural scene, fulfilling certain ritual services for surrounding households. The quantity of nonlocal artifacts at Julien, for instance, could be used in such an argument (see Milner 1984a). Such homesteads demonstrate that rural social life was stable and that certain localities may have been occupied by a set of related households—a "dispersed community"—for considerable periods of time (Emerson 1992). Moreover, these rural farmers and gatherers would have been integrated into local districts or territories managed by local office-holders residing at the secondary centers.

Rural Mississippian population in part of the Northern Bottom Expanse reached a peak during the Stirling phase (Milner 1986). Population subsequently decreased through the Moorehead and Sand Prairie phases (Milner 1986:232–234). The Moorehead-phase rural population of the Northern Bottom Expanse proper, for instance, is thought to have been at most 40 percent of the Stirling-phase levels (Milner 1986:232–233). At the same time, the population of the nearby uplands was probably increasing (Koldehoff 1989:61–62; Pauketat and Koldehoff 1983).

Secondary Political-Administrative Centers

Besides the paramount center of Cahokia, as many as twenty-five archaeological sites in the American Bottom region have or may have had associated Mississippian mounds (figure 4.5). The precise number of sites will vary according to how "site" is defined. For instance, the mounds and associated occupational debris that line the Cahokia Creek bank between

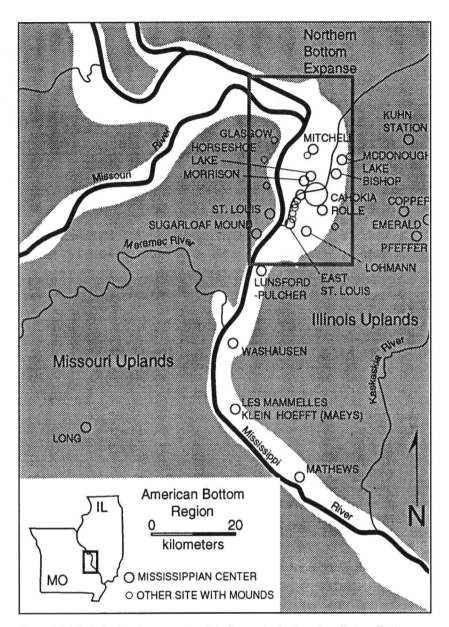

Figure 4.5. Mississippian Centers or Possible Centers in the American Bottom Region

the Cahokia and East St. Louis sites could each be considered separate sites. For this reason, I have introduced the concept of a Central Political-Administrative Complex that incorporates the sprawling St. Louis, East St. Louis, and Cahokia sites.

Outside the Central Political-Administrative Complex, the Mississippian association of the Bishop, Eisely, McDonough Lake, and the southern American Bottom–site mounds is uncertain (cf. Kelly et al. 1979:56; Gregg 1975:79; Harn 1980; Moorehead 1929:62–64; Munson 1971:35–38; Wiegers 1982). In addition, the ages of two adjacent conical mounds (Fox Hill and Sugarloaf) on the bluff top northeast of Cahokia are uncertain. Lastly, temporal affiliation of mounds illustrated by Bushnell (1904) north of the St. Louis site is unknown.

Excluding the central complex, sites with mounds and confirmed components belonging to the eleventh or twelfth centuries A.D. include Mitchell, Hoeffken, Emerald, Lohmann, Horseshoe Lake, and Long (Adams 1949; Chapman 1980:164–169; Gregg 1975; Kelly n.d.; Esarey and Pauketat 1992; Porter 1974; Winters and Struever 1962). The Kuhn Station and Copper sites east of the American Bottom probably date to the Sand Prairie phase, while Emerald and Pfeffer have both Emergent Mississippian and Mississippian components (Fowler and Hall 1978:565; Pauketat and Koldehoff 1983; Koldehoff 1980:8). A Lohmann-phase structure has been excavated at the Pfeffer (a.k.a. "Christ") site (Kelly, Mertz, and Kinsella 1989). Two of the five or more mounds at the Emerald site have produced Moorehead- or Sand Prairie–phase pottery. The Long site in the Big River drainage contained three mounds, at least one of which was a substructural platform (Adams 1949:36–47). Artifacts and features similar to those from the American Bottom's Stirling phase were recovered (cf. Chapman 1980). Milner (1990) believes that its location may have been strategic with regard to nearby galena deposits, and the same may be true of nearby Crescent Hills chert and perhaps even Missouri fire clay.

Two now-leveled mounds and Mississippian artifacts were associated with the Rolle site just to the south of Cahokia (Throop 1928:40–41). The adjacent Olszewski site has produced Lohmann- through Moorehead-phase materials from feature contexts (Hanenberger 1990b; Pauketat and Koldehoff 1988). The excavations and salvage data recovery from the Olszewski site resulted in the documentation of domestic feature clusters in higher densities than the ordinary rural homestead. Moreover, if we assume that the amount of maize kernels relative to cobs or cob fragments in domestic refuse should be higher at an administrative center (where shelled kernels would have comprised a mobilized staple), then the high Olszewski kernel-cob index of 17.91 (Dunavan 1990) may further support the site as a local center or an outlying part of the Central Political-Administrative Complex.

The small-scale excavations at Horseshoe Lake exposed structures and provided information on the internal structure of the mound (Gregg 1975). Gregg (1975:148–151, 179) identified the mound as a Fairmount (now Lohmann) phase platform with two or more terraces built in four or more stages. Besides the mound, there is little in the small excavated sample to suggest administrative activities. Gregg (1975:295, 321) noted that the seemingly high incidence of "field dressed" terrestrial birds and white-tailed deer may be indicative of an elite diet. In a similar vein, perhaps the (unquantified amount of) maize kernels and the absence of cobs in Lohmann-phase features (#5, 16–17, 19–20, 22, 26–28) is suggestive of the shelled-maize provisions received by the Horseshoe Lake patrons by their nonelite clientele.

Excavations at Mitchell have provided abundant clues of a long-term and extensive occupation (Porter 1974). Everything from Emergent Mississippian to Moorehead-phase features was found during excavations. The remains of large buildings were associated with Mitchell-site platform mounds (Porter 1974:147–152). Buildings built and rebuilt frequently below or on top of mounds appear to be affiliated with the Stirling and Moorehead phases (Porter 1974:149–150). There are large post pits with equally large insertion and extraction ramps indicating that enormous logs were hoisted into an upright position and later removed. Indeed, one segment of a bald cypress log measuring three meters in length and nearly one meter in diameter was found resting at the base of a four-meter-deep post pit (Porter 1974:map 29, 1977:145). There also are large quantities of white-tailed deer bones (Porter 1974:129), but no study has yet been undertaken to examine the faunal patterning.

A large material scatter and a now-destroyed mound were associated with the Lohmann site, intermediate between Cahokia, East St. Louis, and Lunsford-Pulcher (Kelly et al. 1979:66–69). Along the eastern periphery of the site excavations related to the widening of a nearby highway were conducted, providing some interesting insights into the structure of a small administrative center. One unusual wall-trench building is "larger than most recorded Lohmann phase structures" and "stands out as the prime example of an extradomestic facility" (Esarey and Pauketat 1992:157). Its long axis is oriented at odds with other domiciles, and it was rebuilt at least once. On its floor were an adze blade, silicified sediment flakes, and an adult male cranial section (Esarey and Pauketat 1992:157). Other seemingly ordinary buildings had extraordinary contents. One building contained on its floor an extended supine interment of an individual missing his right leg below the knee, a heretofore unknown mortuary practice in the American Bottom. On the floor of another building was a cache of unfinished megalithic axeheads. In a separate pit was found a cache of unfinished megalithic axeheads (Esarey and Pauketat 1992:157).

Perhaps the maize kernel-cob index (3.5) of the excavated Lohmann-site Stirling-phase domestic zone is indicative of the shelled-maize provisions received by the local officials. It exceeds the value of the nearby and contemporaneous rural homesteads at the Turner and DeMange sites, even if a cob-filled smudge pit is excluded from consideration (see Johannessen 1991; Whalley 1983). Perhaps the greater quantity of mammalian remains associated with the Lohmann-phase features at the Lohmann site compared to the Lohmann- and Stirling-phase homestead features at the Turner and DeMange sites (see Cross 1983:206–207, 1992) is indicative of the meat provisions with which the Mississippian elite were supplied.[4] Perhaps the lengthy occupation span of the Stirling-phase domestic zone (a pair of structures and associated pits) at the Lohmann site may signal the economic stability of the center of a tributary network of dispersed homesteads (see Pauketat 1989).

Cahokia and the Central Political-Administrative Complex

A number of archaeological features that set Cahokia of the eleventh and twelfth centuries A.D. off from the rest of the communities in the American Bottom have been used to characterize the site and other portions of the Central Political-Administrative Complex as a regional center. Of primary significance, of course, is the sheer magnitude of Cahokia. The Cahokia site is a concentration of mounds, residential areas, plazas, palisade walls, and mortuary remains that has been rather arbitrarily defined

---

4. The Turner-DeMange kernel-cob index = 0.1 (or 1.6 if smudge-pit feature 140 is excluded). No detailed taphonomic study has been made of the faunal assemblages, but it is worthy of note that while mammals comprise 33 percent of a minimum of fifty-eight animals represented in the Lohmann-phase domestic garbage at the Lohmann site (Cross 1992), no individual mammals were identified among the minimum of forty-four animals (fish, birds, and reptiles) found at the Turner and DeMange sites (Cross 1983). The mammal bones that were present in the Turner-DeMange faunal assemblage—perhaps fragments of raccoon, squirrel, and deer—were found in six of the seven homestead feature clusters; there is no reason to suspect that their paucity is a consequence of differential preservation either between the feature clusters at the site or between these clusters and the Lohmann-site features (see Cross 1983:206–7).

to cover approximately fourteen square kilometers (Fowler 1989; cf. Kelly 1991c). However, this fourteen-square-kilometer site area actually consists of a series of moderately discrete clusters of monuments, plazas, mortuaries, and residential subcommunities. There is some indication of planned community structure, organizational axes, baselines, and leveled land at the core of this complex (Fowler 1989:figure 6.31), but the entire site is not so discretely bounded as might be inferred from past descriptions (Fowler 1975a; Gregg 1975a).

For example, the mounds in the vicinity of the Powell Tract stand out as a discrete cluster removed from the majority of Cahokia mounds (figure 4.3). Occupational debris and mounds continue from the Powell mound group in an unbroken line east to the main Cahokia site and south to the East St. Louis site. That is, there is no clear dividing line between the Cahokia and East St. Louis sites. Each mound-and-residential cluster could be isolated as an individual site. The East St. Louis site, with its forty-five or more mounds spread out in a mile-long semicircle, constitutes an extension of this linear mound-and-residential cluster pattern albeit also featuring small mound-and-plaza clusters within this semicircle. The St. Louis site, with its twenty-six mounds, is isolatable thanks to the Mississippi River, but its proximity and uncertain temporal and hierarchical relationship to Cahokia and East St. Louis could be a sign that it also represented a continuation of the sprawling Central Political-Administrative Complex.

Mounds and Plazas

The most visible features of the Cahokia site and the rest of the Central Political-Administrative Complex are its mounds. These include a plethora of rectangular and circular flat-topped platforms, conical tumuli, and a form unique to Cahokia (and perhaps East St. Louis) called "ridgetop" mounds (Fowler 1975a:95–96, 1977:15; Iseminger 1980:3; Pauketat 1993:chapter 10). Over 100 mounds are believed to have made up the Cahokia site (Fowler 1989). Based on the excavations of Moorehead (1922, 1923, 1929), surface collections made by Griffin's Central Mississippi Valley Archaeological Survey (Kozlovich 1953), and other excavations, it is likely that mound construction occurred incrementally throughout the Mississippi period (see Fowler 1989). Incremental construction, notwithstanding marked changes in the size of mantle additions, typifies the Kunnemann Mound (figure 4.6), the Murdock Mound (H. Smith 1977), the Powell Mound (Ahler and DePuydt 1987), Monks Mound (Reed, Bennett,

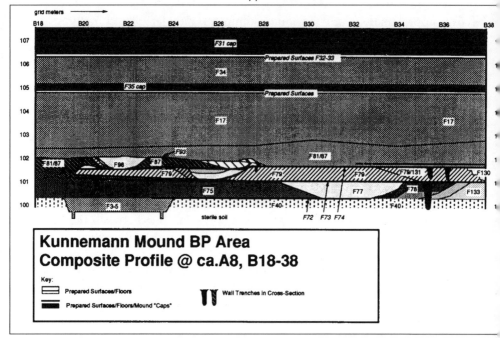

Figure 4.6. A Composite Profile of the Kunnemann Mound, Cahokia

and Porter 1968), and most other Cahokia mounds (Pauketat 1993:chapter 10). The beginning of the construction of Monks Mound, by any measure the largest prehistoric substructural feature of its kind north of Mexico, was thought by Reed, Bennett, and Porter (1968) to date to the Emergent Mississippi period. The final construction episodes of Monks Mound's first terrace are dated to the Moorehead phase (Benchley 1975:20).

The platform mounds, typically truncated pyramids in shape (Reed 1977), appear in most cases to have been substructural monuments (Fowler 1989:192–194). The circular mounds, speculated by some to be conical mortuary facilities, are instead probably flat-topped platforms as well (Pauketat 1993; cf. Fowler 1989:194; Milner 1984c:479). These earthworks are commonly arranged around open plazas rectangular in shape. The eight ridge-top mounds appear to contain elite mortuary facilities that may have been associated with charnel houses (Fowler 1989:194–195; Milner 1984c:479–480). In the case of the Powell Mound and Mound 72, the ridge-top mantle represents the final cap to the mound. This shape, in fact, conceivably could represent the ridge line of a roof of sorts, marking the monument as a house of the elite dead.

Another visible feature of the Cahokia site is the broad, flat land surface upon which the central portion rests. Based on recent electromagnetic survey and limited test excavations, it has been suggested that the central "Grand Plaza" (Fowler 1989:200) might have been constructed sometime around the terminal Emergent Mississippian and earliest-Mississippian interface (Dalan 1989:108; Holley et al. 1990a; Woods and Holley 1989:230). Given the residual nature of the Emergent Mississippian ceramics in the excavated plaza deposits (see Holley et al. 1990a), I suspect that this extensive leveling of the central portion of the Cahokia site points toward a Lohmann-phase construction. Certainly, other borrowing and filling operations at Cahokia have been well documented for the Lohmann phase, leaving such features as the sub-Mound 51 borrow pit (see Bareis 1975a:10–11; Bareis and Lathrap 1962; Chmurny 1973).

Elite Mortuaries

Milner (1984c, 1990:12–13) and Kelly (n.d.) have documented the distinctiveness of the Mississippian elite in mortuary contexts, as opposed to the nonelite both within and peripheral to the Cahokia site and the other large centers. As they conclude, the elite mortuaries in the Cemetery Mound at East St. Louis, the Big Mound at St. Louis, the large Mitchell site mound, and at least four Cahokia-area mounds (Powell, Harding, Mound 72, and the Wilson or Junkyard Mound) are representative of a class of facilities that appear to hold the highest echelons of the elite dead. For instance, the Cemetery Mound reportedly contained two large burial pits. In one pit, burials were accompanied by marine whelk shells, marine shell beads, whole pots, groundstone tools, a chert ceremonial axehead, chert adze blades, arrow points, and one or probably two copper-covered limestone earspools. The other pit, based on a newspaper account of the time, appears to have been full of women and contained pottery vessels only (Kelly n.d.).

The Big Mound in St. Louis similarly was reported to have contained a large tomb near its base. In this were articulated human remains interred in a row. Accompanying them were marine shell disk "beads and shells in prodigious numbers, though in no instance were both deposited with the same individual" (Conant 1877 cited by Chapman 1980:166; see Williams and Goggin 1956:21–23). Elsewhere was a pair of burials, perhaps male and female, with which were placed marine-whelk columellae, nine columnar or barrel-shaped marine shell beads "one inch in length and nearly one-half in diameter," and two copper long-nosed god maskettes (Conant

1877 cited by Chapman 1980:166). Also associated with the mound were small marine snail-shell beads (*Marginella* sp.), woven cloth, an earspool, and arrow points (Chapman 1980:166).

The large Mitchell Mound, destroyed in 1876, contained a long rectangular pit or "trench" six to eight feet wide and full of human bones and numerous copper and marine shell artifacts. The artifacts included copper tortoise-carapace objects, copper awls or needles, copper-covered bone earspools, a copper-covered deer mandible, and other copper-covered wooden items most of which apparently had been wrapped in animal skins and fabric prior to burial. Marine whelk shells, a whelk-shell dipper, and marine-shell beads were found along with mollusc shell pendants and a Ramey knife (Howland 1877; Winters 1974).

Materials associated with the Powell-Mound mortuary included biconical copper earspools, marine-shell bead-and-pendant necklaces, and what may have been fabric studded with small *Marginella*-shell beads (Ahler and DePuydt 1987; A. R. Kelly 1931; Titterington 1938, n.d.). The Wilson or Junkyard Mound excavations of Preston Holder in 1954 uncovered a large mortuary facility in which scores of individuals are represented (Milner 1984c:figure 5). Copper-covered bone earspools and large numbers of marine whelk shells, columellae, and disk beads were found associated with this feature.[5]

Similarly, in Mound 72 large amounts of marine-shell disk and columnar beads were found. The lavish accoutrements in this mound also included over 1,000 finely chipped stone arrow points, many of which had been mounted on bundles of arrows, antler projectile points, a rolled tube of sheet copper, chunky stones, and a pile of mica (Fowler 1991; Fowler and Anderson 1975). The human remains in this mound appear to have been interred during a series of mortuary episodes, some of which involved the mass burial of honored dead (extended burials on cedar litters and a pit full of some forty fully articulated females) and dishonored dead (including the haphazardly entombed burials beneath the cedar litters and another group of beheaded and behanded males). Another portion of the mound contained an important male surrounded by what seem to be likely material (and human) offerings (Fowler 1974:20–22; Fowler and Anderson 1975).

Mound 72 and perhaps the Wilson Mound have been dated to the Lohmann phase. As these features illustrate, "an elite social stratum had

5. Field notes of Preston Holder, on file at the Museum of Anthropology at the University of Michigan. The Wilson Mound artifacts are curated by the Illinois State Museum, accession number 1957–14.

developed at Cahokia that is distinguishable by segregated and elaborate mortuary areas. There was differential access to unusual items, many presumably signifying high-status positions, that were often finely crafted, fashioned from exotic materials, and occasionally disposed of in considerable numbers" (Milner 1990:12). It also should be added that, in the case of dishonored males, warfare-related deaths may be implicated. The evidence for later Stirling-phase and Moorehead-phase elite burials at Cahokia and elsewhere is less certain, given that the excavations of these features occurred prior to the implementation of formal archaeological techniques in the region (Milner 1984c:484). It is likely, however, that some ridge-top mound mortuaries date to the Stirling phase.

It is important to note that objects in nonelite mortuaries peripheral to the American Bottom proper in bluff-top cemeteries (and in the lower Illinois River valley) include low numbers of the craft items also found in the elite mortuaries (Milner 1984c). Copper-covered earspools, rolled copper beads, chunky stones, and marine-shell beads were found at the Kane Burial Mound and McCain cemeteries (Fugle 1962; Melbye 1963; Milner 1984c; Pauketat 1986:appendix). These same things were also found at the Schild cemetery in the lower Illinois River valley (Perino 1971). A fire-clay figurine pipe was found at Schild and at a bluff-top location in the American Bottom (Emerson 1983:259). Marine-shell beads, chunky stones, and long-nosed god maskettes were found in a bluff-top cemetery at the Booker T. Washington site in the Northern Bottom Expanse (Perino 1971:141). A chunky stone, Ramey knives, and an exotic long-stemmed axehead were found at the Soucy Cemetery site (Pauketat 1983; F. Terry Norris, personal communication, 1986). A pipe, shell beads, and chunky stones may have been associated with a nonelite cemetery on Walker's Island, Horseshoe Lake (Norris 1975). In the instance of the Kane Burial Mound, the nonelite interments date to the Moorehead phase. On the other hand, in the case of Mound 72, the elite mortuary dates to the late Lohmann phase (see Fowler 1991; Milner 1984). Perhaps the distribution and temporal affiliations of these objects may be related to the dispersal of prestige goods from core elite to peripheral nonelites over a period of one to two centuries (cf. Brown et al. 1990).

Central Residential Subcommunities

As opposed to many rural homesteads and farmsteads of the eleventh and twelfth centuries A.D., domestic remains at Cahokia and other political-administrative centers provide evidence for the extended use of house sites or domestic zones over many years. Structures were rebuilt in the same spot over and over. While the best estimates of the duration of rural sites average only a few years (Pauketat 1989:301–302), a Stirling-phase domestic zone at a secondary Mississippian center is estimated to have been occupied for fifteen to twenty years (Esarey and Pauketat 1992:159). The rebuilt houses excavated at Tract 15A, 15B, the Powell and Merrell Tracts, and the Interpretive Center Tract-II were likely occupied for equally long spans of time.

The large excavated tracts of the Cahokia site along with the surface evidence from the Kunnemann Tract provide possible evidence of what may have been discrete "subcommunities" (Collins 1990; Fowler 1975:100, 1978:466; 1989:202; O'Brien 1972). At the Interpretive Center Tract-II, for instance, the (late) Lohmann-phase subcommunity arrangement appears to have consisted of a series of buildings at orthagonal angles to each other surrounding a well-built and larger-than-average T-shaped structure and adjacent to a possible plaza containing large post pits (Collins 1990:figure 5.2). The Stirling-phase occupation of the Powell tract seems to include a similar group and a large rectangular building of around 180 square meters (O'Brien 1972:figure 13; Mehrer 1988:160). The Lohmann-phase evidence from Tract 15A and the Dunham Tract also features two building size modes and a subcommunity plaza (see chapter 5). The arrangement of domiciles on the Kunnemann Tract has not been documented except by Preston Holder's excavations beneath Kunnemann Mound and the surface indications of domestic debris (Holley 1990; Pauketat 1993).

As noted by a number of researchers in the past (see Milner 1990:13–14), it has been suspected that the central subcommunities may have been involved to variable extent in craft-goods production. It is certainly reasonable to suspect that, given the extended occupancy of Cahokia domestic zones relative to many rural sites, Cahokian households would have been supported to some extent by their linkage to high-ranking subgroups at the site, linkages that might have entailed reciprocation by "attached" households in terms of the production of craft items (*sensu* Brumfiel and Earle 1987).

The production of shell beads at Cahokia in particular has been characterized as a craft intensively practiced by a limited number of Cahokian households (Yerkes 1983, 1989, 1991). Shell-working tool debris and marine shell scrap are by no means rare at Cahokia and have been found in a number of excavated contexts (e.g., Ahler and DePuydt 1987:24–29; Pauketat 1987a, 1991:table 2). However, the densities of microlithic shell-bead manufacturing tools and tool-making debitage are quite high on a fairly small portion of the Kunnemann Tract (Holley 1990; Mason and

Perino 1961; Yerkes 1991), while they are lower among other sectors of the community (e.g., the Lohmann- and Stirling-phase subcommunities at ICT-II). The high-density deposits of unfinished or broken beads, microlithic artifacts, and sandstone files from a single building and midden adjacent to an early stage of the Kunnemann Mound, along with the scattered beads and microlithic tools on the mound itself, illustrate the close relationship between craft production and the elite activities and architecture on and around the mound (Pauketat 1993). From this debris we may infer that shell working and necklace manufacture were subsidized or performed by the Cahokian elite during the Lohmann and Stirling phases (Pauketat 1993:chapter 10). Importantly, the craft activities documented in these excavations and in the surface indications from the Kunnemann Tract stand out as qualitatively distinct from the small-scale shell working and bead manufacture outside Cahokia (e.g., Prentice 1983; Yerkes 1992).

Monumental Architecture

A series of extraordinary wall-trench buildings has been documented at the Cahokia site, most dating to the Stirling phase. These include huge rectangular or circular structures atop Monks, Murdock, and Kunnemann Mounds and on Tracts 15A and 15B (see Fowler 1975b:figure 31; H. Smith 1977; Pauketat 1993). Both Kunnemann and Murdock provide sequential information on nondomestic architecture. About twelve mantles were identified in the Murdock Mound, each surmounted by a wall-trench building. The largest of the rectangular buildings had a floor area of 150 square meters and large roof support posts (see H. Smith 1977:figures 34–37; cf. Pauketat 1993:chapter 10). Similarly, a total of forty-four distinct platform-mound enlargements and mantles comprise the construction history of the Kunnemann Mound (Pauketat 1993). A total of eighteen elaborate buildings with black- or red-plastered floors, circular puddled hearths, and unusual internel features were documented in the limited excavations on top of the mound's various stages. These buildings were usually large, the rectangular forms covering from 25 to over 96 square meters and a circular example covering an area of 58 square meters.

A series of features excavated on Tract 15B in 1960 appears to have been gigantic circular buildings or rotundas dating to the Lohmann or Stirling phases (see Wittry 1960a; Wittry and Vogel 1962). They superimpose Emergent Mississippian house basins and are superimposed by large rectangular structures elsewhere dated to the Moorehead and Sand Prairie phases (see chapter 5; Salzer 1975:7). The 15B rotundas include an ill-defined early version consisting of narrow wall trench segments of which only the southern portion is visible in the exposed surface; it may have measured 15 to 18 meters in diameter (figure 4.7a). An extraordinarily large circular building with a 60-plus-centimeter-wide wall trench measures 24 meters in diameter and covers an area of 452 square meters (figure 4.7b). Three other arcs of large postmolds are located around the exterior of the wall trench feature. The northern and southwestern arcs consist of postmolds about 30 to 60 centimeters in diameter (few obvious insertion ramps) spaced some 30 to 120 centimeters apart (figure 4.7c). A third arc of post pits (postmolds with insertion ramps) is found regularly spaced about 120 centimeters apart along the eastern exterior of the wall trench feature (figure 4.7d). These arcs of post molds and post pits may represent separate, albeit ill-defined, circular structures. However, given their concentricity with the circular wall trench feature 238, it is possible that the post depressions represent the rebuilt walls of this same wall-trench building; there also is some indication that the southern wall trench feature 238 diverges at one point, perhaps a consequence of a rebuilding episode. Three perhaps sequential post pits are located in the approximate center of the largest rotunda, presumably for the support of a roof (figure 4.7e).

Unlike these circular rotundas is another form of circular construction called "woodhenges" by Wittry (1964, 1977, 1980), Hall (1985:183–184), and Smith (1992) but hereafter referred to as Post-Circle Monuments (figure 4.8). These monuments were recognized by Wittry based on his 1961 excavation of Tract 15A. Later 15A excavations located additional component post pits associated with four identified circles that range from 72 to over 140 meters in diameter and were made up of from 21 to 48 perimeter posts. Central posts of the larger post-circle monuments, offset one to two meters east of center, were delineated by Hall's work in 1963 (Hall 1964). These were offset, according to Wittry (1977:47), to allow a human observer of astronomical alignments to sight along the center post and the perimeter posts.

There are indications of other Post-Circle Monuments in the form of sets of two or three adjacent post pits. These suggestive sets of post pits include features found just south of Tract 15A in the Dunham Tract. Based only on the sample of Tract 15A and the Dunham Tract in hand, it might be speculated that ten or more Post-Circle Monuments (rather than just four)

Figure 4.7 (facing page). A Portion of Tract 15B, Plan View

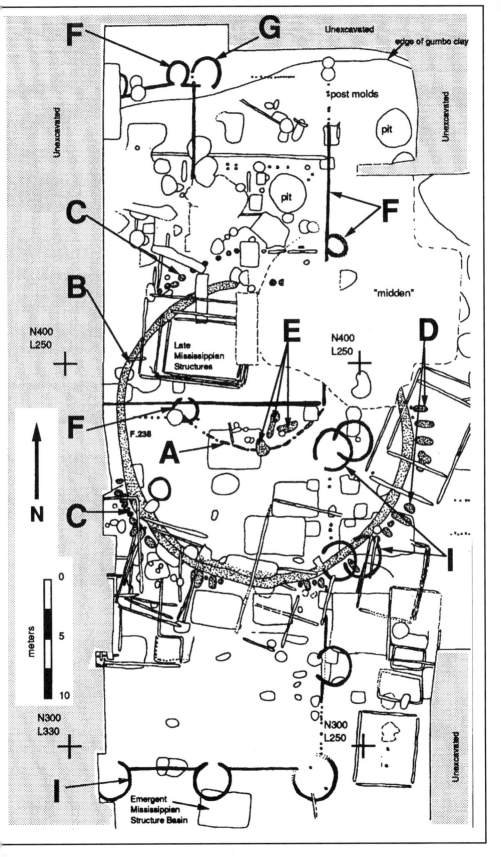

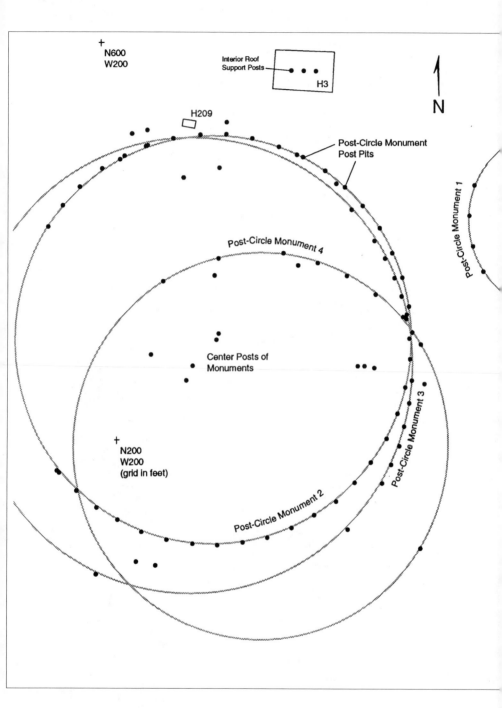

Figure 4.8. The Post-Circle Monuments at Cahokia

could have been constructed over a period of time in the vicinity of Tract 15A. If correct, the sequential reconstruction of the Post-Circle Monuments may be reminiscent of the mode of mound construction at the site (see above).

Palisades and Compounds

The principal identified palisade at Cahokia is a large wall with evenly spaced bastions that encircled the central precinct of Cahokia (figure 4.3). This feature initially was constructed during the late Stirling phase and was wholly rebuilt at least three times during the late Stirling and early Moorehead phases (Anderson 1977:92; Pauketat 1987a, 1990:72). Iseminger (1990:35) has estimated that about 20,000 logs were used during each of these four primary construction episodes. During this time, the size of the wall posts and the shape and spacing of bastions and entryways evolved (Iseminger 1990; see also Anderson 1977; Holley et al. 1990b). Iseminger (1990) argues that, because of the 20-meter spacing of bastions (a reasonable distance for the effective use of bows and arrows), the use of screened entrances, and the possible presence of catwalks along the inside of walls, all constructions had a defensive intent. Koldehoff (1990b:92) also suggests that the quantity of arrow points with impact and bend fractures found around the palisade wall indicates that the wall actively served a defensive function.

Subsequent to the prehistoric removal of the circular rotundas on Tract 15B, it appears that at least two and perhaps four rectangular compounds were constructed (figure 4.7). These had open-backed circular bastions spaced along their walls and at their corners like the bastions associated with the earliest (late Stirling-phase) central palisade wall (Anderson 1977; Iseminger 1990). Wittry (1960) observed that the compound's posts averaged 12 centimeters in diameter and "were set at intervals of one foot or less on center. The fill of the post molds indicated that the walls had been covered with orange-colored clay" (Wittry 1960:6; also Wittry and Vogel 1962:28).

The rectangular enclosure represented in the northern exposed portion of Tract 15B measures about 25 meters across its north-south axis; the incompletely exposed east-west dimension exceeds 18 meters (figure 4.7f). The small round bastions associated with this compound are about 1.5 meters in diameter. A single wall and bastion (2 meters in diameter) of a possible second rectangular compound in this northern area superimposes a wall of the first feature (figure 4.7g). Another large rectangular compound(s) was constructed south of the first one, its eastern side represented by two sets of superposed bastions (figure 4.7h). The north-south dimensions of the southern enclosure match those of the northern compound, although the bastions of this southern feature are large, measuring 2.7–3.0 meters in diameter.

If we assume that the rectangular compounds on Tract 15B were in fact square in plan shape, then the area enclosed by them is 625 square meters. The interior division of space is not clear, but it is possible that one wall-trench building or more was located inside the southern rectangular compound. The function of these extraordinarily large walled enclosures is speculative. Their size and the existence of possible mud-plastered walls and bastions may indicate that whatever was inside not only took up a considerable amount of space but required protection. It is possible that these compounds screened off elite sanctum sanctorums. Alternately, the enclosures might have been storage areas for the material accumulations of the central residents of Cahokia. If the latter was true, then we might reasonably wonder who the potential marauders of the enclosed contents might have been, and we might suspect that the legitimacy of the paramount claims to the contents was being called into question at some level and by some element of the population.

Craft Debris and Exotic Artifacts in Mississippian Refuse

While the excavated sample of sites dating to the eleventh and twelfth centuries in the American Bottom is perhaps among the most extensive in North America, this sample consists mostly of small rural sites. There is available information from Mississippian centers, but its quality and comparability are variable. In order to establish a baseline of the regional political economy, I will here summarize current information on the distribution of certain artifact classes among the rural homesteads and political-administrative centers in terms of both qualitative and quantitative considerations.

A variety of nonperishable materials is recovered from Mississippi-period sites in the American Bottom region. Sandstone, limestone, silt-stone, igneous and metamorphic cobbles, and chert are by and large obtainable within 10 to 20 kilometers of any site in the region. Other lithic materials, minerals, mineraloids, and metal ores originated from nonlocal sources. Nonlocal finished objects and raw materials found in assemblages of Mississippian refuse in the American Bottom region include a variety of cherts, large bifacial tools, small bifacial arrow points, minerals, copper, igneous rocks, pots, and marine shells (Griffin 1984:xvi; Kelly 1991a, 1991b; Milner 1990:23–27).

Exotic Siliceous Raw Materials and Tools

The vast majority of siliceous artifacts in Mississippian refuse consists of Burlington, St. Louis, Ste. Genevieve, Salem, and glacial gravel cherts all found in the uplands within 30 kilometers of Cahokia (see Kelly 1984; Koldehoff 1990a, 1990b). The exotic cherts associated with Mississippian deposits include Fort Payne (Dover or Elco) chert, a black chert, several Union County cherts, and a silicified sediment. Fort Payne chert has been reported from the Interior Low Plateau Province of southern Illinois and the Tennessee and Cumberland drainages of Kentucky and Tennessee (Koldehoff 1990c:84; Nance 1984). It is most often found in the form of amorphous flakes or flake-tools and occasionally in the form of projectile points in the refuse of American Bottom Mississippians (e.g., Koldehoff 1990c:91). The black chert from Tract 15A may be Pitkin chert from the Ouachita Mountains in southwestern Arkansas (see House 1975) or a dark variety of Fort Payne. This may be the same material out of which was made a cache of "Black stemmed" projectile points from Mound 72 (see Fowler 1991:figure 1.15).

The Union County cherts, from Union County, Illinois, include the so-called Kaolin, Cobden or Dongola, and Mill Creek types (Kelly 1984:27–33; Koldehoff 1990c:78–85; Mays 1984). Of these, Cobden or Dongola chert appears primarily as projectile points. Mill Creek chert is represented primarily in the form of hoe blades and, along with Kaolin chert, a whole range of large bifaces including "Ramey" knives, polished nonutilitarian axe blades (or "spuds"), and adze blades (figure 4.9; see Pauketat 1983; Titterington 1938:figures 17–24). Artifacts made from a silicified sediment similar to Hixton from Wisconsin and other varieties from southwestern Illinois and perhaps the Missouri Ozarks (cf. Griffin 1984:xvi; Koldehoff 1990c:84, personal communication, 1991; Porter 1974:908–909) include primarily flakes and flake tools. Silicified-sediment artifacts also include projectile points and in one case a polished nonutilitarian axehead (Emerson and Jackson 1984:243; Pauketat 1983:4).

Large Mill Creek and Kaolin chert bifaces apparently were produced in the Mill Creek valley of extreme southern Illinois, not in the American Bottom region (Brown et al. 1990; Cobb 1988; Kelly 1984; Koldehoff 1990b, 1990c; Pauketat 1983; Winters 1981). Recycled Mill Creek chert tool fragments often were used as expedient implements or were remanufactured

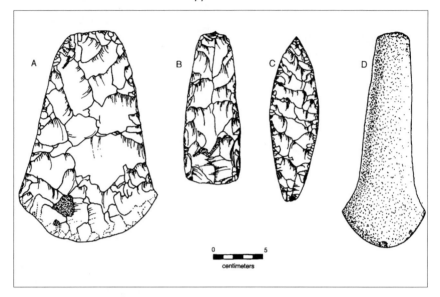

Figure 4.9. Chert Hoe, Adze, Knife, and Axe Blades (a–c, adapted from Milner 1984a; d, adapted from Moorehead 1929)

into cores, drills, and projectile points. Kaolin chert cores may have been used expressly for the manufacture of flake tools and projectile points, not unlike that described for Fort Payne chert. It is also important to note that a large biface industry similar to that located in the Mill Creek valley of southern Illinois existed in the Crescent Hills area of the northern Ozark fringe just 30 kilometers southwest of Cahokia. Based on what little archaeological evidence is available from sites in the Meramec and Big River drainages, we may surmise that Burlington hoe blades, Ramey knives, and adze blades found in the American Bottom were manufactured in Missouri (see Adams 1949; Ives 1984; Watts and Watts 1980). This same Burlington chert was a mainstay of Mississippian lithic technology in the American Bottom, oftentimes accounting for 90 to 100 percent of chert debitage at archaeological sites. Yet it is most often involved in the expedient-tool ("informal" core-and-flake) industry and a microlith industry (Kelly 1984; Koldehoff 1987, 1990a).

In addition to the large-biface, expedient-tool, and microlith industries, Burlington chert also was used in "small biface" or projectile point production (Koldehoff 1987, 1990a). Projectile points and arrows undoubtedly were a common local product. There also are numerous examples of exotic projectile points identified on the basis of both their formal attributes and the nonlocal cherts used in their manufacture. Hayes, Agee,

Alba, Homan, and Bayogoula points have been illustrated in published reports of American Bottom Mississippian remains (Milner 1984a:figure 46; Moorehead 1929:plate 13, lower row [three on the left]; Titterington 1938:figure 13:bottom row; Grimm 1980:56, upper left section, lower row).[6] Most of these are forms originating from the mid-South and appear to have been made in many cases from mid-southern cherts and jaspers. Examples of nonlocal points manufactured from silicified sediment also are known (Emerson and Jackson 1984:243; Titterington 1938:figure 15, top row).

It is significant to note that, based on my own macroscopic examination, many of the nonlocal forms among the caches of Mound-72 projectile points actually were produced from local Burlington cherts. Equally significant is the presence among the Mound-72 assemblage of local point forms made from silicified sediment and exotic Fort Payne, Mill Creek, and Kaolin cherts. There are nonlocal point forms manufactured using exotic cherts among the Mound-72 specimens, but most of the 1,000 or so finely chipped arrow points in Mound 72 probably were local products (Fowler 1991:14).

Minerals and Copper

Found among Mississippian occupational remains from the American Bottom are a number of minerals, mineraloids, and metal ores—fluorite, barite, quartz, hematite, galena, fire clay, and copper—presumably derived from distant sources (Kelly 1991a, 1991b). Fluorite crystals infrequently are recovered in Mississippian assemblages and originate from southeastern Illinois near the Ohio River. Quartz crystals are known from geodes in limestone strata to the north, south, and west of the Northern Bottom Expanse (Porter 1974:935), but the crystals in these geodes are small. Large crystals (from geodes) the size of the illustrated example from the BBB Motor site (Emerson and Jackson 1984:figure 68e) probably originated from central Arkansas or perhaps northern Missouri or southeastern Iowa (see Porter 1974:935–936). Quartz-crystal flakes found at Tract 15A and rare quartz-crystal projectile points would seem to have been knapped from these large nonlocal crystals (see Titterington 1938:figure 15b).

Hematite and copper can be found in the glacial tills of the uplands to the east of the American Bottom (Kelly 1980, 1990a; Milner 1990:24). However, hematite also is abundant in the Missouri Ozarks (Porter

6. As these types have been defined by Bell (1958:8, 32), Justice (1987:220–22, 235–37), Perino (1968:4, 34, 1985:29), and Williams and Brain (1983:222).

1974:937). It could have been obtained near the galena source. Walthall (1981) has demonstrated the origin of most American Bottom galena to be the Potosi source in the eastern Ozarks. It is not certain whether the copper found in Mississippian contexts in the American Bottom was acquired via human channels from the Lake Superior region, or whether float copper in the glacial tills of Illinois was relied upon (Goad 1980; Goodman 1984:7–9). Fragments of Ramey Incised pottery vessels were found at the Lakes-phase Sand Point site located on the Lake Superior shoreline (Dorothy 1980) a discovery that, although not constituting evidence for direct control of the copper sources by Cahokians, probably does signal the point of entry for a substantial quantity of copper into Upper Mississippian and perhaps Middle Mississippian exchange networks (Milner 1990:25). Copper shows up in the form of finished ornamental items at the Cahokia, St. Louis, East St. Louis, and Kane Burial Mound sites. Long-nosed god maskettes, cover-covered and biconical earspools, small copper beads, needles, awls, and other copper-covered items have been associated with mortuary remains (Ahler and DePuydt 1987; Kelly n.d.; Melbye 1963; Milner 1984; Titterington 1938; Williams and Goggin 1956). Perino (1971:138) suspects that a surface beneath Mound 34 at Cahokia shows signs of copper working.

Fire clay is found in central Missouri; it earlier had been assumed to be bauxite from Arkansas (McQueen 1943; Perino 1971:139; Valeton 1972). This typically is a dull red or maroon color sometimes featuring patches of white (described as "ferruginous mudstone" by Fuller and Fuller 1987). Fire clay seems to have been used at or around the Cahokia site in the manufacture of figurines, figurine pipes, and earspools (Emerson 1982, 1983; Emerson and Jackson 1984; Farnsworth and Emerson 1989; Fuller and Fuller 1987; Hanenberger 1990b; Jackson et al. 1992:chapter 9; Kelly et al. 1987; Koldehoff 1990c; Milner 1984a; Watts and Watts 1980). Carved figurines and pipes of the "Cahokian effigy style" have been found at a restricted number of sites in the mid-South (figure 4.10; *sensu* Emerson 1983). In the American Bottom region, they have been associated with special mortuary or "mortuary temple" contexts (Emerson 1982, 1983; Emerson and Jackson 1984; Farnsworth and Emerson 1989; Jackson et al. 1992).

Sandstone Tablets

The distribution of engraved sandstone tablets, of which eleven are known, appears restricted to Cahokia proper. These have been found

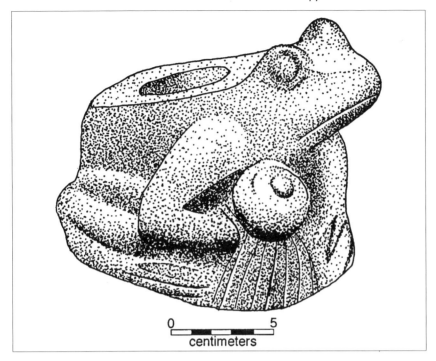

Figure 4.10. Cahokia-Style Figurine

associated with mounds and domestic refuse in at least three cases dating to the Moorehead phase, one of which was House 35 at Tract 15A (see Collins 1990; Emerson 1982:figures 17 and 18; Moorehead 1929:plates 16, 18, and 22; Williams 1975; Pete Bostrom, personal communication). The tablets usually feature cross-hatched lines on one surface. Anthropomorphic or zoomorphic characters are featured on two tablets (see Emerson 1982:26–32). While these appear to be local products, it seems equally clear that few if any were permitted to leave the bounds of the center.

St. Francois Igneous Rock

Igneous rocks are available from most every upland stream bed surrounding the American Bottom. Nonetheless, a substantial amount of aphanitic-igneous rock from the Precambrian-age St. Francois Mountains of the northeastern Ozarks is associated with Mississippian political-administrative centers in the American Bottom (Esarey and Pauketat 1992;

Pauketat 1991). This rock takes the form of utilitarian axeheads and unfinished megalithic axeheads, or roughly shaped celts much larger than any previously recovered utilitarian version (figure 4.11b), manufactured from weathered blocks of aphanitic igneous rock presumably derived from exposed geological dikes some 100 kilometers south of Cahokia.

Unfinished utilitarian celts and large quantities of debitage have been found with the Lohmann-phase domestic refuse at Tract 15A (figure 4.11a). Thirty-six megalithic celts were found at the Lohmann site, thirty-two in a pit and four (along with some igneous debitage) on the floor of a wall-trench building (Esarey and Pauketat 1992).[7] Based on written descriptions or photographs, the other caches of megalithic celts from Cahokia, East St. Louis, and an unknown site probably were manufactured from similar aphanitic igneous rock presumably derived from the St. Francois Mountains (see Titterington 1938:7; Hoehr 1980:43; Moorehead 1929:98; Pearson 1979:160; Rau 1869). It is not known whether this exotic item was imported in similar quantities during any other Mississippian phase. It seems likely, in fact, that many of the celts represented in the tool kits of American Bottom Mississippians were manufactured from igneous erratics obtained from the glacial till of the nearby uplands.

War Clubs

A number of nonutilitarian clubs and axes have been reported from the American Bottom. One unique wooden club studded with both sharks' teeth and imitation chert sharks' teeth was found near Mound 34 by Gregory Perino (Perino 1980:67). Another "sceptor," or unusual chert axehead made from a "clear white flint" was recovered from "a low mound near Cahokia" (Throop 1928:36).

Other spatulate axeheads found include polished-chert specimens manufactured in southern Illinois, long-stemmed metamorphic-rock varieties from the Tennessee Cumberland or South Appalachians regions, and igneous-rock specimens perhaps locally made (Brown 1976b; Kelly 1991a:72; Pauketat 1983:3). These nonutilitarian axeheads have been re-

7. The majority of these exhibit plagioclase phenocrysts and reddish-brown or yellow-brown patina on unfinished surfaces. Given these attributes and the large size of the cached objects (up to 10 kilograms in weight), it is relatively clear that the raw material did not originate in the local glacial tills. Instead, it seems as if massive blocks of rock, perhaps already finished to some degree, were hauled to the American Bottom (Esarey and Pauketat 1992).

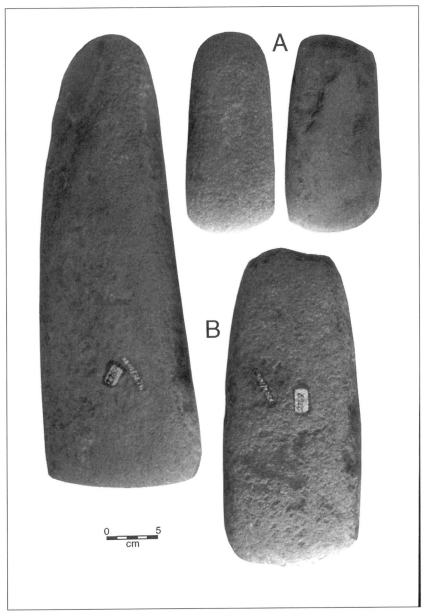

0 —— 5
cm

Figure 4.11. Unfinished Utilitarian and Megalithic Axeheads: a, Tract 15A; b, Lohmann Site

ported only from the Cahokia, East St. Louis, Mitchell, and Soucy Cemetery sites (Kelly n.d.; Pauketat 1983; Titterington 1938). Outside of mortuary contexts, broken examples are known only from Cahokia (Pauketat 1983:5).

Ceramic Vessels

Like the Emergent Mississippian ceramic assemblages (see chapter 3), grit- and grog-tempered Yankeetown Filleted, Kersey Incised, Dillinger Cordmarked, and Baytown wares along with shell-tempered Varney Red Filmed and Mississippi Plain wares and fine grog- and bone-tempered Coles Creek pottery have been identified in Mississippian refuse (Emerson and Jackson 1984; Holley 1989; Kelly 1980; Koldehoff 1982; O'Brien 1972; Pauketat 1984). Shell-tempered vessels made in distant regions often are not readily identified because of the difficulty in distinguishing their pastes from local Mississippian wares. Complicating matters is the likelihood that high-ranking marriage practices and demographic centralization at Cahokia resulted in the incorporation of potters with diverse manufacturing-tradition backgrounds. This may have led to a situation where exotic styles were locally produced.

The reproduction of nonlocal ceramic traditions in the American Bottom might account for the adoption of shell-tempered pastes there, especially if this nonlocal tradition was associated with prestigious distant or esoteric knowledge. The same process may have resulted in many of the fine grog-tempered and decorated bowls and beakers associated with Cahokia Mississippian refuse (Esarey and Pauketat 1992:101; Holley 1989:403–404; Pauketat 1993). Some of these appear to be Coles Creek wares from the lower Mississippi and Arkansas River valleys (Kelly 1990b:80). However, many of those tempered with fine grog and fine shell that have a brownish paste, a reddish-brown slip, polished surfaces, thin walls, and exterior fine incisions and excisions (made after the pastes had dried leather hard) have a local appearance (figure 4.12; see Holley 1989:107–108).

Clearly, some decorated Cahokia Mississippian vessels probably functioned in contexts similar to the above-described finewares. Ramey Incised jars are foremost among these local containers and were most likely produced under centralized conditions by a limited number of potters (Pauketat and Emerson 1991; Emerson 1989). In like manner, Monks Mound Red ceramics, reviewed in chapter 3, were produced perhaps under the aegis of central authority through the Stirling phase. Trailed and

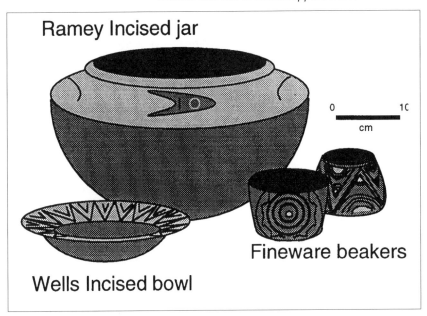

Figure 4.12. Decorated American Bottom Mississippian Pottery

incised plates and bowls comprise another category that might conform to these same centralized production and distribution patterns. In the end, the significance of local versus nonlocal origin is reduced relative to the meanings conducted by the pots and their decoration or the social context in which they were employed. For instance, the Ramey Incised pot, while a local product, conveyed supralocal or supernatural meanings (Pauketat and Emerson 1991; see chapter 6).

Marine Shell

The quantity of marine shell artifacts among the Mississippian-elite mortuaries at East St. Louis, St. Louis, Mitchell, and Cahokia is astounding. Among the artifacts are columnar and disk beads, whelk dippers, columella pendants, and even simple unmodified columellae primarily manufactured from *Busycon* spp. from the Gulf of Mexico (Kelly 1991a:72). At Cahokia's Kunnemann Tract, an array of beads and pendants was manufactured from marine and fresh-water gastropods and mollusc shell, along with other stone, bone, and possibly wood (Pauketat 1993). The sandstone and microlithic tools for cutting, smoothing, and perforating beads are found in profusion (Holley 1990; Pauketat 1993; Yerkes 1991). All were probably related to the Kunnemann Tract manufacture of necklaces, an activity that occurred in close proximity to the nearby ritual temples and platform mounds.

Limited numbers of disk beads and columellae also occur at rural Mississippian sites in the American Bottom, and there is some indication that the manufacture of disk beads or perhaps the final disposition of the beads among these same rural folks also was somewhat restricted (see Milner 1983, 1984a; Koldehoff 1990a; Prentice 1983, 1985; Yerkes 1992). Microlithic shell-working tools are found at rural sites in the American Bottom region, and microscopic examinations of these tools have revealed that almost all were used to drill shell (see Koldehoff 1990a:50–57, 1990b:84–90; Prentice 1983:35–40; Yerkes 1989, 1991, 1992). Such rural bead manufacturing or disposition, however, may not be a quality or intensity similar to Kunnemann Tract shell-craft production.

Distributional Patterns of Craft Items and Exotic Materials

Locally crafted goods and nonlocal raw materials or finished products seem most common to Cahokia (table 4.1). However, the samples upon which this statement is based are not entirely comparable. Few controls are available over such things as artifact density or even from what sorts of features these artifacts originated. A comparison of a suite of exotic artifacts illustrates the sampling problems (table 4.2). Few adequate samples are available from the large sites, and the short-term occupations at homesteads engender refuse diversity simply because of the lack of correspondence between site occupation span, item use life, and post-depositional alteration (Pauketat 1987c, 1989). There is some support for the statement that more kinds and higher densities of exotic materials and craft goods are found nearer to Cahokia and perhaps also nearer to Lunsford-Pulcher (figure 4.13).[8] Unfortunately, definitive statements are not possible at the present time.

We also might speculate that other finished copper, mollusc shell, and lithic items recovered from sites to the distant north of the American Bottom had been manufactured at Cahokia (see Emerson and Lewis 1991).

8. Data reported by Emerson and Jackson (1984, 1987), Esarey and Pauketat (1991), Finney (1985), Fortier (1985), Gregg (1975), Hanenberger (1990a, 1990b), Jackson (1990a, 1990b), Kelly (n.d.), Mehrer (1982), Norris (1978), Prentice (1985), Prentice and Mehrer (1981), and Yerkes (1980).

Table 4.1 The Qualitative Distribution of Exotic or Locally Crafted Sumptuary Goods

Site	En-graved Tablets	Ceremonial Clubs/Celts	Chunk Stones	Fire-Clay Items	Mica	Non-local† Points	Nonlocal† Adzes/Knives	Copper	Source
Cahokia and Sites within 3 km of Cahokia									
Cahokia	x	x	x	x	x	x	x	x	Grimm 1980; Perino 1971; Titterington 1938; Koldehoff 1990b; Pauketat 1983; Throop 1928
BBB Motor	-	-	-	x	x	x	-	-	Emerson and Jackson 1984
R. Schneider	-	-	-	x	-	-	-	-	Fortier 1985
Olszewski	-	-	-	x	-	-	-	-	Hanenberger 1990b; Pauketat&Koldehoff 1986
Other Mississippian Centers									
St. Louis	-	-	-	-	-	-	-	x	Chapman 1980; Peale 1862
Horseshoe Lake	-	-	-	-	-	-	x	x	Gregg 1975; Kelly 1991b
Mitchell	-	x	-	x	-	-	x	x	Howland 1877; Porter 1974; Winters 1974
Lohmann	-	-	x	-	-	-	x	-	Esarey and Pauketat 1991; Kelly et al. 1979
Pulcher	-	-	-	-	-	x	x	-	Freimuth 1974; personal reconnaissance
East St. Louis	-	x	-	-	-	-	x	x	Kelly n.d.
*Other Mississippian Rural Sites**									
Esterlein	-	-	-	-	-	-	x	-	Jackson 1990a
Karol Rekas	-	-	-	-	-	-	-	-	Hanenberger 1990a
Turner	-	-	-	-	-	-	x	-	Milner 1983; notes on file, Univ. of Illinois
Julien	-	-	x	x	-	x	x	-	Milner 1984a
Sandy Ridge	-	-	-	-	-	-	-	-	Jackson 1990b
Lily Lake	-	-	-	-	-	-	x	-	Norris 1978
Labras Lake	-	-	-	-	-	-	x	-	Yerkes 1980
Range	-	-	-	-	-	x	-	x	Mehrer 1982
Carbon Dioxide	-	-	-	-	x	-	-	-	Finney 1985
George Reeves	-	-	-	-	-	-	-	-	McElrath and Finney 1987

note: *list constructed as the rank order distance from Cahokia
†in the case of points, nonlocal in form and/or chert type; in the case of adzes and Ramey knives, Mill Creek or Kaolin cherts

Table 4.2 Density of Select Exotic Items in Early Mississippian Domestic Garbage

Site[*]	N of Jars	grams/jar				n/jar		Source
		Galena	Ft. Payne	Sil. Sed.	Kaolin	Quartz Xstal	Fineware[††] Bowls	
BBB Motor	112	0.29	0.00	†	0.57	0.045	-	Emerson & Jackson 1984
Olszewski	14	-	2.58	-	2.64	-	-	Hanenberger 1990b
R. Schneider	6	0.03	-	-	-	-	0.167	Fortier 1985
HorseshoeLake	33	?	?	?	-	-	0.030	Gregg 1975**
East St. Louis	23	?	?	?	-	?	0.261	Kelly n.d.
Karol Rekas	4	0.03	-	-	0.65	-	-	Hanenberger 1990a
Esterlein	8	0.64	-	-	14.01	-	-	Jackson 1990a
Lohmann	230	0.13	0.06	0.03	0.00	0.004	0.026	Esarey and Pauketat 1991
Turner-DeM.	186	?	?	?	0.99	0.005	0.005	Milner 1983
Lab Woofie	54	-	?	?	?	-	0.019	Prentice and Mehrer 1981
Sandy Ridge	4	-	-	-	-	-	-	Jackson 1990b
Marcus	6	-	-	-	-	-	0.167	Emerson & Jackson 1987
Lily Lake	275	-	-	-	-	-	0.019	Norris 1978
Labras Lake	30	-	-	-	-	-	0.067	Yerkes 1980
Range	167	1.62	?	?	?	0.024	0.012	Mehrer 1982
Carbon Dioxide	10	-	-	3.44	?	-	-	Finney 1985
George Reeves	17	?	-	-	-	-	-	McElrath & Finney 1987

notes:
*   listed in rank order distance from Cahokia
** features 5, 16-17, 19-20, 22, 26-28
†   a nonlocal-style (Hayes) projectile point was made from this
†† tempered with finely crushed grog (and shell); polished surfaces present but not quantified

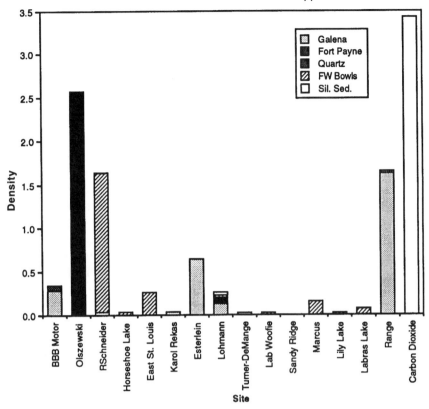

Figure 4.13. The Density of Exotic or Craft Goods in the Northern Bottom Expanse

It does seem apparent that items crafted at Cahokia, particularly Ramey Incised pots and marine shell beads, were dispersed to the populations to the north and south of the American Bottom (see Anderson 1987; Conrad 1989; Emerson and Lewis 1991; Henning 1967; Kelly 1991a; Milner 1990:24–27; Williams and Brain 1983).

Conclusions

Regional sampling and quantification problems aside, it is possible to depict in broad strokes the Mississippian regional, community, and household patterns in the American Bottom region as these are presently known. These patterns include a distinctive regional settlement hierarchy, marked differences in community size and organization among the three loosely defined settlement-hierarchical tiers, and refuse distribution patterns suggestive of centrifugal and centripetal economic forces or region-wide asymmetries.

Many of the Mississippian archaeological remains are not well understood, even given the large-scale archaeology of the American Bottom region. This lack of understanding probably stems from the historical pursuit of site-based salvage and contract archaeology rather than from problem-oriented regional archaeology. The large or unusual architecture, monuments, plazas, palisades, and mortuaries of Cahokia and the Central Political-Administrative Complex reflect the highly centralized character of public or elite activities and the sacred qualities of this core complex. The residential occupation at Cahokia includes social entities termed subcommunities that appear to have produced craft goods made from exotic raw materials. Among the possible centrally produced articles are shell bead-and-pendant necklaces, fire clay figurines, copper ornaments, and a variety of lithic, mineral, and ceramic objects. Local imitations of exotic fineware and the Ramey Incised jars featuring elite or religious motifs exemplify the importance of esoteric knowledge and distant symbols in the local domain. Other markers of status or badges of office like sandstone tablets, war clubs, and megalithic unfinished axeheads found exclusively in Mississippian centers or with the dead further illustrate the importance of such symbols. In fact, the Mississippian centers themselves—their monuments, plazas, and architecture—may have connoted important symbolic meanings to American Bottom Mississippians.

Cahokia, East St. Louis, St. Louis, and perhaps Mitchell overshadow the secondary political-administrative centers in the American Bottom, pale microcosms of the former. The tertiary tier of the settlement hierarchy consists of the rural homesteads and farmsteads scattered around and beyond the Mississippian centers. The people occupying the peripheral locales presumably would have contributed to the Mississippian central developments, the construction of mounds, palisades, plazas, and the like. These same people presumably would have produced the bulk of the subsistence and, to a limited extent, craft goods upon which core subgroups at least in part might have relied. Only suggestive clues of the centripetal mobilization of comestibles exist, and rural craft production data also remain equivocal. Likewise, the regional exotic-artifact distribution data are not amenable to definitive statements regarding the exchange or redistribution of nonlocal objects. The sum total of various separate lines of evidence does support the contention that craft-goods production and exotic-goods importation were centralized and thus controlled to an uncertain degree by the Mississippian elite.

In order to shed additional light on this problem and refine our observations about the diachronic development of Cahokia, a detailed analysis will be undertaken of the architectural and community-organizational patterns and artifact-density data from excavated residential tracts at Cahokia. These are presented in chapters 5 and 6 and serve as the basis for comprehending the generation of the Cahokian Leviathan in chapter 7.

Chapter 5

Diachronic Community and Architectural Evidence

Household and community form and size provide essential information about social forms and cultural structures (Kus 1983). This information lies at the heart of the present study of the region-wide transformation of local ranked groups into a regionally consolidated political entity and cultural hegemony. In order to measure the rate and scale of social and political changes over the Emergent Mississippian-to-Mississippian continuum, and thus to evaluate the rise of the Cahokian Leviathan, diachronic architectural and community-organizational data are necessary. The architectural and community-organizational data sets used in this study were excavated at Tract 15A and the Dunham Tract at Cahokia (figure 5.1). These data have been broken down into the 15A-DT subphases described in chapter 3. The subphases provide temporal resolution at a scale as fine grained as is currently available. The EM-2 through L-3 subphases represent an occupation continuum confined to a span of about a hundred years (calibrated to A.D. 1000–1100). Since each of these subphases represent periods of time averaging about two decades, within-generation changes may be monitored. Less resolution is offered by the Stirling and Moorehead subphases.

Excavations of Tract 15A undertaken in 1961, 1963, 1977, 1978, and 1985 exposed an area of about 10,000 square meters (Wittry 1961; Hall 1964; Hall and Wittry 1980; Iseminger 1985). A total of about 750 features were defined during the Tract-15A field work, including the remains of 240 buildings (or substantial rebuildings), 282 pits, 138 post pits, and 90 hearths, trenches, artifact concentrations, isolated postmolds, and ill-defined or amorphous deposits of cultural fills (figure 5.2). Additionally, a series of 5-by-5-foot test squares excavated in 1961 near the low marshy Cahokia Creek floodplain (about 30 to 60 meters northeast of the northern end of the primary Tract 15A excavations) contained midden presumably derived from the Tract 15A occupation (figure 5.3). This midden was excavated in arbitrary 6- or 12-inch levels, some of which are included in the present analysis.

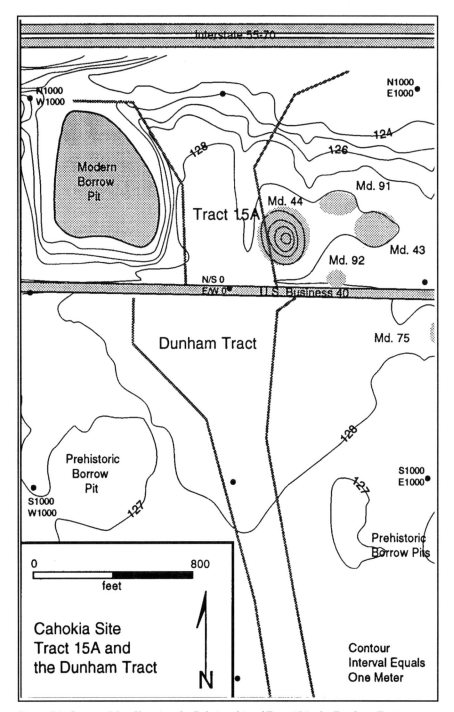

Figure 5.1. Contour Map Showing the Relationship of Tract 15A, the Dunham Tract, Mississippian Mounds, Borrow Pits, and Modern Features

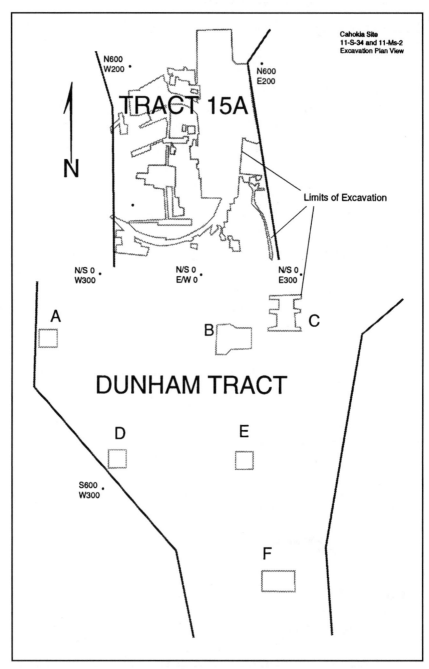

Figure 5.2. The Tract 15A and Dunham Tract Excavation Blocks (grid in feet)

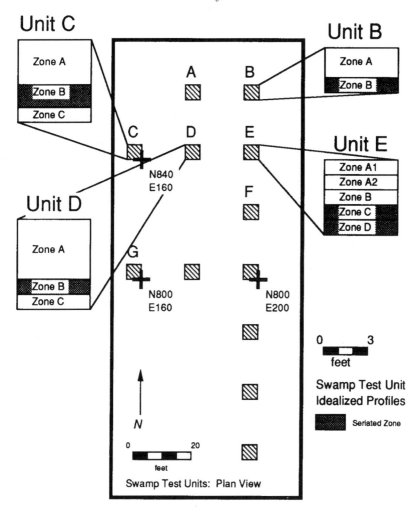

Figure 5.3. Swamp Test Units Used in 15A-DT Sample

Approximately 90 percent of the Tract-15A nonbuilding features were hand-excavated in their entirety; basin fills of building remnants were all excavated although wall trenches and postmolds selectively were excavated. Feature fills excavated during 1961 and 1963 were hand excavated with shovels and trowels. No fills were screened as these excavations were carried out under urgent salvage conditions, and of course the flotation method of sampling feature fills had not been realized at that time.

Unfortunately, these conditions necessitated the machine-aided removal of midden and occasionally building basin fills and the incomplete excavation of some features. Mapping of features in plan view was conducted using a grid system in units of feet. The same grid established in 1960 at Tract 15A was used for all subsequent work at the tract and at the Dunham Tract just to the south (Bareis 1967; Wittry 1960, 1961; Hall 1964). Features were usually excavated in halves, with a profile being drawn prior to the excavation of the second half. For Tract 15A, the documentation of feature fill composition, zonation, and in some cases metric details, when recorded, was not done with consistency and has limited value.

The Dunham Tract blocks were excavated under less urgent conditions. The University of Illinois 1966 block excavations on the Dunham Tract immediately south of Tract 15A exposed 4,617 square meters of the subsurface area and 174 features or "fill areas" (Bareis 1967). Twelve percent of the Dunham-Tract features were excavated, including the remains of seven buildings and fourteen pits (Bareis 1967:12). Nevertheless, the considerable size and scattered placement of the excavated blocks provide valuable insight into the spatial distribution of features in this part of Cahokia.

The limitations associated with the excavated 15A-DT sample to a large extent preclude an in-depth spatial analysis, particularly of artifact distribution. A series of built-in biases exists in the spatial dimension of the artifact sample. For instance, numerous residential features in portions of the tracts are not represented in terms of volumes of excavated fills. On the other hand, the distinctive size and shape attributes of seriated features do permit the interpolation of community patterns even though diagnostic artifacts may not be associated with feature fills. Such interpolation permits the pace and scale of community-organizational change to be monitored.

Architecture and Community by Subphase

The numbers and kinds of features grouped as individual subphases differ between each of the eleven subphases defined. The number of building remnants associated with each subphase ranges from one to fifteen, while the number of pits per subphase ranges from one to thirty-six (table 5.1). Obviously, the proportions of buildings, pits, or other feature types from different subphases are not necessarily comparable. In fact, certain subphases have many more buildings per pit (or other non-building feature) or house-basin-fill volume per pit-fill volume than do others

Table 5.1 Summary of 15A-DT Features and Fill Volume by Subphase

	A	B	C	D	E	F	G	H	I	J	K	L
Subphase	N of Bldg.	N of Bldg. With Vol.	Bldg. Fill (m³)	N of Pits	Pit Fill (m³)	N of Other	Total N	Tot. Vol. (m³)	C/B	E/D	C/E	A/(D+F)
EM 1	1	1	0.98	1	0.170	0	2	1.15	0.98	0.17	5.76	1.00
EM 2	10	4	5.84	33	13.503	3	46	19.343	1.46	0.41	0.43	0.28
EM 3	15	7	12.58	17	5.861	2	34	18.438	1.80	0.35	2.15	0.79
L 1	13	3	10.99	36	17.846	5	54	28.836	3.66	0.50	0.62	0.32
L 2	5	2	2.61	9	5.957	0	15	9.117	1.31	0.66	0.44	0.56
L 3	8	3	10.28	16	4.430	1	25	14.71	3.43	0.28	2.32	0.47
S 1	1	0	-	4	1.570	3	8	1.57	-	0.39	-	0.14
S 2	1	1	5.93	3	1.280	4	8	7.21	5.93	0.42	4.63	0.14
M 1	6	4	21.53	1	1.459	0	7	22.989	5.38	1.46	14.8	6.00
M 2	4	2	15.12	2	0.570	2	8	15.69	7.56	0.29	26.5	1.00
Total:	64	27	85.86	122	52.646	20	207	139.593	-	-	-	-

(table 5.1k–l). This pattern may be a by-product of the seriation method or excavation biases, or it could be an accurate reflection of community development.

Emergent Mississippian 1

The remains of a single building and its interior pit may be identified as belonging to the earliest Emergent-Mississippian subphase identified (figure 5.4). The two EM-1 Tract-15A features do not constitute an adequate sample for comparisons with other subphases except perhaps that they represent a less extensive occupation of the Cahokia site. The first extensive usage of Tract 15A appears to have occurred during the early Edelhardt phase (EM-2), perhaps due to the location of Tract 15A and the Dunham Tract marginal to the central portion of the Cahokia site.

Emergent Mississippian 2

A total of ten buildings and thirty-six pits or (ill-defined) fill areas located on Tract 15A comprise the archaeological features seriated as the EM-2 subphase. No EM-2 features were identified on the Dunham Tract. The EM-2 buildings as a group have comparable dimensions, averaging

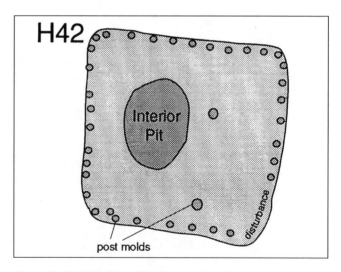

Figure 5.4. EM-1 Building Plan (2.4 m in length)

Table 5.2 EM-2 Building Attributes

Building	Length (m)*	Width (m)*	LxW	W/L	Basin Vol (m³)	Average PM Spacing (cm)	Average PM Depth (cm)
Principal Courtyard Cluster							
H75	2.7	1.6	4.3	0.593	-	30	24
H80	3.4	2.1	7.1	0.618	-	30	12
H89	2.5	2.0	5.0	0.800	1.30	24	12
H90/92	3.7	2.1	7.8	0.568	-	20-24	18
H115	4.0	2.3	9.2	0.575	-	17-24	?
Other Buildings							
H47	2.7	1.8	4.9	0.667	0.87	28	21
H63	4.6	1.7	4.3	0.370	2.46	30	?
H81/82	3.7	1.9	7.0	0.514	-	25	18
H98/129	3.9	2.0	7.8	0.513	-	20	14
H105	4.1	2.1	8.6	0.512	1.21	25-32	12
Mean	3.53	1.96	6.6	0.573	-	26	16.4
s.d.	0.69	0.212	1.83	0.113	-	4.1	4.6

note: *as measured from row of postmolds.

3.5 meters in length and 2.0 meters in width (table 5.2; figure 5.5). The wall posts in these buildings usually were spaced between 20 and 30 centimeters apart. Two buildings in the southern portion of the main 15A excavation block are longer than most but are similar in width. It is not clear whether these buildings were contemporaneous with the other EM-2 structures.

Five of these other buildings are found in what may be a courtyard cluster, the remains surrounding a central open area of about 150 square meters (figure 5.6). An EM-2 bell-shaped pit (F179) with a volume capacity of 0.77 cubic meters lies near the center of the courtyard. Additionally, there are three possible EM-2 post pits (F173, 180, 202) in the central area of the courtyard. These are superimposed by other pits that postdate the EM-2 subphase. Feature 180 especially seems a likely candidate for a central post. While not drawn in profile, a post mold 20 centimeters in diameter was noted by the excavators on the plan of this shallow pit.

Seventeen other building remains excavated at Tract 15A share the morphological characteristics of the EM-2 buildings and may be tentatively identified as dating to the early Edelhardt phase. These include four building remnants that are located in the primary EM-2 courtyard feature cluster. The basin fills of three of these (H74, H76, and H79) were seriated to the EM-3 subphase. It is possible that these three buildings were

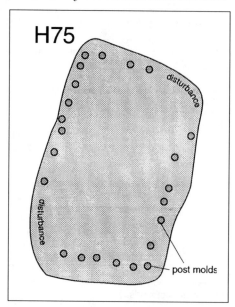

Figure 5.5. EM-2 Building Plan (2.7 m in length)

components of the EM-2 courtyard and either remained standing into the EM-3 subphase (thereby having outlasted the other EM-2 buildings) or simply happened to function as EM-3 garbage receptacles while other EM-2 building basins did not. In either case, the deposition of EM-3 garbage in basins of houses that appear to have EM-2 attributes may provide some evidence of habitation continuity. The possibility of uninterrupted occupation of the area is important to note, since the subsequent EM-3 community plan appears to involve a shift in the location of courtyards.

Emergent Mississippian 3

The fill from a total of sixteen separate zones within fifteen buildings has been seriated to the EM-3 subphase. Nineteen pits or fill areas were assigned to the EM-3 subphase, an increase in both the number of buildings per nonbuilding feature and the volume of building-basin fill versus pit fill compared to the EM-2 subphase (table 5.1). The volume capacities of pits remained fairly constant relative to the preceding subphase, but the sizes of buildings and thus volume of building-basin fills increased noticeably (table 5.3). House form remained the same as in EM-2, rectangular in outline with wall posts set in individual postmolds (figure 5.7).

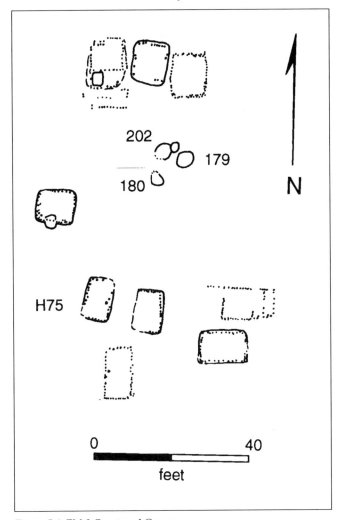

Figure 5.6. EM-2 Courtyard Group

At least one courtyard feature cluster may be identified in the spatial distribution of domicile remnants (figure 5.8). At least six and perhaps more than ten buildings were arranged around an open area of over 300 square meters. A larger-than-normal building (H93) with deeper-than-normal postmolds was located at the northern end of the courtyard (figure 5.9). A possible postmold or small pit (F192)—53 centimeters in length and 43 centimeters in width with a supposed depth of 20 centimeters—superimposes a small rectangular EM-2 pit (F191) and may have marked the

Table 5.3 EM-3 Building Attributes

Bldg.	Length (m)*	Width (m)*	LxW	W/L	Basin Vol (m³)	Average PM Spacing (cm)	Average PM Depth (cm)
Principal Courtyard Group							
H18	4.1	2.4	9.8	0.585	-	30	30
H19	4.5	2.2	10.0	0.489	-	25	30
H44	3.3	1.9	6.3	0.576	0.94	20-25	>12
H79†	3.5?	2.7?	9.5	0.771	-	-	23
H93	4.5	3.1	14.0	0.689	4.59	30	49
H96	4.0	1.8	7.2	0.450	-	20	30
Other Buildings							
H43	4.9	2.5	12.2	0.510	2.92	20-25	15
H48a	4.2	2.2	9.2	0.524	0.70	30	24
H64†	3.7	2.3	8.5	0.622	1.22	28	18
H74a†	2.9	1.6	4.6	0.552	0.567	25	24
H74b†	"	"	"	"	-	-	"
H76†	3.2	1.9	6.1	0.594	-	15-30	18
H100	4.0	2.2	8.8	0.550	-	20-25	24
H121	3.2	2.3	7.4	0.719	2.42	25	27
H139	5.1	-	-	-	0.44	25-30	-
H213	-	-	-	-	-	-	-
Mean	3.94	2.24	8.74	0.587	-	25	26
s.d.	0.67	0.85	2.54	0.09	-	-	8.78

notes: * Measured from row of postmolds.
     † Probably originally an EM-2 structure.
     Dimensions are those of basin; no interior postmolds defined.

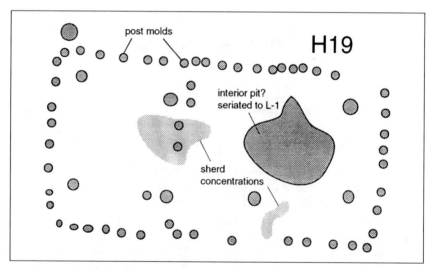

Figure 5.7. EM-3 Building Plan (4.5 m in length)

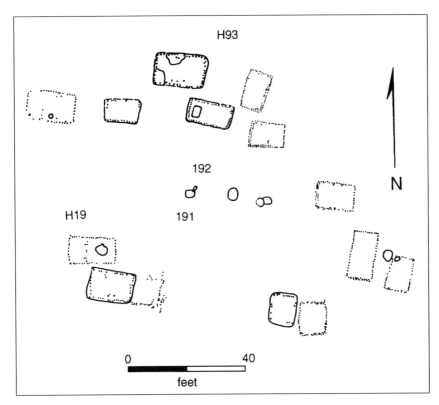

Figure 5.8. EM-3 Courtyard Group

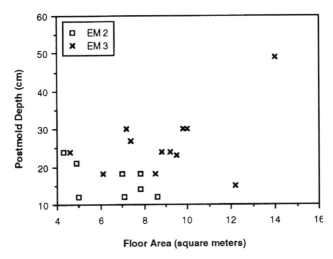

Figure 5.9. EM-2 and EW-3 Building Sizes

location of an EM-3 center post. Unfortunately, no sherds or other diagnositic materials were recovered from it. Two other post pits in this area are components of a later Mississippian Post-Circle Monument.

Based on the size and shape of the definite EM-3 buildings, the remains of twenty-one other buildings (or substantial rebuildings) excavated on Tract 15A are suspected to date to the EM-3 subphase; none were identified on the Dunham Tract. These probably were also arranged around courtyards. For instance, another larger courtyard covering about 450 square meters may have flanked the principal identified EM-3 courtyard feature cluster to the northeast. A series of likely post pits was located in the center of this proposed courtyard.

Three of the single-post buildings (H48b–c, H101, H109) suspected to have been constructed during the EM-3 subphase have basins that contained refuse associated with the subsequent L-1 subphase. This may indicate occupational continuity, although post-depositional mixing might also account for this pattern. In the case of H48, the L-1 fill had been deposited in the upper levels of the basin while the lowest zone contained EM-3 refuse. In the case of H101, it is unclear whether the associated basin fill represents some or all of the refuse associated with an ill-defined Mississippian building that superimposed H101.

Lohmann 1

The subphase that follows EM-3 has been labeled Lohmann 1, although it could be further subdivided as L-1a and L-1b. Lohmann 1a includes the (upper) basin fills of H48, H101, and H109 (cf. Hall 1975:22–23), seven wall-trench buildings, and four pits. Only three (or perhaps four) wall-trench-building basin fills and thirty-seven pits were seriated to the L-1b subphase (table 5.1).

The discrepancy between the proportions of L-1a and L-1b buildings and pits might be an artifact of the postdepositional mixing of Edelhardt-phase fills with Lohmann-phase fills. By the early Lohmann phase, there probably would have been much accumulated Emergent Mississippian midden that easily might have washed into Lohmann-phase depressions, particularly the shallow basins of abandoned buildings. The smaller pit features presumably were filled rapidly by surrounding domestic groups. Hence, the L-1b pits might date as early in the Lohmann-phase as anything at Tract 15A.

The number of L-1 building basins (n = 13) and pits or fill areas (n = 41) is comparable to the subphases that precede and follow the L-1 subphase. In their distribution across the excavated Tract 15A surface, the early

Table 5.4 Lohmann-1 Building Attributes

Building	Length (m)*	Width (m)*	Area LxW	W/L	Basin Vol (m³)	Wall Trench/PM Depth (cm)
L-1a						
H48, zone b-c	-	-	-	-	2.80	-
H66	5.0	2.6	13.0	0.520	-	34
H85	4.5	2.5	11.3	0.556	-	6
H101	4.9	2.5	12.3	0.510	3.68	40
H102	3.2	2.2	7.0	0.688	-	21
H103	4.0	2.1	13.4	0.328	-	30
H109	2.7	2.7	7.3	1.000	-	30
H156	4.8	2.1	10.1	0.438	-	30
H172	-	-	-	-	1.46	-
H210	3.6	3.0	-	-	-	-
L-1b						
H145	4.6	2.4	11.01	0.522	-	21
H157	4.7	2.5	13.2	0.532	4.51	24
H165	6.25	3.9	24.6	0.624	-	55
H204†	5.00	2.5	12.5	0.500	-	?
Mean	4.44	2.58	12.34	0.565	-	31.5
s.d.	0.94	0.49	4.63	0.171	-	10.09

notes: * measured from the center of opposing wall trenches.
        † considered only as a possible L-1b structure basin.

Lohmann-phase building basins and pits begin to hint at a very different community plan than witnessed in the EM-2 or EM-3 remains. As a group, the L-1 building floor areas are only slightly larger than their EM-3 counterparts. However, one of the rectangular L-1b buildings (H165) had a floor area twice that of any other L-1 building (table 5.4). H165 appears to be representative of a class of large rectangular buildings that appear more commonly in later Lohmann subphases.

Besides the buildings and pits, other features from this earliest Mississippian subphase include a long and winding ditch (F171) appearing to have drained an open area that may have been a subcommunity plaza. There are two large post pits (F222 and F243) in the middle of this possible plaza that could date to the Lohmann phase. Massive post impressions were defined at their bases, set at least 1.5–2.0 meters below the ground. Feature 222 provided hints that its post had been about 50–60 centimeters in diameter. Feature 243's post was probably about 75 to 100 centimeters in diameter; one of the insertion or extraction ramps for this post pit was 7 meters long.

Lohmann 2 and 3

The Lohmann-2 and Lohmann-3 subphases are represented by the remains of twelve buildings and thirty pits scattered across Tract 15A and the Dunham Tract (table 5.1). A number of L-2 buildings and pits are clustered in the northwestern portion of Tract 15A. One of the L-2 pits is a large amorphous fill area excavated on the Dunham Tract that contained 4.1 cubic meters of fill. Two L-2 features mentioned in the EM-3 discussion, features 87 and 88, may be post pits (though morphologically distinct from the Post-Circle Monument features) like the EM-3 features (89 and 90) adjacent to them. If so, then it seems a possibility that the northeastern courtyard tentatively identified as an EM-3 feature was in fact maintained as such into the Lohmann phase. In fact, the two large post pits mentioned above (F222 and F243) are located in the same open space.

Circular buildings first appeared at Cahokia during the L-2 and L-3 subphases. The single L-2 circular building (H41) measures 4.1 meters in diameter and has a superposed sequence of central hearths on its floor. Another circular building (H111) associated with the L-3 subphase measures 2.7 meters in diameter and contains a central hearth. An L-3 concentration of cracked igneous rock (3,210 grams) and limestone (1,040 grams) immediately south of this building may be the discarded materials associated with the use of this building as a sweat house.

Most of the L-2 and L-3 rectangular buildings are small (table 5.5). However, like the L-1 H165 building, there are five large L-2 and L-3 rectangular buildings represented among the seriated features. One of the four L-2 rectangular buildings (H33) is twice the size of any of the other L-2 features. It superimposes the L-2 circular building H41 (figure 5.10). Four of the seven L-3 buildings (D12, D18, H21, and H61) are large, having floor areas between 17 and 27 square meters.

Most buildings documented in the excavations of rural sites in the American Bottom correspond to the sizes of the smaller 15A buildings (Milner et al. 1984:figure 61a). Two large Lohmann-phase buildings from the small Mississippian center at the Lohmann site have floor areas in excess of 25 square meters (Esarey and Pauketat 1992:table 7.3). The largest Lohmann-phase rectangular building from the ICT-II at Cahokia falls into this large-size mode, having a floor area of 23 square meters (Collins 1990:78). Consequently, we may speak of two primary size modes of rectangular Lohmann-phase buildings (figure 5.11), both amply represented in the 15A-DT sample and reaffirmed by their presence elsewhere at Cahokia and at a secondary Mississippian center.

Table 5.5 Lohmann-2 and Lohmann-3 Building Attributes

Building	Length (m)*	Width (m)*	Area LxW	W/L	Basin Vol (m³)	Wall Trench Depth (cm)	Notes
L-2							
H33	6.9	4.3	29.8	0.623	-	12	-
H41 (zone a)	4.1	4.1	13.2	-	1.52	30	circular; area= r^2
H69	3.8	2.4	9.1	0.632	1.09	46?	-
H206	4.5	2.5	11.3	-	-	?	-
H211	4.1	2.4	9.8	0.585	-	?	-
L-3							
D12	7.4	3.5	25.9	0.470	6.66	11	-
D18	7.1	3.7	26.3	0.520	-	?	-
H21	7.2	3.7	26.6	0.514	-	34	-
H61	5.2	3.4	17.7	0.654	-	24	-
H108 (a-c)	3.4	1.8	6.1	0.529	2.83	21	-
H110 (northern and southern "rooms")							
northern	>4.3	-	-	-	-	6?	open-ended
southern	5.0	2.7	13.7	0.540	-	6?	-
H111	2.7	2.7	5.7	-	-	24	circular; area= r^2
H176	-	-	-	0.800	-	?	ill-defined partially excavated bldg.
Mean	5.12	3.1	16.27	0.587	-	24	6's excluded in calculation
s.d.	1.64	0.78	8.71	0.096	-	10.97	-

note: *as measured from the center of opposing wall trenches.

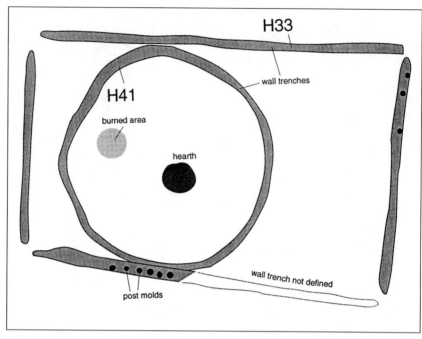

Figure 5.10. Lohmann-2 Building Plans (H33 is 6.9 m in length)

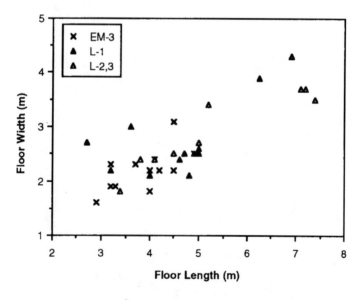

Figure 5.11. Edelhardt- and Lohmann-Phase Building Sizes

Stirling 1 and 2

The Lohmann phase comprises the maximum extent of residential use of Tract 15A and probably the Dunham Tract. In contrast, the subsequent Stirling-1 component at Tract 15A and the Dunham Tract is represented by a paucity of features and related refuse. The basin fill of only one building and the fills of four pits, one post pit, and two arbitrary levels of the swamp test units contain Stirling-1 ceramics (figure 5.12). The four pits include two within the bounds of an extraordinarily large rectangular building (H3) covering an area of 229 square meters.

Nearby lies H209, a small S-1 building morphologically similar to Lohmann-phase buildings. In fact, the S-1 artifacts associated with H209 are believed to derive from the basin fill, given their high density. Except for the darker coloration of vessel surfaces and the presence of Ramey Incised jars (figure 5.13), even the shell-tempered ceramic vessels represented in the refuse share the morphological qualities of late Lohmann-phase ceramics. Thus the H209 vessels and other refuse may well be the earliest Stirling-1 deposit on the tract.

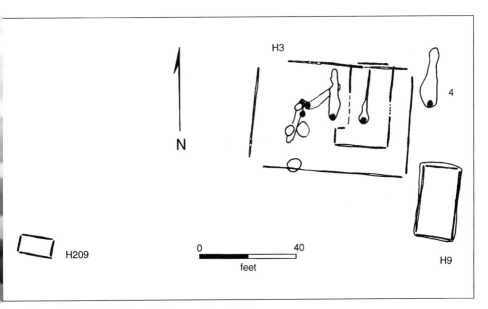

Figure 5.12. Stirling-Phase Features on Tract 15A

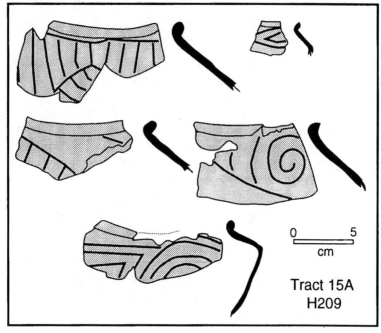

Figure 5.13. The Ramey Incised Pottery from H209

No Stirling-1 features were identified south of the grid line N500 and north of the Dunham Tract except for the post pits of the Post-Circle Monuments (see chapter 4). None of the post pits belonging to any one of the known circles have been found to contain Stirling-phase ceramics. Rather, most post pits contain a mixture of Edelhardt-phase and Lohmann-phase refuse. If these had been constructed after a Stirling-phase residential occupation in the area, then Stirling-phase domestic refuse probably would have been included in at least some of the post pits. Its absence, however, in conjunction with the lack of Stirling-phase residential remains and the fact that at least three Lohmann-phase buildings were superimposed by Circle posts indicates that the first monument was constructed during the Stirling phase. If the H209 deposit demarcates this earliest monument, then construction may be placed at the Lohmann-Stirling phase interface.

Radiocarbon assays of uncarbonized red cedar wood recovered from post pit features 548, 601, and 618 may be used more precisely to date Circle 2. While assays from F548 yielded ages that appear too early

(1085±55 B.P. [WIS-948] and 1060±55 B.P. [WIS-969]), the F601 assays yielded ages that calibrate to the early Stirling phase. These include samples dated to 940±60 B.P. (WIS-1128) and 920±60 B.P. (WIS-1133) that may be calibrated to about A.D. 1110 and 1115, respectively. The first of two assays from F618 (890±60 B.P. [WIS-1133] and 990±60 B.P. [WIS-1136]) may be calibrated to A.D. 1130. The three dates that cannot be calibrated to the early Stirling phase may not be in error, but may date the older inner rings of the original tree, predating the actual construction of the earliest Post-Circle Monument by up to a century.

There is no indication that any Post-Circle Monument dates as late as the Moorehead phase. In fact, there are seven clear instances in which post pits associated with Circles 1, 2, and 3 are superimposed by Moorehead-1 and Moorehead-2 buildings. In other words, the four or perhaps many more Post-Circle Monuments were constructed during the Stirling phase. To the north outside the bounds of these circles, at least one large rectangular building and perhaps two marker posts occupied the space between the standing Post-Circle Monument and Cahokia Creek. The reconstructed vessel assemblage associated with the internal post pits and pits of this huge building (F18, 361–365, and 375 within H3) include fourteen undecorated jars, three decorated (Ramey Incised) jars, four beakers, a bowl, a bottle and two funnels. This assemblage may indicate that the building served domestic purposes. The size of the H3 building and its proximity to the Post-Circle Monument may indicate the importance of the person(s) who resided there.

There is some evidence that a Post-Circle Monument was standing during the Stirling-2 subphase. One pit (F348) has been dated to the S-2 subphase *within* the bounds of Circles 2, 3, and 4. This pit may be associated with the floor of a large square building (H148) that has a floor area covering 94 square meters and presumably a large internal roof support post. If this building dates to the S-2 subphase, it probably would not have been located within the bounds of Circles 2, 3, or 4. It is, of course, possible that another Post-Circle Monument, such as Circle 1, was in use at the time the building was standing.

Except for the pit F348, one post pit (F365) inside H3, and three arbitrary zones within the swamp test units (Cb, Dc, and Ed), S-2 subphase occupational debris derives from the Dunham Tract. The post-abandonment fills in the basin of at least one building and two pits from three separate Dunham-Tract block units date to the Stirling-2 subphase. Based on these remains, the use of the tract is suspected to have continued largely unaltered from the S-1 subphase. In all likelihood, this residential use bordered the Post-Circle Monument and perhaps one or more extraordi-

narily large buildings between the monument and the Cahokia Creek
floodplain.

Moorehead 1 and 2

There is ample architectural evidence from Tract 15A that the Post-
Circle Monuments had been removed and the area had been reconverted
into a residential neighborhood. Fill from six rectangular buildings and
three pits on Tract 15A represent the Moorehead-1 subphase (tables 5.1
and 5.6). There are no circular buildings associated with the Moorehead
phase remains, and there are no Moorehead-phase remains of any kind
found on the Dunham Tract. Moreover, no Moorehead-phase garbage was
recovered from the swamp test units to the north of Tract 15A. A single M-
1 pit, feature 63, was excavated on the sloping bank between the Tract 15A
community remains and the creek bottom.

The Moorehead-phase buildings are large with width-length indices
occasionally greater than 0.80 (table 5.6). The buildings on Tract 15A are
spaced widely apart. It is not certain whether this spacing involved some
sort of courtyard; perhaps the large posts erected in post pits F222 and F243
marked the center of a Moorehead-1 courtyard rather than a Lohmann-
phase plaza. It may be significant to note that the upper fills of a Lohmann-
phase house basin adjacent to Mound 44 contained Moorehead-phase
refuse presumably washed down the mound. This may help date the latest
stages of Mound-44 construction to the Moorehead phase. The unusual
orientation of one M-1 building (H2), with its long axis about 20 degrees
east of north, may indicate the importance of facing Mound 44 rather than
conforming to a "community grid" (cf. Collins 1990:230). Nonetheless,
most of the other Moorehead-phase buildings approximated the orienta-
tions of buildings that date to the Edelhardt, Lohmann, and Stirling
phases.

Three of the six Moorehead-1 buildings exhibit evidence that incinera-
tion represented the final act of abandonment. This is quite different from
anything seen in the Edelhardt- and Lohmann-phase architectural remains from Tract 15A and the Dunham tract; burning might have been a
cultural practice that developed at Cahokia during the Stirling phase as a
means of sealing off a particular location from further residential usage
(see Collins 1990:150–153; Pauketat 1987a, 1987b). It further affirms the
observed wide spacing of Moorehead-phase domiciles (burning
Lohmann-phase buildings conceivably could have accidentally ignited a
number of the tightly-spaced adjacent buildings). This practice seems to

Table 5.6 Moorehead-1 and Moorehead-2 Building Attributes

Building	Length (m)*	Width (m)*	Area LxW	W/L	Basin Vol. (m³)	Wall Trench Depth (cm)	Notes
M-1							
H2	5.9	4.9	28.9	.831	-	37	burned
H9	8.0	4.4	35.2	.550	6.26	40	maybe a Stirling-phase building
H32	9.3	5.2	48.4	.559	-	24	burned; northwest portico
H77	7.0	4.3	30.1	.614	2.71	42	burned
H95/99	-	-	-	-	0.96	-	structural dimensions not defined
H143a1	4.13	3.86	16.0	.935	-	24	complex superpositioning ill-defined
M-2							
H10	10.3	4.9	50.5	.476	12.25	37	without rebuilt east wall, length=8.4 m central portico (like H32)
H35	5.7	4.2	23.9	.737	-	24	superimposes H32
H108d	-	-	-	-	-	-	upper zone related to Md. 44 wash zone
H302	5.3	3.9	20.7	.736	-	30	-
H305	8.1	6.6	53.5	.815	-	55	-
Mean	7.08	4.7	34.13	.695	5.55	34.78	-
s.d.	2.01	0.85	13.72	.150	4.98	10.43	-

note: *as measured from the center of opposing wall trenches.

account for the end of two other Moorehead-phase buildings on the tract not assigned to a subphase. Large sections of broken pots, anvil stones, and miscellaneous artifacts typically are associated (as abandonment refuse) on the floors of these buildings (see also Milner 1984a; Pauketat and Woods 1986).

The Moorehead-2 features include only four wall-trench buildings, the upper zone of a Lohmann-phase building basin, two pits, and a possible postmold and a post pit. The buildings are isolated in the northern, eastern, and southern portion of Tract 15A. There appear to be two sizes of buildings: H10 and H305 (itself a rebuilding of the unseriated H301) comprise a large mode with floor areas around 50 square meters; H35 and H302 comprise a small mode with floor areas around 20 to 24 square meters (figure 5.14).

The 15A-DT Community in Diachronic Perspective

A number of general trends over the Emergent Mississippian-to-Mississippian continuum have been identified with variable degrees of

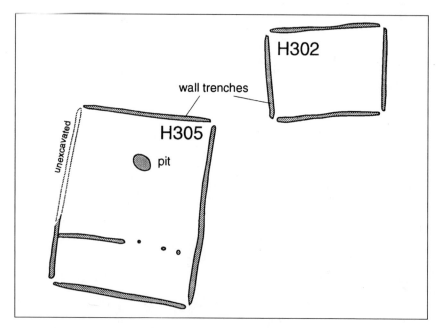

Figure 5.14. The Moorehead-2 Building Plans on Tract 15A (H305 is 8.1 m in length)

certainty using the subphase feature groups. By the early Edelhardt phase (EM-2) within the bounds of Tract 15A, community patterning involved groups of single-post buildings arranged around courtyards that in some cases may have featured a central post. No Emergent Mississippian features have been identified in the Dunham tract excavations. Beginning with EM-2, buildings were small, their floors covering an average area of 6.6 square meters. The courtyard feature clusters also were small, the small buildings being arranged around what were probably central posts in open areas. One open courtyard covered an area of about 150 square meters (figure 5.15).

This community organization continued through the late Edelhardt phase (EM-3), with the development of the community seemingly involving the construction of new courtyards and new buildings all at about the same time. This is comparable to what has been argued to exist at the Range site (Kelly 1990b). It is quite likely that a series of EM-3 courtyards and their component single-post buildings flanked one another, each with a central post. The buildings and the courtyards themselves were increased in size. House floor areas averaged about 8.7 square meters. EM-3 courtyards covered about 300 and 450 square meters. One larger-than-normal building with deeply set regularly spaced wall posts may represent the domicile of an important householder who resided at the northern end of an EM-3 courtyard.

The last evidence of single-post buildings is associated with the Lohmann-1a subphase. As one of the three L-1a single-post buildings clearly illustrates, these were probably *not* occupied during the L-1a subphase but had been abandoned during the EM-3 subphase subsequently to serve as L-1a garbage receptacles. Importantly, from the earliest Lohmann subphase onward, building posts were set in linear wall trenches rather than in individual post holes. Moreover, the average size of buildings increased to 12.3 square meters (11.1 square meters if H165 is excluded). L-1 community patterns are difficult to discern but may reflect a new emphasis on supracourtyard community order. There is one possible early Lohmann-phase courtyard feature cluster that may be highlighted using the projected Tract-15A building distribution. Two of the seven or more buildings of this possible cluster have been dated to the L-1 subphase. Another small building (H88) at the eastern end of this possible courtyard underlies a series of later Lohmann-phase buildings. The position of this potential early Lohmann-phase courtyard feature cluster just to the southwest of an identified EM-3 courtyard feature cluster may signal it as the succeeding residential location of the same or a related series of households. Such successional development of flanking courtyards might ac-

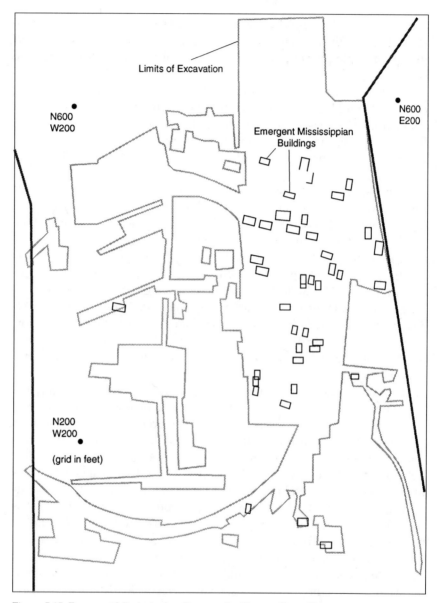

Limits of Excavation

N600
W200

N600
E200

Emergent Mississippian
Buildings

N200
W200

(grid in feet)

Figure 5.15. Emergent Mississippian Community Plans at Tract 15A

count for the EM-2 to EM-3 community-developmental patterns. If this early Lohmann-phase courtyard did exist as an organizational entity (by no means a certainty), then it covered an area of 360 square meters, comparable to the adjacent EM-3 courtyard.

At the same time, another large EM-3 courtyard tentatively identified in the northeastern portion of Tract 15A may have been maintained or enlarged as a Mississippian plaza during the subsequent L-1 subphase. A number of post pits in this area are the possible remnants of both EM-3 and L-1 marker posts. Certainly, no Lohmann-phase wall-trench buildings were found in this possible plaza area of more than 850 square meters, and only two to four probable Lohmann-phase wall-trench buildings (of which one is circular and dates to the L-3 subphase) are located in a much larger open area covering 1,500 square meters (figure 5.16). This area seems to have been drained by a newly dug ditch (F171) that dates to the L-1 subphase. At the eastern end of this proposed plaza is a large and possibly T-shaped (partially exposed) wall-trench building (H37) of uncertain pre-Moorehead-phase temporal affiliation. Its north-south walls are oriented approximately 13 degrees east of north as are most Lohmann-phase buildings. This large building may have served a special purpose or personage.

To the south on the Dunham Tract are a number of superimposed rectangular wall-trench structures (figure 5.17). Many of these were only roughly defined in 1966 and remain unexcavated. It is clear from the ceramics from specific feature and general excavation contexts that all buildings date to either the Lohmann or Stirling phases. No Emergent Mississippian or Moorehead-phase features were defined in the Dunham Tract excavations. In many cases, phase or subphase assignations more detailed than this are not possible. Nonetheless, the sample can be usefully employed to obtain a gross measure of community-organizational change in this part of the Cahokia site.

The placement of buildings of different sizes and shapes across Tract 15A and the Dunham Tract illustrates that the Lohmann-phase community had expanded to cover more areas and to include more households than its EM-3 predecessor. Two rectangular building size modes are apparent. Seventy-six percent of the 15A-DT sample of twenty-one rectangular Lohmann-phase buildings have floors that range from 2.7 to 5.2 meters in length and 1.8 to 3.4 meters in width, defining the small mode. The other 24 percent of the building sample includes large, similarly shaped L-1, L-2, and L-3 buildings ranging from 6.25 to 7.4 meters in length and 3.5 to 4.3 meters in width (tables 5.4 and 5.5).

Circular buildings appeared during this time and are associated on Tract 15A with the larger rectangular houses, in turn found clustered to the

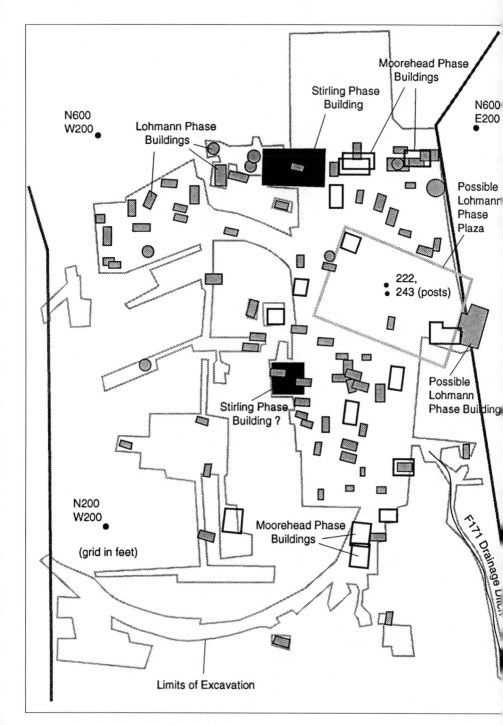

Figure 5.16. Mississippian Community Plans at Tract 15A

S147
W480

A

S490
W280

D

S500
E100

E

S197
W430

S540
W230

S550
E150

S150
E 50

Lohmann

Stirling

B

S210
E150

S840
E170

F

S900
E270

Figure 5.17. Lohmann- and Stirling-Phase Community Remains at the Dunham Tract

north and south of smaller rectangular buildings. A total of nine circular buildings are on Tract 15A, eight of which have their central floor areas exposed and contain hearths. At least two of these date to the Lohmann phase. One such building superimposed the L-1 building H165; another large example with an apparent walled western entrance was superimposed by feature 245, an apparent Stirling-phase post pit. There are no circular buildings represented in the Dunham-Tract excavation blocks. In addition to the restricted location of these circular sweat houses along the northern fringe of Tract 15A, at least four circular buildings are isolated several meters from the nearest rectangular building.

Thus the Lohmann-phase community configuration as a whole is drastically different from its Emergent Mississippian antecedents. Rather than a series of flanked courtyard feature clusters, the Lohmann-phase features—while hinting at some continuity with the EM-3 remains—bespeak of one integrated, large-scale, and internally complex community plan. Not only does the Lohmann-phase community plan appear to be reflective of some kind of larger-scale order, but it corresponds with the appearance of wall-trench building foundations. There is some chance that two single-post buildings were standing during the earliest Lohmann subphase, but, excluding these, all subsequent buildings built on Tract 15A and the Dunham Tract were wall-trench construction. Moreover, there may have been many more people occupying this portion of the Cahokia site than had earlier been the case, given the increased number and size of Lohmann-phase buildings.

Using the total number of seriated and projected Emergent Mississippian and Lohmann-phase buildings, it may be estimated that 27 EM-2, 36 EM-3, and 100 L-1, -2, and -3 buildings occupied Tract 15A alone. Assuming the fifty-year spans currently assigned to the Edelhardt and Lohmann phases and for the moment considering only Tract 15A, it would appear that nearly twice as many Lohmann-phase buildings as Edelhardt-phase buildings were constructed. Using the mean floor areas of the Edelhardt and Lohmann subphases and multiplying these figures by the projected number of buildings per phase, we can estimate that approximately 495 square meters of floor area are represented by the Edelhardt-phase buildings, while 1,440 square meters are represented by the Lohmann-phase buildings. By this measure then, the Lohmann-phase building area on Tract 15A is greater than that of the Edelhardt phase by a ratio of nearly three to one. Adding the Dunham Tract into this equation could greatly increase this ratio.

In order to eliminate, however, the biases of the Tract 15A sample, a result of irregular excavation limits, and take the Dunham Tract features into account, we may recalculate building density. Based on three large rectangular blocks within the Tract 15A excavated area (N500–220, E0–120; N315–250, W150–70; N530–465, W205–90) and the Dunham Tract blocks (total area = 6,048 square meters), we may conclude that Lohmann-phase buildings covered three times the surface area of Edelhardt-phase houses (figure 5.18). We may translate the 15A-DT architectural data as supporting a substantially increased population size for this segment of the Cahokia site. While other factors require consideration, it is possible that the population of this Cahokia locale had tripled over a period of a few decades at most. If such growth can be projected for the site as a whole, then the 15A-DT evidence clearly attests to demographic centralization, not to mention community reorganization.

Based on an analysis of buildings and associated features from the ICT-II, Collins (1990:228–235) has identified three important diachronic trends pertaining to Cahokia-community living and storage space over the late Lohmann-to-Stirling phase continuum. First, external storage pit volume decreased while the number and volume of pits within buildings (along with building floor area) increased. The changes in the location and size of storage facilities may reflect an "increased privatization of storage practices" (Collins 1990:221) whereby residents "resist the expropriation of

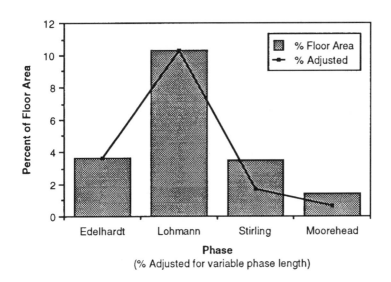

Figure 5.18. Percent Building Floor Area at Tract 15A and the Dunham Tract

their goods" (DeBoer 1988:10). Second, the size of supposed domestic zones (i.e., the areal extent of groups of buildings and exterior facilities) contracted over this same period. The changes in the size of domestic zones at the ICT-II might reflect the increased prominence of households as socioeconomic units as opposed to suprahousehold Lohmann-phase units (Collins 1990:229). Last, the Lohmann-phase community with its domestic buildings neatly arranged according to a north-south axis and/ or cardinal directions gave way by the late Stirling phase to variable building orientation aligned relative to a nearby platform mound (Collins 1990:220–230). The reduced diversity of Stirling-phase feature forms may be evidence of a restricted range of domestic activities in the ICT-II vicinity relative to the preceding Lohmann phase (Collins 1990:229).

The Stirling-phase Post-Circle Monument remains on Tract 15A and part of the Dunham Tract bespeak of elaborate nonresidential usage. The Post-Circle Monument, like Cahokia mounds, illustrates the importance placed on the maintenance of a monument. At least four and perhaps more than ten Post-Circle Monuments may have been constructed in the 15A-DT area during the Stirling phase. Perhaps the building, dismantling, and rebuilding of the Post-Circle Monument may have been conducted within the context of a ritual calendrical cycle along with other Cahokia monuments. Stirling-phase mound constructions, modifications, and small incremental enlargements along with the regular construction and renewal of temples and hearths on mound summits better illustrate the regularity of monument maintenance (see chapter 4).

Large domiciles or special-purpose buildings similar to other temples and elite houses at Cahokia were located on Tract 15A adjacent to the Post-Circle Monuments. A Stirling-phase residential area did exist on the Dunham Tract south of the Post-Circle Monument (perhaps half the buildings represented in the excavated sample). The concomitant reduction in the residential population of this portion of Cahokia (figure 5.18) may not characterize all of Cahokia (cf. Collins 1990). It may nonetheless be telling of the elaboration of public and elite monuments and architecture in the center of Cahokia and the Central Political-Administrative Complex during the Stirling phase.

As recognized at the ICT-II, the Moorehead-phase community was "strikingly different" from preceding community arrangements (Collins 1990:230). It seems as if the "population at the site may have been free to occupy any convenient, preferably high location, unencumbered by the cultural or political constraints of the past" (Collins 1990:230). Additionally, increasing storage potential out-of-doors relative to the preceding Stirling phase (at the same time that building floor area continued to

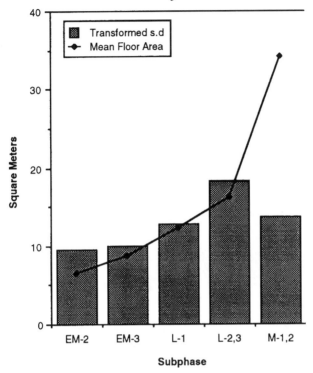

Figure 5.19. Structure Mean Floor Area and Size Diversity through Time

enlarge) may indicate the removal of social or political factors that had earlier made subterranean storage within buildings desirable.

The average Moorehead-phase building on Tract 15A covers much more area than the average Emergent Mississippian or Lohmann-phase building, and thus the standard deviation will also be larger. In order to compare standard deviations we may transform them by multiplying each standard deviation by the quotient of the mean Moorehead-phase floor area/mean other-phase floor area. Having performed this transformation, we observe that (while mean building size increased through time) the variance of Moorehead-phase building size decreased compared to the L-2 and L-3 subphases (figure 5.19).

The Moorehead-phase building bimodal distribution is reminiscent of the Lohmann phase except for a potentially important spatial difference: the Lohmann-phase building-size modes were segregated at the scale of the community, suggesting that community-social variability may account for the different-sized Lohmann-phase dwellings. However, the Moorehead-2 remains, if the proximity of H302 and H305 is a reliable indicator, might be interpreted to suggest that these different-sized buildings were functionally complementary components of a household's domestic zone; the sizes may not have been segregated at the scale of the community. Undoubtedly, elite residential areas existed at Cahokia during the Moorehead phase. Nonetheless, the 15A-DT pattern illustrates a reduction of the internal complexity of the social order in the late-prehistoric American Bottom.

Chapter 6

Diachronic Artifactual Evidence

Domestic refuse can provide integral insights into the identities and activities of community members. As identities change through time, we may infer that the cultural hegemony has transformed the consciousness of the populace. As activities change through time, we may argue that the relationship of subgroups or households to horizontal or vertical social structures has been altered. Both lines of evidence are integral for evaluating political, social, and economic transformations throughout the American Bottom region. The 15A-DT evidence will be argued in chapter 7 to reflect an abrupt consolidation of political power, a realignment of social order and identity, and the coalescence of sacral chiefly authority and a nonstate class hegemony.

At a populous site like Cahokia, domestic garbage might have included discarded household possessions and residues from subsistence activities, tool production and use, craft goods manufacture, household ritual, and communal or public gatherings. These discarded items and residues might have been consistently deposited in specific locations, as Mehrer (1988) has concluded occurred at rural Mississippian sites. Unfortunately, the palimpsest of superimposed pits and buildings at Cahokia inhibits the recognition of discrete refuse deposits belonging to individual households or subgroups (Mehrer 1988; Pauketat 1987c:79, 1989). Even discovering which pits were used by a given domestic group usually is not possible.

Buildings and the refuse found in their basins are not necessarily contemporaneous or attributable to the same household. In addition to the garbage that might have been allowed to accumulate on house floors (see Deal 1985; Hayden and Cannon 1983), additional refuse may have been deposited in abandoned house depressions by households unrelated to the earlier occupants. This postabandonment deposition is especially likely in the case of deep basins at Cahokia that might have required more than one or two years to fill completely. Pits, on the other hand, are much smaller and may have been filled over the course of a season or, at most, a year or two (Mehrer 1988:128–130). Post pits are also distinct from either building basins or pits and, since they were most often backfilled with extraneous soil and debris after the post had been emplaced, contain refuse-poor matrix or a mixed bag of midden and feature fill predating the feature itself (Porter 1974:106–111).

Compounding these depositional problems are the limitations of the archaeological excavations themselves. Most feature fills were not screened. In some cases, the areal extent and depth of fill from Tract-15A building basins and floor deposits were not recorded, preventing the measurement of excavated fill volume. Many of these features could not be incorporated into the present analysis. Nonetheless, the potential error introduced into the excavated data set due to the depositional variability and recovery problems may be controlled to an extent by including various feature types into subphase assemblages and by differentially weighting the measures of artifact quantity to reflect the differential proportion of feature types that contributed to the subphase quantity.

Quantification and Controls over Assemblage Variability

Unlike the calculation of percentages, artifact density provides a measure of item quantity in domestic refuse independent of the other artifacts among the same refuse. Two separate means of calculating artifact density will be employed. These density figures in turn will be supplemented by the calculation of artifact ubiquity, which is to say the percentage of features per subphase that contain the artifact of concern. Ubiquity, while not a precise means of quantification, does provide insight into the distribution of an artifact type. This information complements density and assists in the comparisons of artifact classes.

For those features where all necessary metric information is available, artifact density may be expressed in terms of the number or weight of a particular material item per cubic meter of excavated feature fill. Where no such volumetric data are available, an ad hoc measure of feature volume must be employed. It has been demonstrated elsewhere that the number of ceramic jars at rural Mississippian homesteads positively correlates with the volume of feature fill (Pauketat 1989:table 6). A similar correlation may be observed in the 15A-DT sample. The number of jars in the 15A-DT sample is highly correlated with both pits and buildings (figure 6.1). This positive correlation is only slightly weaker when considering only Emergent Mississippian and Lohmann-phase building basins (*Pearson r* = .88, *df* = 5, *p* < .05) or pits (*Pearson r* = .92, *df* = 5, *p* < .05). It is important to note,

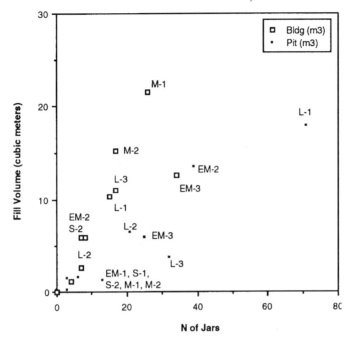

Figure 6.1. The Relationship between Feature-Group Volume and Number of Jars

however, that while number of jars positively correlates with both building-basin fill and pit fill volume, the density of sherds representing individual containers in pits is on average two to four times as high as the density of such sherds in building basins (table 6.1). This pattern is not surprising if we acknowledge that the depositional trajectories of variable feature types may differ.

Other refuse exhibits the same density pattern as does the number of jars. Sandstone, limestone, and expedient-tool chert debitage (not including Mill Creek chert debitage or any broken tools not recycled as expedient-tool cores) in pits or other fill zones is usually about twice as dense as in the basin fills of buildings (figure 6.2). Positive correlations between building-basin volume and chert debitage (*Pearson r* = .44, *df* = 6, *p* > .10) or sandstone (*Pearson r* = .18, *df* = 8, *p* > .20) are weak to absent. On the other hand, strong positive correlations exist between pit volume and chert debitage (*Pearson r* = .87, *df* = 8, *p* < .01) or sandstone (*Pearson r* = .82, *df* = 8, *p* < .02). In short, it appears that there was considerable variability in the deposition of garbage in abandoned house basins. Limestone quantities do not correlate with either house-basin volume (*Pearson r* = .21, *df* = 8, *p* > .20) or pit volume (*Pearson r* = .14, *df* = 8, *p* > .20).

Table 6.1 Pottery Jars and Fill Volume

Subphase	A N of Jars in Bldgs.	B Building BasinVol(m³)	C N of Jars in Pits	D Pit Vol (m³)	E A/B	F C/D	G F/E
EM 1	4	1.15	0	0.170	3.48	0	0
EM 2	7	5.84	39	13.503	1.20	2.89	2.41
EM 3	34	12.58	25	5.861	2.70	4.27	1.58
L1	17	10.99	71	17.846	1.54	3.98	2.58
L 2	7	2.61	21	5.957	2.68	3.53	1.21
L 3	15	10.28	32	3.780	1.46	8.47	5.80
S 1	0	0	6	4.700	0	1.28	0
S 2	8	5.93	13	1.280	1.35	10.16	7.53
M 1	26	21.53	3	1.459	1.21	2.06	1.70
M 2	17	15.12	3	0.210	1.12	14.29	12.76
EM/L Mean	13.3	7.05	31.3	7.8	1.82	4.56	2.93
EM/L s.d.	10.9	3.7	19.9	5.9	0.77	1.98	1.80
Grand Mean	13.1	8.5	21.3	5.5	1.62	5.52	4.40
s.d.	10.4	6.4	19.9	5.4	0.68	4.13	3.80

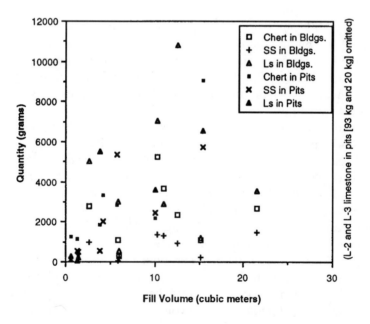

Figure 6.2. Quantities of Chert, Sandstone, and Limestone in Features

Since the average density of general refuse classes is at least twice as high in pits as in the basins of buildings, it is necessary to control for this density differential when comparing subphases that are represented by more or less pit or building-basin fill. A weighted density measure will be used for present comparative purposes calculated by dividing by two the quantity of artifacts (weight or count) in pits, then adding to this quotient the quantity of artifacts in building basins, and finally dividing the sum by the total cubic meters of fill volume. When using the proxy quantity/jar density measure (instead of quantity/cubic meter of fill), no adjustments need be made. Both density measures are used for graphic presentation. The use of the weighted density measure is selected where possible over quantity/jar in the statistical evaluations of diachronic density patterns.

Artifact Density and Ubiquity Through Time

With the aid of density and ubiquity measures, the diachronic patterns of cherts, sandstone, silicified sediment, microlithic tools, beads, mineral crystals, mineraloids, metal ores, large imported bifaces, axehead-making igneous-rock waste, projectile points, and pottery vessels in the 15A-DT refuse may be elucidated. These time-series data are largely independent of the architectural and community-organizational evidence presented in chapter 5. Additionally, certain classes of artifacts vary independently of other classes. These multiple lines of artifactual evidence are summarized at the end of this chapter and comprise an important component of the inferential arguments in chapter 7.

Sedimentary-Rock Refuse, Debitage, and Large Bifaces

Even though the chert and sandstone densities correlate with volume of fill, there are significant diachronic trends. For instance, chert debitage, sandstone, and limestone artifacts exhibit high weighted density values for the L-2 subphase (figure 6.3). Paired one-tailed *t*-tests of local chert and sandstone in refuse reveal that statistically significant increases occurred only between EM-3 and L-1 (t-value = 12.5, df = 1, p = < .03) and L-1 and L-2 (t-value = 4.6, df = 1, p < .08).

Siliceous artifacts like chert are an especially useful means of evaluating diachronic archaeological trends, not only because of their durability, but also because chert and other siliceous material was extensively used as a raw material for many expedient tools which during late prehistory had

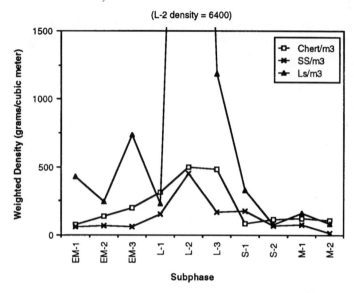

Figure 6.3. Diachronic Density Patterns of Local Cherts, Sandstone, and Limestone

brief use-lives. Hence, there tends to be a great quantity of chert debitage about. Also, if the cherts were used in everyday sorts of tasks (i.e., expedient-tool production and use), the time between the acquisition of the cherts and the discard of chert artifacts should not have been long, making them an acceptable means of monitoring exotic goods in circulation.

The six exotic siliceous types (silicified sediment and Cobden, Fort Payne, unidentified-black, Kaolin, Mill Creek cherts) are obtainable at outcrops 100 kilometers or more away from the Northern Bottom Expanse. Except for Mill Creek and Kaolin cherts, most 15A-DT exotic-chert artifacts represent expedient-tool and small-biface production debitage. Cobden chert has been identified from only one 15A- DT feature dating to the L-2 subphase. Kaolin chert is found throughout the 15A-DT sequence, albeit in varying densities. It appears as a minor component of the EM-2 lithic assemblage, is absent in EM-3, and then appears in more substantial amounts in the L-1 and especially L-2 subphases. Kaolin chert appears in abundance in the 15A-DT sample during the Moorehead subphases (figure 6.4). While barely represented in the artifacts of the 15A-DT Stirling subphases, it is represented as early as the early Stirling phase elsewhere at Cahokia (Pauketat 1993).

Much Kaolin and Mill Creek chert derives from large southern-Illinois

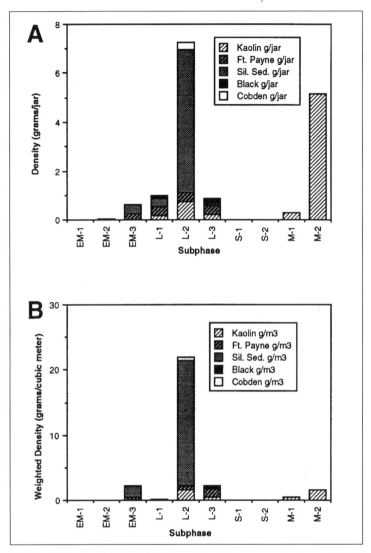

Figure 6.4. Exotic Chert and Silicified Sediment Density: a, grams/jar; b, weighted density

bifaces (adze blades, Ramey knives, hoe blades). A significant quantity of the 15A-DT Kaolin debitage also appears to be a by-product of an expedient core-and-flake industry. Only fragmentary adze and knife blades, recycled hoe blades, and hoe-blade resharpening flakes are quantified for the present time-series analysis. No complete or nearly complete hoe blades are included in the present quantification although several were found on the floors of Moorehead-phase buildings. If they had been included, the distribution would have been inordinately skewed towards the Moorehead phase, since the Mill Creek tools typically were included among the de facto remains on structure floors.

Fort Payne chert artifacts first appear during the EM-3 subphase and, using the quantity/jar index, increase in density through the Lohmann subphases. The black chert, possibly a dark Fort Payne variety, was recovered from three features, two of which are included in the present sample and date to the L-1 and L-3 subphases. The silicified-sediment diachronic-density pattern is skewed by the high L-2 density (a single 130-gram core in an L-2 feature would have further skewed the high L-2 density but has not been included in the present figures). Like chert density in general, there is some statistical significance associated with the increased densities of exotic cherts from the EM-3 to L-1 and the L-1 to L-2 subphases (table 6.2).

Mill Creek chert biface-resharpening flakes, recycled hoe blades, and expedient tools and debitage are common in the fills of EM-2 features but uncommon in the subsequent EM-3 fills. Mill Creek chert density rebounds by the beginning of the Lohmann phase but drops during the Stirling subphases (figure 6.5). If this density is a reasonable measure of hoe-blade numbers, then Mill Creek chert hoe blades were scarce during the EM-3 subphase, more common throughout the Lohmann phase, and slightly less common afterwards (although judging by the ubiquity index, Mill Creek chert hoe blades were most widely dispersed during the Moorehead phase).

As opposed to hoe blades, it is possible to monitor the density of individual adze blades and Ramey knives. Assuming, based on macroscopic comparisons, that each fragment or resharpening flake from an individual feature constitutes a single tool, then a total of fifteen Burlington chert and Mill Creek chert adze blades and three Ramey knives are represented in the 15A-DT lithic assemblage (table 6.3). While the tools are found throughout most of the Mississippian sequence, there are few adze blades and no Ramey knives dating to the Emergent Mississippi period. The tools, however, figure prominently into the L-1 subphase refuse and into each succeeding Lohmann subphase. The density is markedly reduced by the end of the 15A-DT Lohmann phase occupation. However, like Mill Creek chert hoe blades, adze and knife blades are found in over half of the M-2 features. The weighted density of Moorehead-phase adze and Ramey knife blades, on the other hand, shows that the tools are just slightly more prevalent than in the Lohmann phase (table 6.3; figure 6.6).

An examination of exotic chert ubiquity (or percent of features per subphase containing a particular chert type) reveals a divergent trend

Table 6.2 Paired One-Tailed *t*-tests of Exotic Cherts, Minerals, and Other Tools

Subphase	Exotic Chert†	Exotic Minerals††	Tools†††
EM 2			
t-value	1.37	1.0	1.0
p	>.12	>.20	>.20
EM 3			
t-value	**1.759**	.333	**2.219**
p	**<.08**	>.35	**<.08**
L 1			
t-value	**1.546**	**3.0**	3.69 E-20
p	**<.10**	**<.11**	>.49
L 2			
t-value	1.4	.375	.896
p	>.10	>.35	>.20
L 3			
t-value	**2.742**	.085	**2.982**
p	**<.03**	>.45	**<.05**
S 1			
t-value	1.0	1.0	1.0
p	>.18	>.20	>.20
S 2			
t-value	1.0	1.0	1.0
p	>.18	>.20	>.20
M 1			
t-value	1.0	-	1.692
p	>.18	-	>.10
M 2			

† d.f.=4; includes Cobden, Black, Ft. Payne, Kaolin, and silicified sediment (weighted grams/m3)
†† d.f.=1; includes copper and mica (weighted item/m³)
††† d.f.=2; includes adzes, ramey knives and projectile points (weighted tool/m3)

(figure 6.7). First, paralleling the diachronic-density data, more kinds of exotic chert are found in a higher percentage of Lohmann-phase features. Three to four of the six exotic cherts consistently were associated with between 3 to 15 percent of the Lohmann-phase features. By the S-1 subphase, exotic cherts were almost absent except for Mill Creek. In later subphases, however, Mill Creek and Kaolin cherts are the only represented exotic varieties in the 15A-DT sample. That is, while overall exotic chert density and ubiquity decreased, two S-1 types (usually associated with large bifacial tools) diverged from the pre-Stirling phase pattern.

With the conversion of the 15A-DT area from a residential location to

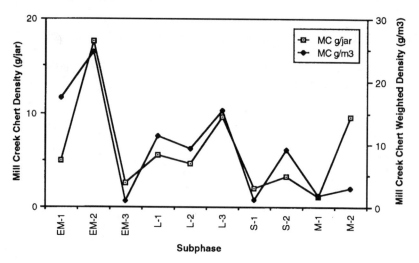

Figure 6.5. Mill Creek Chert Density

Table 6.3 Large Bifacial Chert Adze Blades and Ramey Knives

Subphase	Feature	Wt. (g)	Chert Type
Adze Blade Fragments and Resharpening Flakes			
EM 2	H81/82	94.6	Burlington
EM 2	185	32.5	Burlington
EM 3	H213	7.2	Burlington
L 1a	H48c	5.8	Mill Creek
L 1a	H109	31.9	Mill Creek
L 1b	157	62.0	Burlington
L 1b	427	20.9	Mill Creek
L 2	425	34.0	Burlington
L 2	H69	77.8	Mill Creek
L 3	297	7.3	Burlington
L 3	401	3.6	Mill Creek
M 2	H10	125.5	Burlington
M 2	H35	100.9	Burlington
M 2	H302	15.0	Burlington
M 2	H302/303	10.0	Burlington
M 2	H305	11.6	Burlington
Ramey Knife Fragments			
L 1b	427	17.4	Burlington
L 3	102	65.3	Burlington
M 2	309	9.1	Mill Creek

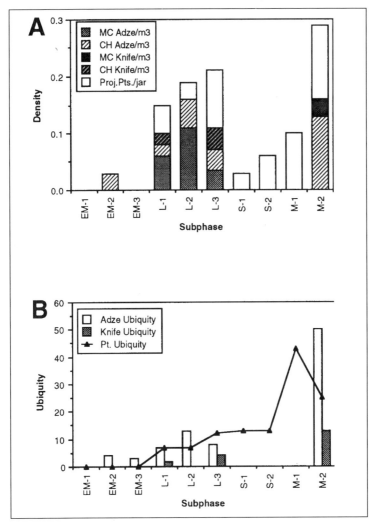

Figure 6.6. Adze Blade, Ramey Knife, and Projectile Point Density and Ubiquity

the site of the Post-Circle Monument, it is not surprising that, given a much reduced sample and hence a higher probability of sampling error, we see a reduction in the density and ubiquity of exotic cherts. On the other hand, nonsiliceous exotic materials are well represented in the Stirling-1 fills (see below), as might be anticipated where elite activities would have been prominent. The subsequent residential refuse associated with the Stirling-2 and Moorehead-phase components of the Dunham Tract and Tract 15A

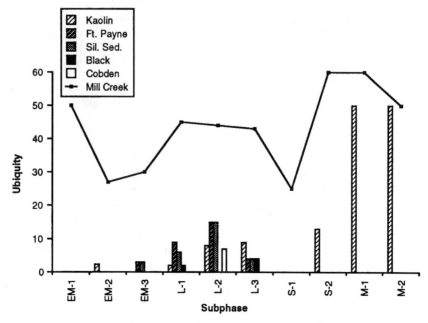

Figure 6.7. The Ubiquity of Exotic Cherts

does not contain any exotic cherts besides Mill Creek and Kaolin, a pattern that also is duplicated in other American Bottom data sets. All other excavated Stirling- and Moorehead-phase components in the American Bottom in which a thorough and well-documented chert analysis has been conducted record only Mill Creek and Kaolin chert as the exotic types (Pauketat 1992:table 2.1).

Projectile Points

While there were examples of nonlocal projectile points recovered from general contexts at Tract 15A and the Dunham Tract and from elsewhere at Cahokia (see chapter 3), the twenty-three projectile points in the present sample are considered local products. All but one, a marginally retouched point from an M-1 building (H2), are triangular in shape. Most have side notches, and some have basal notching. No projectile points were recovered from the Emergent Mississippian subphase features at Tract 15A. Instead, projectile points (and then only the Mississippian triangular variety) make an abrupt appearance in the earliest Lohmann-subphase refuse. There are hints that point density and ubiquity increased slightly through the Lohmann phase. As early as the S-2 subphase and certainly through the Moorehead phase, projectile points clearly become an increasingly common component of refuse (figure 6.6).

All but four of the Mississippian projectile points were manufactured from Burlington chert. One L-2 specimen was made from Mill Creek chert, one S-2 point was made from a reddish-tan gravel chert, and one L-3 item and an M-2 specimen were manufactured from an unidentified reddish-brown chert. The Burlington chert of the other nineteen projectile points displayed some variation in color, thermal alteration, and flaking patterns. Specimens were grouped according to color, presence of pressure flakes over one or both faces, and thermal alteration (identified as a waxy texture and glossy appearance).

Given these classification criteria, a distinct finely made point form was identified as Type A. Type-A points display pressure-flake scars on both faces and are made from thermally altered white Burlington chert. It should be noted that this intentional thermal alteration might have been a technique for obtaining this white coloration using a chert that, unless treated, often has an off-white (bluish) appearance in its natural state. If this was the reason for thermal alteration, the potential symbolic significance of the color might be an important consideration (Kelly 1980; the avoidance of a high-quality and locally available red chert of the Ste. Genevieve formation might also require explanation in symbolic terms.) Seven of the eight Type-A specimens are associated with Lohmann-phase features; a fragment of an eighth artifact in M-1 building H32 is probably tertiary admixture ultimately derived from Lohmann-phase garbage. Five of the six specimens associated with the L-1 subphase are Type-A points; the sixth also is made from a white-colored Burlington chert.

Microlithic Artifacts and Shell Beads

As discussed in chapter 4 and based on the surface-collection and excavated samples, high densities of microlithic tools and debitage are associated with domestic remains and elite activities on the Kunnemann Tract at Cahokia. In addition, many sandstone files or saws; bead-smoothing abraders; chisels; *Busycon* marine-shell finished and unfinished disk and columnar beads; pendants; *Olivella, Marginella,* and *Anculosa* snail shells and shell beads; and modified marine-whelk shell (scrap) were found amidst the Lohmann- and Stirling-phase debris from Kunnemann-Tract features (Pauketat 1993). Indeed, the excavated sample, while small, comprises the most complete shell-bead and ornament-making assemblage from Cahokia available to archaeologists. The density of microblades, microblade cores, and shell beads exemplifies the distinctiveness of the material assemblage. The Kunnemann-Mound Lohmann-phase feature 40 produced 4 microblade cores per eighteen ceramic jars; early Stirling-phase deposits yielded 121 microblade cores and twenty-two beads per fifty jars; the late Stirling-phase feature 48 on the mound (probably incorporating some earlier admixture) produced thirteen beads per eleven jars (Pauketat 1993). Bead-and-pendant necklaces were produced by elite households or households closely tied to these Cahokian elite.

By comparison, the entire 15A-DT Lohmann-phase sample produced only one microblade core and one (bone) bead per 208 jars; the Stirling-1 15A-DT sample included no such objects, while the Stirling-2 15A-DT materials include three shell beads per 36 jars. Only two artifacts resembling microdrills were found with L-1 and L-2 features, and these are not the classic microdrill form as described by Mason and Perino (1961). Two other similar microperforators were associated with the M-1 and M-2 samples (figure 6.8). In short, there is scant evidence that shell-working ever occurred at Tract 15A or the Dunham Tract. It is abundantly clear, however, that such activities were integral components of Kunnemann Tract household activities.

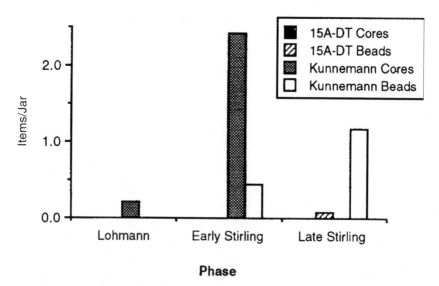

Figure 6.8. The Density of Microblade Cores and Beads in the Kunnemann Mound and 15A-DT Samples

Exotic Minerals and Copper

Small residual mica (i.e., muscovite) flakes, copper, galena cubes (ground and unmodified), unmodified hematite chunks, and whole crystals and knapped flakes of quartz, fluorite, and plagioclase constitute the mineral, mineraloid, and metal-ore artifacts recovered from Tract 15A and the Dunham Tract. While few of these exotic artifacts are abundant, the 15A-DT density and ubiquity indices may be compared to the exotic chert and bifacial tool data.

Mica is first associated with a single pit (F353) dating to the EM-3 subphase at Tract 15A and the Dunham Tract and has elsewhere been associated with Edelhardt-phase fill below the East Palisade (Koldehoff 1990b:87). Mica is absent from L-1 and L-3 subphase fills and is found in only one L-2 feature (D5). Clearly, while mica probably circulated within the Mississippian social networks at Cahokia, it was rarely acquired or disposed of by Lohmann-phase households at Tract 15A and the Dunham Tract. Contrariwise, it may have been one of the common exotic materials associated with the 15A-DT Stirling subphases although still found in only one feature per Stirling subphase (figure 6.9).

Copper first appears in the 15A-DT material assemblage during the L-1 subphase; it also has been found in the late Merrell or early Edelhardt-phase fill of a building below the East Palisade wall (Koldehoff 1990b:87). In any case, the density and ubiquity of copper in 15A-DT feature fills increased during the L-2 and L-3 subphases. Importantly, no copper is associated with any subphase later than Lohmann-3 in the 15A-DT sample (figure 6.9). Of course, it is known from other Mississippian contexts at Cahokia and the Central Political-Administrative Complex (see chapter 4).

Like copper and mica, few mineral crystals were found among the 15A-DT domestic refuse (table 6.4). Three flakes of large quartz (SiO_2) crystals in L-1 subphase contexts were apparently a result of knapping activities. It is unknown whether this knapping of quartz crystal was done as a means of making more of the few crystals available or if the debitage derives from knapping quartz-crystal projectile points, rare but documented at Cahokia (see Titterington 1938). Smaller quartz crystals perhaps derived from geodes like those available within a thirty-kilometer radius of Cahokia were found in individual L-1 and L-3 features. One plagioclase (Na-feldspar) crystal and a single fragment of a large rubbed or ground fluorite (CaF_2) crystal were found in Lohmann-phase features. Otherwise, fluorite crystals were restricted to the Moorehead-2 subphase (figure 6.10).

Galena (PbS) and hematite (Fe_2O_3) artifacts in the form of irregular

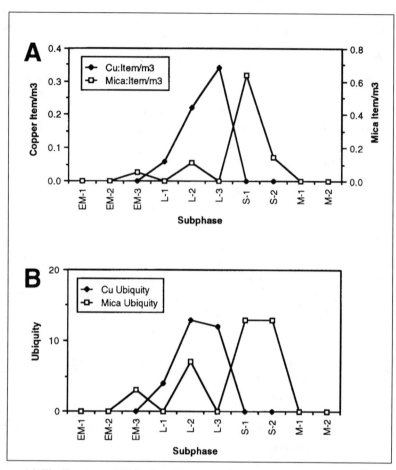

Figure 6.9. The Density and Ubiquity of Copper and Mica Artifacts

Table 6.4 Quartz, Fluorite, and Plagioclase Crystals

Subphase	Feature	Wt. (g)	Description
L 1b	H157	1.1	1 quartz crystal flake
L 1b	163	2.7	2 quartz crystal flakes
L 1b	171	11.8	small quartz crystals from ("local"?) geode
L 1b	190	2.1	1 plagioclase crystal
L 3	D12	16.3	small quartz crystals from ("local"?) geode
L 3	130	6.4	1 rubbed fluorite crystal fragment
M 2	H35	13.4	1 fluorite crystal
M 2	H302	8.0	1 fluorite crystal
Total:		61.8	9

chunks or rubbed pieces (probably used for pigment) were found in 15A-DT features that postdate the EM-3 subphase (figure 6.11). Hematite was associated with earlier Emergent Mississippian features at the Merrell Tract, but galena was restricted to Merrell Tract features dating to the Edelhardt phase (Kelly 1980:table 25). The distribution and density of 15A-DT hematite was fairly uniform through time, while the density (grams/jar) of galena significantly increased from the EM-3 through L-3 suphases (table 6.5). The ubiquity of galena, however, decreased subsequent to the L-1 and prior to the S-2 subphases. Both galena and hematite are ubiquitous components of Stirling-2, Moorehead-1, and Moorehead-2 garbage. However, the weighted densities of these minerals are often less than Lohmann-phase levels. This ubiquity pattern finds some verification in

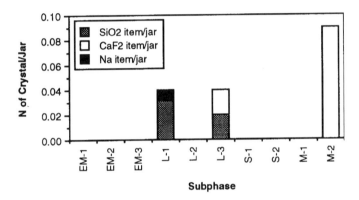

Figure 6.10. Mineral Crystal Density

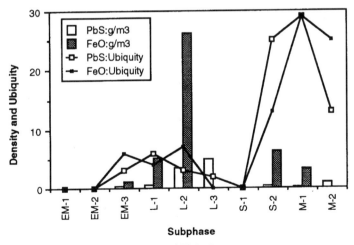

Figure 6.11. Galena and Hematite Density and Ubiquity

Table 6.5 Paired One-Tailed *t*-tests of Galena and Hematite

Subphase	Galena	Hematite
EM 2 and 3		
t-value	1.0	0.934
p	>.20	>.25
L 1		
t-value	**10.053**	0.876
p	**<.04**	>.25
L 2 and 3		
t-value	**7.198**	0.609
p	**<.05**	>.35
S 1 and 2		
t-value	2.76	0.328
p	>.10	>.35
M 1 and 2		

note: degrees of freedom =1

other Moorehead-phase mineral assemblages from Cahokia (Koldehoff 1990b:87) and outlying sites (e.g., Pauketat and Woods 19 86:table 2) and suggests that, while more galena may have been available to a few people during the Lohmann phase at Cahokia, less galena was available to more people during the Moorehead phase.

Exotic Igneous Rock and Axehead Production

Aphanitic igneous rock from the St. Francois Mountains is abundantly represented in the 15A-DT refuse. This 15A-DT igneous rock was used in the manufacture of axeheads and includes knapping debitage (i.e., shatter and flakes), celt-preform fragments (fractured during the initial knapping or during later surface-pecking stages of shaping), and two whole unfinished celt preforms embedded in the upper level of a pit (F298) in the floor of a Lohmann-phase building (H125; not tabulated with the totals). The recovered Tract-15A rock includes primary (decortication-like) flakes that show an iron-stained patina on the weathered angular exterior. This iron-stained angular surface is typical of weathered blocks of intrusive igneous rocks from the St. Francois Mountains, especially in dikes of diabase and basalt. It is not a common feature of cobbles deposited as glacial erratics in the tills of the Illinois uplands to the east of the American Bottom.

The diachronic rock-debitage data show that axehead manufacture is represented in the EM-3 subphase; the few EM-2 rocks may represent fire-cracked cobbles. The density of axehead-manufacturing refuse increased through the L-3 subphase while rock-debitage ubiquity decreased after the L-1 subphase (figure 6.12). A one-tailed t-test of the EM-2 and L-1 subphases relative to those of Lohmann 2 and 3 subphases illustrates that weighted-density increases are statistically significant (t-value = 3.87, df = 1, $p < .10$). The ubiquity pattern, in turn, may indicate that a larger number of people were involved in celt making during the L-1 subphase but that fewer people were so involved during the L-2 and L-3 subphases. That is, while the density of celt-knapping debitage reached extreme amounts by the L-3 subphase, the proportion of features containing such refuse steadily decreased. No signs of axehead production remain with the cessation of Lohmann-phase residential usage of Tract 15A and the Dunham Tract; the weighted densities of L-2 and L-3 versus S-1 and S-2 features are significantly different (t-value = 4.306, df = 1, $p < .08$). The low density but widely dispersed scatter of this material in S-2, M-1, and M-2 features is likely a consequence of these later features intruding upon the earlier Lohmann-phase fills. There is no evidence that celts were made in the area beyond the end of the Lohmann phase.

Pottery Containers

Emergent Mississippian and Mississippian pottery-vessel assemblages are uniform with respect to the percentage of the minimum number of jars and bowls or beakers from particular subphases. One exception is the L-2 subphase, where fewer jars are complemented by a large number of seed

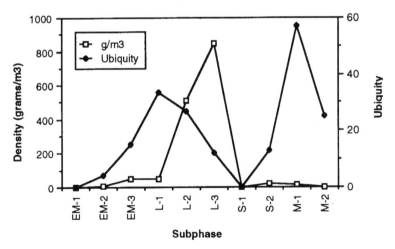

Figure 6.12. The Density and Ubiquity of Igneous-Rock Celt-Making Waste

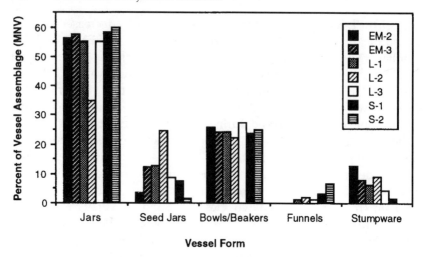

Figure 6.13. The 15A-DT Ceramic Vessel Assemblage

jars. Otherwise, seed jars exhibit a near-normal diachronic distribution. The numbers of stumpware vessels declined as funnels, their apparent functional descendants, increased in frequency (figure 6.13). Because of their relative uniformity through time and because they include distinct subsets of decorated wares, jars, bowls, and beakers are employed to track the appearance and densities of pots that may have been part of or functioned within social interactions.

Except for Monks Mound Red seed jars and other miscellaneous vessel forms, grog-tempered fineware bowls and beakers and Ramey Incised jars constitute the principal types of decorated containers in the 15A-DT ceramic assemblage. The frequencies of each are examined separately because each vessel type was probably intended for distinct groups or social audiences. Each also probably is characterized by different production and distribution trajectories.

There are three ways of monitoring density of fineware vessels through time, each affecting the interpretation of the Lohmann-phase trends. Tabulating the number of vessels as identified using distinctive rim sherds or examining the ubiquity of fineware sherds in refuse results in the observation that the L-2 and S-1 subphases represent peaks of fineware deposition (figure 6.14). However, by examining the weight of vessel fragments per cubic meter of fill or per jar, we see a low density of containers in the EM-2 and EM-3 subphases and significant density peaks at L-1 and S-1. A directional *t*-test illustrates the significant differences between the EM-2 and EM-3 weighted densities and the L-1 and L-2 densities (*t*-value =

6.909, $df = 1$, $p < .05$), and between the L-2 and L-3 subphases and the S-1 and S-2 subphases (t-value = 7.0, $df = 1$, $p < .05$). Fineware vessels remain common through the M-1 subphase; decreased densities (S-1 and S-2 versus M-1 and M-2) are not statistically significant (t-value = .749, $df = 1$, $p > .25$).

In summary, the availability of the fancy beakers and bowls (serving and eating containers) increased after the Edelhardt phase and again after the Lohmann phase. It is noteworthy that the density of fineware vessels in Stirling-phase garbage mirrors that seen on the Kunnemann Mound (Pauketat 1993). In all likelihood, the amount of fineware used, broken, and discarded depended in large measure upon the social status of the household or the location of elite-sponsored activities and rites at Cahokia.

Ramey Incised jars may not have been linked with social status in the same way as fineware beakers and bowls. Emerson (1989) and I (Pauketat and Emerson 1991) have argued that the context, regional distribution, physical characteristics, and standardized design elements of Ramey Incised jars support the contention that these pots were manufactured under centralized conditions and dispersed from Mississippian centers into the immediate hinterlands (and beyond). The pots are found at most Stirling-phase rural sites but are relatively uncommon, comprising a small proportion of any homestead refuse assemblage (e.g., Emerson and Jackson 1984;

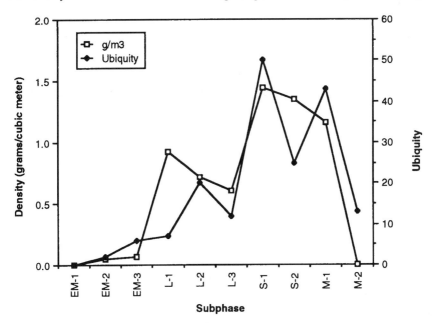

Figure 6.14. Fineware Vessel Density and Ubiquity

Fortier 1985; Hanenberger 1990a, 1990b; Jackson 1990a, 1990b; Mehrer 1982; Milner 1983, 1984a; Pauketat 1986, 1989). Ramey Incised jars were not small serving and eating containers, like fineware dishes. Some were capable of containing large volumes (more than fifty liters) of foodstuffs and probably were not used on a daily basis in the ordinary consumption of foods. If Ramey Incised jars were centrally made, then it is reasonable that the pots were produced initially for use in centralized gatherings or ritual events, where a large storage or cooking pot might have been required. Subsequent to such an event, the containers could have facilitated the redistribution of foods or medicines (Emerson 1989; Pauketat and Emerson 1991).

Thus the simple and redundant representations and synecdoches of mythical sky-world deities, the sky arch, sun/fire, and perhaps serpentine form of Ramey iconography would have engaged the Mississippian commoner initially in a different context than the complex iconography of a fineware pot. These motifs, arranged according to a quadripartition of the vessel design field, are inferred to have expressed basic cosmological principles not unlike those associated with other late-prehistoric and historic Native American groups of eastern North America and the Plains. The pots so embellished are interpreted as a medium for elite-commoner communication, the design and the mode of dispersal defining in effect the relationship between the elite, the nonelite, and the cosmos (Pauketat and Emerson 1991). Given this symbolic interpretation, the appearance of these jars during the Stirling-1 subphase is quite important as it correlates with the initial construction of the Post-Circle Monument at Tract 15A (figure 6.15). Their frequency in the 15A-DT refuse of the Stirling-1 through Moorehead-1 subphases, consistently making up around 20 to 22 percent of the jars, bespeaks their prominent and long-standing place in Cahokian vessel assemblages.

Time-Series Summary

One means of summarizing the artifact-density time-series information is by converting the weighted density figures into z-scores ([observed value–mean value]/standard deviation). The z-scores provide a standardized perspective into raw-value diversity. The standardized scores of the 15A-DT exotic artifacts and craft-goods residues that exceed the value of one standard deviation (i.e., a z-score 1.0) indicate occurrences of extreme density value.

The 15A-DT z-scores illustrate four principal patterns (table 6.6). First,

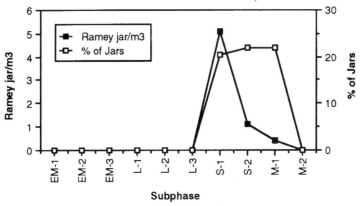

Figure 6.15. Ramey Incised Jar Density and Percent of Total Jars

there are few artifacts in the EM-2, EM-3, and L-1 material assemblages that stand out against a standardized background: Mill Creek chert density fluctuates wildly between the EM-2 and EM-3 subphases; fineware vessels (and many other exotic goods and craft items) are few in number. Second, the high densities of many items in the L-2 and L-3 subphases are indicated as positive z-scores greater than or equal to 1.0. Exotic cherts, silicified sediment, copper, galena, hematite, basalt debitage, large bifacial tools, projectile points, and mineral crystals in the L-2 and L-3 subphase fills all exceed the mean values for these items by more than one standard deviation. Third, a limited array of items (mica and fineware vessels) stands out as Stirling-phase high-density items. Last, a few artifacts (Kaolin chert, large bifacial tools, and fluorite crystals) characterize the high-density objects of the M-2 subphase. Fineware is a conspicuously low-density M-2 item, as are a number of other items (not unlike the EM-2 subphase).

The numerous seed jars, the extreme high density and ubiquity values of some items, and the low density of projectile points that characterize the L-2 subphase may be indicative of relatively high-status garbage. On the other hand, the high L-2 artifact densities are not that different from L-3 density values. Perhaps the low density of Stirling-1 exotica is a function of sampling error, given the small size of the S-1 sample. Of course, it is doubtful that a larger S-1 refuse sample would be entirely comparable to that of the Lohmann subphases, since the S-1 refuse might well be the garbage of elite households. This difference would explain the relatively high density and ubiquity values of mica and fineware vessels along with the low density of Mill Creek chert hoe-blade maintenance debitage.

Social variability, however, does not explain the absence or extreme low density of copper, exotic cherts, and nonlocal minerals in S-1 features.

Table 6.6 Z-scores of Weighted Artifact Densities

Sub-phase	Cobden Black	FtPay	Kaolin	MCk	SilSed	Cu	Mica	PbS	FeO	Basalt	Adze	Knife	FWare	Points	Xstals
EM 2	-.333	-.635	-.622	**2.039**	-.487	-.561	-.503	-.687	-.555	-.542	-.347	-.632	**-1.15**	-.673	-.624
EM 3	-.333	.546	-.719	**-.955**	.802	-.561	-.214	-.483	-.414	-.386	-.839	-.632	**-1.1**	-.673	-.624
L 1	-.333	-.517	-.719	.352	-.417	.057	-.503	-.365	.05	-.358	.31	.632	.388	-.481	.713
L 2	2.667	**1.089**	**1.609**	.106	**2.42**	**1.087**	-.021	**1.259**	**2.554**	**1.144**	**1.787**	-.632	.033	.384	-.624
L 3	-.333	**2.057**	.109	.858	-.37	**2.22**	-.503	**2.136**	-.555	**2.24**	.31	**1.897**	-.179	**2.307**	**2.049**
S 1	-.333	-.635	-.719	-.92	-.487	-.561	**2.58**	-.687	-.555	-.554	-.839	-.632	**1.309**	-.673	-.624
S 2	-.333	-.635	-.672	.066	-.487	-.561	.171	-.438	.201	-.485	-.839	-.632	**1.149**	.673	-.624
M 1	-.333	-.635	-3E-4	-.854	-.487	-.561	-.503	-.563	-.173	-.504	-.839	-.632	.813	-.192	-.624
M 2	-.333	-.635	**1.734**	-.693	-.487	-.561	-.503	-.172	-.555	-.553	**1.295**	**1.265**	**-1.24**	-.673	.98

Given the similar patterns recognized in other Stirling-phase assemblages associated with the Kunnemann Mound, outlying rural sites, and even the Stirling-2 15A-DT remains, the sparsity of these exotics in the 15A-DT Stirling-1 subphase remains may reflect a regionwide pattern of decreased exotica diversity. The Stirling-1 remains, then, could represent the first of a series of subsequent subphases in which exotic possessions were largely restricted to galena, hematite, marine-shell beads, and Kaolin and Mill Creek chert tools.

By simply plotting the incidence of exotic chert or mineral type per subphase, a graphic image is provided that complements the description of the z-score matrix above (figure 6.16). Since the EM-3 through L-3 subphases each contain a diversity of exotic material goods, especially prevalent in the L-2 and L-3 subphases (and slightly less so in the L-1 or EM-3 subphases), this simple tabulation is in some ways an adequate summary of the 15A-DT diachronic-density patterns. However, the incidence summary leaves out an important dimension of the time-series analysis. Not only did the amounts of local and exotic cherts, projectile points, large bifacial tools, fineware, and quartz crystals increase markedly from the EM-3 to L-1 subphases, but also the density of almost *all* exotica and craft goods increased over that same short span. Additionally, the densities of some items decreased subsequent to the L-1 subphase.

As a means of bypassing the smoothing effect of standardized data while focusing on change (not density per se), a tally is made of the number of times that the density values of a total of fifteen possible artifact

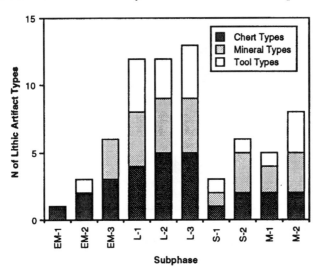

Figure 6.16. Numbers of Exotic or Finely Crafted Lithic Types per Subphase

classes increased or decreased from one subphase to the next excluding instances of no change. This summary provides a very different diachronic picture of artifact density change (figure 6.17). The brief period of the EM-3 subphase to the earliest Lohmann subphase witnessed the most instances out of the entire 15A-DT sequence of increased densities and concomitantly the fewest instances of decreased densities. Subsequent to the L-1 subphase, artifact densities did not uniformly increase. In other words, the total array of exotic items and craft-goods residues that emerged across the board as a component of the L-1 refuse did not keep emerging as a unit. Everything had increased at once after the EM-3 subphase, although L-1 density values in general are not usually as great as certain L-2 values. The density values of many items did increase markedly during the L-2 and L-3 subphases, but this increase occurred on a more isolated basis. The uniformity of directional change displayed by the L-1 subphase artifact densities steadily decayed thereafter, perhaps reaching some sort of Stirling- or Moorehead-phase equilibrium.

The time-series information is analyzed in the next chapter in conjunction with architectural, monumental, and community-plan data, reducing the reliance upon any particular artifact type or subphase assemblage.

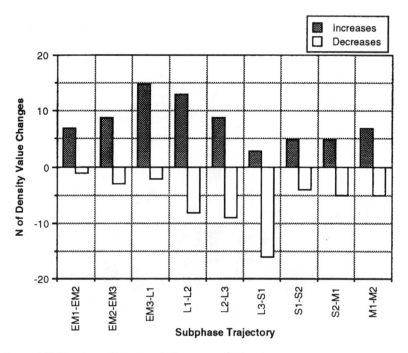

Figure 6.17. Number of Directional Changes in Artifact Density

Thus sampling error as it affects the 15A-DT interpretations will be minimized. Of course, it remains possible that specific time-series observations made using the 15A-DT data might not be replicated using some other Cahokia sample. On the other hand, it is difficult not to have some confidence in the principal qualitative patterns apparent in the 15A-DT sample. There appears to be artifactual and perhaps iconographic evidence for (1) a dramatic social and political-economic transformation at the end of the EM-3 subphase, (2) the intensification of Cahokian production-and-exchange during and subsequent to the L-1 subphase, and (3) a transformed political economy and altered political-religious representation during and subsequent to the Stirling-1 subphase.

Chapter 7

The Generation
of the Cahokian Leviathan

I saw the lesser mounds which round me rose;
Each was a giant heap of mouldering clay;
There slept the warriors, women, friends and foes,
There side by side the rival chieftains lay;
And mighty tribes, swept from the face of day,
Forgot their wars and found a long repose.

(Flint 1826:168)

The ascent of chiefs from modest communal beginnings to the high offices of region-wide stratified domains can best be understood as a long-term historical process. Recourse to an abstract political approach to chiefdoms is necessary but not sufficient to explain the generation of the Cahokian Leviathan. In addition, we must view the late-prehistoric political world of competing high-ranking factions within the context of the commoner sense of the world at any point in time as the cultural hegemony enabled or constrained human actions. As traditional common sense was appropriated and transformed by the dominant ideologies of elite Cahokian subgroups, as commoners were estranged from their own social reproduction, so the powers of a ruling elite were enhanced and the American Bottom political economy expanded. A rank hegemony was transformed into a class hegemony.

How did this hegemonic transformation occur? Did the regional transformation of political structure and social relations occur at a gradual pace or result from an abrupt political consolidation of the region? The subphase data from Tract 15A and the Dunham Tract provide the resolution to answer these questions, and in so doing we will better comprehend the significance of particular political actions, historical events, and punctuated transformations that gave rise to the Cahokian Leviathan.

Lohmann-Phase Political Consolidation

The development of the Tract-15A Emergent Mississippian community followed a course much like that identified elsewhere in the American
Bottom (Kelly 1990a, 1990b). Single-post buildings were arranged around
small flanking courtyards. The EM-2 and EM-3 structural remains along
with the Merrell- and Edelhardt-phase remains from elsewhere at Cahokia
are indicative of a substantial Emergent Mississippian population. Hun-
dreds of Edelhardt-phase households, perhaps members of a number of
separate communities each with component courtyard groups, may have
occupied the south bank of Cahokia Creek. While not demonstrable using
the data at hand, it is likely that the Emergent Mississippian occupation at
Cahokia was one of a number of local political-administrative centers in
the American Bottom (see chapter 3).

The EM-2 refuse includes little in the way of nonlocal items. Union
County chert hoe blades from southern Illinois and a small amount of
nonlocal fineware from the mid-South are among the EM-2 exotica. The
high density of Mill Creek chert may be a signature of the extensive tillage
of the surrounding soils by these EM-2 households using chert hoe blades.
A whole range of exotic items is found in the 15A-DT EM-3 sample.
Among them are Fort Payne chert, silicified sediment, mica, galena, and
hematite. However, the residue of few of the Union County tools so
abundant in the EM-2 subphase was deposited in EM-3 garbage, especially odd since the overall density of chert in refuse actually increased
from the EM-2 to EM-3 subphase. Random variation in the size (and hence
weight) of Mill Creek chert artifacts cannot be ruled out as a source of
sampling error since, in terms of the ubiquity of Mill Creek chert, the EM-
3 sample has a value comparable to the EM-2 sample. Conversely, it
remains possible that the low EM-3 Mill Creek chert density is an accurate
reflection of a community-wide trend. Union County chert does not seem
rare at the nearby Edelhardt-phase site of BBB Motor (Emerson and
Jackson 1984:97, 107), although not entirely comparable to the 15A-DT
EM-3 subphase. The percent of Mill Creek chert in the Edelhardt-phase
chert assemblage from the Merrell Tract is slightly less than the earlier
Merrell-phase figure, perhaps duplicating the 15A-DT evidence (Kelly
1980:table 32). Unfortunately, the Merrell Tract phases are not entirely
comparable with the 15A-DT EM-2 and EM-3 subphases, both of which
fall primarily within the Edelhardt phase.

In some ways, the exotic-material assemblage of the EM-3 subphase
represents the first of a series of comparable subphase assemblages (EM-3
through L-3). The exotic artifact types of the later subphases like Fort

Payne chert, silicified sediment, mica, galena, hematite, fineware, and St. Francois Mountain igneous rock are associated with the EM-3 subphase, albeit in often low densities. If nothing else, the kinds of exotic materials in EM-3 refuse may indicate that the *configuration* of EM-3 long-distance exchange relations was comparable to the configuration that characterized the subsequent Lohmann subphases. There are some differences and important changes in density subsequent to EM-3, but in terms of the exotic artifact assemblage, EM-3 seems more similar to L-1 than to EM-2. However, none of the examined differences between the material densities of the EM-2 versus EM-3 subphases may be argued to be different with much statistical certainty. The array of nonlocal items changed, and quantities increased, but these developments do not represent a clear break with the EM-2 patterns.

At the same time, if the density reduction of Mill Creek chert artifacts is an accurate reflection of reduced usage (and not simply sampling error), then the Cahokian households may have been doing less farming with stone-bladed hoes (or otherwise had less access to Union County tools). As the absence of Mill Creek chert hoe-blade maintenance debitage may indicate a change in the agricultural activities of Cahokian households, so the absence of arrow points in the 15A-DT Emergent Mississippian refuse may be explained as the absence of much need for hunting devices or weaponry. Emergent Mississippian projectiles without stone tips might account for the apparent absence of arrow points, but stone points do show up in other Emergent Mississippian contexts (e.g., Kelly et al. 1984, 1990; Koldehoff 1990a).

It should be recalled that, during the period covered by the Patrick through Range phases at the Range site, the quantities of arrow points and large mammalian species in refuse decreased while the quantities of maize increased. These patterns were interpreted to indicate a decreased reliance upon large mammals (particularly deer) as sources of protein and an increased reliance upon maize agriculture (L. Kelly 1990b:511). Given this change, Lucretia Kelly's (1979, 1990a) documentation of the steadily increasing amounts of white-tailed deer through the Emergent Mississippi period should correlate with increased numbers of projectile points if Cahokia residents were doing most of this hunting. However, based on the complete absence of stone projectile points in the EM-1, EM-2, and EM-3 fill samples analyzed here, the most reasonable conclusion seems to be that the meat brought to Cahokia was acquired via a social network (e.g., tribute to high-ranking subgroups).

While exchanges of prestige goods between high-ranking individuals and the mobilization of staple goods in support of high-ranking Cahokians appear to have been increasing during the Emergent Mississippi period, the EM-3 domestic zones, community plan, and architectural style mirror those of the earlier EM-2 arrangements. That is, the EM-3 subphase at Tract 15A saw the continuation of the same community organization as the EM-2 subphase, although the size of domestic buildings and courtyards increased noticeably as did the overall numbers of buildings per unit excavation area. At least one EM-3 domicile was more substantial than the rest, perhaps the first sign of what seems to have been a divergence of domestic architecture size in the subsequent Lohmann phase.

In sum, the EM-3 remains from Tract 15A and the Dunham Tract are indicative of an enlargement of Cahokia's Emergent Mississippian community and political economy. Undoubtedly this enlargement included the high-ranking sector of the community; the increased densities of an array of nonlocal goods in refuse probably are indicative of the extensification of certain Emergent-Mississippian sociopolitical alliances and an intensification of emergent tributary relations between central and peripheral subgroups. This may properly be considered a consequence of gradual political-economic developments, a necessary but not sufficient precursor for what was to follow. At a certain point in this gradual development, regional consolidation became a means for a small number of high-ranking Emergent-Mississippian individuals to reproduce its claim to authority. By reproducing this claim, however, social relations were transformed.

The Pace of Consolidation

There are a number of indications—the location of buildings, garbage inside abandoned buildings, and the location of an L-1 plaza and perhaps an L-1 courtyard group—that the earliest Lohmann subphase represents a continuation of the EM-3 residential occupation. There also are indications in the sorts of exotic artifacts associated with the L-1 refuse that the configuration of Cahokia's external relations may not have changed drastically from the EM-3 artifact assemblages.

Nonetheless, there is sufficient evidence in the 15A-DT sample to conclude that the L-1 subphase features and artifacts represent a qualitative political-economic shift and a restructuring of social organization. This is inferred to be the political consolidation of an unknown portion of the American Bottom region in the form of a complex chiefdom. At this point in time (calibrated to circa A.D. 1050), it would appear that an office-holder(s) at Cahokia was able to extend his or her authority across the

American Bottom and perhaps into the adjacent uplands by subjugating or incorporating neighboring chiefships within his or her domain. The size of the region under the new paramountcy probably included or would have soon included much of the Northern Bottom Expanse, as perhaps indicated by the extent of the Lohmann-phase architectural and rural settlement-pattern shifts (see Emerson 1992; Mehrer 1988; Milner et al. 1984; Porter 1974). The continued existence of a Pulcher ceramic tradition (i.e., Lindhorst phase), alongside the Cahokian (Late Bluff) tradition may mean that the Cahokian consolidation was limited at first to the Northern Bottom Expanse and did not incorporate the central American Bottom.

A reliable means of measuring the size of the consolidated Cahokian polity might be through the quantification of the staple goods moving into Cahokia. However, given the present dearth of such data, a rough idea may be obtained by measuring the extent of the transformation of Cahokian community order (since laborers undoubtedly were fed using staple-goods stores or compensated using material wealth, ultimately derived via the transformation of food-energy sources). It is evident that the earliest Lohmann subphase is characterized by what may well have been a thorough restructuring of community organization. There may have been one L-1 courtyard group similar in size and layout to the Emergent-Mississippian feature clusters, but otherwise the arrangement of 15A-DT Lohmann-phase buildings suggests that the tightly clustered courtyard groups of preceding subphases were gone. There are reasons to suspect that a large open plaza was created in place of what probably had been a smaller EM-3 courtyard. That is, this plaza appears to have been an enlargement of an established open ground, its transformation further confirmed by the L-1 drainage ditch.

The L-1 subphase also witnessed the complete disappearance of single-post building construction. It is likely that, after the initial implementation of wall-trench technology, all buildings at Cahokia were built using wall trenches. It is not certain whether this represents any substantial changes to the above-ground building itself. Lohmann-phase buildings were larger than EM-3 examples, but the latter were also larger than EM-2 buildings. In the very least, the seemingly complete and abrupt L-1 transition to wall-trench foundations at Cahokia implies that work crews were not organized on a familial or subgroup basis. That kind of work-crew organization probably would have resulted in the retention of traditional single-post construction techniques beyond the L-1 subphase at Cahokia. Rather, construction crews probably were organized relative to the changed macrostructural political-kinship bases of community organization. The conversion to wall-trench foundations, as it corresponds to the restructuring of community space, makes likely the inference that many old (Emergent Mississippian) buildings systematically were removed over a brief span of time.

This explanation begs the question of why wall trenches were adopted across a large portion of the American Bottom region during the Lohmann phase or its southern Lindhorst-phase variant (cf. Bareis 1976; Kelly et al. 1989; Mehrer and Collins 1989; Milner et al. 1984). Even if we accept that a top-down reconstruction of the Cahokian community occurred as explanation of the appearance of wall-trench buildings, there also appears to have been a regional acceptance of this new mode of house-foundation construction that can hardly be explained as the work of roving work crews from Cahokia. The view of a top-down restructuring of the community (and reconstruction of buildings) and the regional adoption of a mode of digging building foundations suggest to me that Lohmann-phase changes involved as well a cultural element that spread rapidly, perhaps through the collaborative political tactics and the centralization of agricultural or fertility ritual suspected to have been sponsored by the new Cahokian paramountcy.

Along with seemingly abrupt changes in community organization and mode of house construction, there are recognizable changes in the artifact assemblage of the L-1 subphase. The densities of L-1 chert debitage, adze, and Ramey-knife blades and projectile points may be interpreted to be substantially different from EM-3 assemblages. These density increases are of a larger magnitude than the more subtle increases between EM-2 and EM-3 or subsequent subphases. The density and ubiquity of Mill Creek chert surged higher than the low EM-3 levels. Copper artifacts and mineral crystals in L-1 features constitute the earliest such occurrences in the 15A-DT sequence. The densities of both galena and hematite in L-1 features represent an increase, albeit not statistically recognizable, over the EM-3 densities. The weight of fineware sherds in features rose substantially by the L-1 subphase, although the number of features in which they are found is only slightly higher.

In fact, the density of almost every type of exotic (and local) artifact increased from the EM-3 to L-1 subphases. As this across-the-board density increase corresponds to the subphase in which the mode of building construction and the spatial arrangement of the community appear to have been radically altered, a punctuated change in the political economy and the social organization of the American Bottom around A.D. 1050 may be beyond question. The large-scale earth-moving activities of the

Lohmann phase (leveling of the central plaza, mound construction, and the sub-Mound 51 borrow) provide us with further evidence of the Lohmann-phase transformation of the Cahokian community.

It can be expected that a concomitant of the physical and social transformation of Cahokia was substantial demographic change. Indeed, the Lohmann-phase population of Cahokia was perhaps three to four times that of the Edelhardt-phase population, based on the number and size of buildings on Tract 15A and the Dunham Tract. Extending this population increase to the Cahokia site as a whole, we move from a population guessed to include a maximum of a thousand people to one of perhaps several thousand people or more (not counting the rest of the sprawling Central Political-Administrative Complex). The Lohmann-phase evidence from elsewhere at Cahokia provides further evidence that population had been substantially enlarged (see Collins 1990; O'Brien 1972).

A population increase of such magnitude and within a span of a few decades indicates that people were being drawn into the center of Cahokia. Most of these folks probably came from the American Bottom proper, although some probably originated outside the region if the distinct local and nonlocal ceramic traditions and the rapid ceramic techno-morphological changes are any guide. The implications of the centralization of the population from the surrounding floodplain and uplands include the likelihood that Cahokian patrons reshaped the social landscape of the rural countryside as well. That is, the centralization of people also would have amounted to the centralization or articulation of the social networks of these former peripheral subgroups now relocated at Cahokia. This would have given the high-ranking Cahokian subgroups full and direct access to low-ranking networks along with indirect access to each rural farmer as he or she was socially linked into these networks.

Demographic and political centralization also would have been the centralization of ritual sponsored by the chiefly individuals (and perhaps even the usurpation of low-ranking subgroup or household ritual by high-ranking Cahokian patrons). The necessary fertility rites, of which Emergent Mississippian chiefs or officeholders probably would have been traditional sponsors, were most likely performed under even more centralized circumstances at Cahokia or other political-administrative centers after regional consolidation. The rural farmer could have frequented Cahokia and other Mississippian centers at regular intervals for a variety of ritual occasions or social functions, again providing high-ranking families and elite officeholders access to the consciousness of the nonelite farmer.

The Products and Symbols of the New Order

In developing a dynamic construct of complex chiefdoms, Wright (1984:49) suggests that "ritual and political control of production, warfare, and other aspects of societal life" by chiefs were inseparable elements of nonstate political economy. One might propose that for regional consolidation to succeed, chiefly office must already have been sanctified by an association with cosmic powers. The continued development of an elite ideology promoting class divisions might be expected to have proceeded along with political centralization (Wright 1984:49ff.). That is, subsequent to regional consolidation, the "ritual prerogatives" of the paramount officeholder would have been bolstered with claims to additional cosmic powers (cf. Wright 1984:50).

If the regional consolidation of political authority in the American Bottom had been accomplished in a series of small-scale expansions or if several quasi-autonomous chiefships had remained intact during the Lohmann phase in close proximity to Cahokia, we might expect to find that the Stirling-phase iconographic expression of divine chiefship or a nonstate class hegemony corresponds to the artifactual, architectural, and community-organizational evidence for regional consolidation. Instead, however, the 15A-DT evidence points toward a large-scale consolidation as having truncated the Emergent Mississippi period. Furthermore, except for the simple designs of seed jars, there would appear to be a dearth of iconographic evidence from the Lohmann phase symbolizing the elevated sanctity of Cahokian lords. There may yet prove to be some iconographic expression of an emerging elite ideology in the form of locally produced decorated fineware. Other than fineware, the best iconographic indicator of an elite ideology espousing the supernatural qualities of Mississippian high office is found on Ramey Incised pots. These pots, however, were manufactured first during the Stirling phase some four or five decades after the regional consolidation of the American Bottom polity.

There may be a similar instance of lag in the iconographic manifestation of a class ideology in the Deh Luran Plain of southwestern Iran. There, "the residential indications of class segregation and the settlement pattern features indicative of tribute extraction appeared . . . earlier than the material correlates of the ideology that would justify support of such a political economy" (Wright 1984:68). Perhaps, where a class hegemony had not penetrated tradition to a substantial degree, elite iconography should not be anticipated; sacral authority based on aristocratic and commoner classes would not yet have coalesced. The common sense of the populous would still have been rooted in a rank hegemony, even though substantial cosmic powers might have been recognized to be a component of political office. Thus the materialization of an ideology touting elite separateness would have presented the consciousness of the nonelite with an unacceptable challenge to common sense and subordinate ideologies.

Given a situation in which large-scale regional consolidation occurred relatively early within the long-term cultural-hegemonic process, an elite iconography is not to be immediately expected. Under such conditions, a collaborative chiefship may have been the primary means of reproducing the regional polity. A certain amount of time might have been required between the point at which the office of paramount was established—when the cosmic powers vested in political office and conceded to by the masses were sufficient to permit regional political consolidation—and the consolidation of the cosmic powers within a class hegemony or the coalescence of a divine chiefship. Regional political consolidation in the American Bottom—the establishment of the paramountcy or a complex chiefdom centered at Cahokia—need not be seen as the equivalent of a divine chiefship. The collaborative tactics of a Lohmann-phase paramount, perhaps acceptable and understandable to the low-ranking subgroups, could have provided a backdrop for the high-ranking claims to additional cosmic powers.

Chiefly largesse and paramount generosity theoretically should have been prominent components of a collaborative chiefship. Centripetally mobilized goods would have been largely dispersed or redistributed in a centrifugal manner. Perhaps the large numbers of seed jars, if these were centrally manufactured and subsequently used to redistribute comestibles, constitute an indirect and preliminary measure. In the absence of evidence for the redistribution of comestibles, the volume and diversity of exotic artifacts in the Lohmann-phase 15A-DT refuse also may indicate not just the extent or configuration of the long-distance elite alliance network but also the willingness on the part of whoever controlled the local distributions of exotic items to give them away.

This is not to say that the new Cahokian paramountcy would have been generous to anyone but loyal followers within the local domain. In a larger political arena, warfare might have played a key role in the consolidation of power. It is not clear whether the actual events that might have led to the consolidation of the American Bottom included military actions, but such an abrupt and large-scale consolidation without some sort of warfare, assassination, or high-stakes feuding would appear unlikely if Mississippian political arenas were in any way comparable to ethnohistorically known chiefly arenas.

The first projectile points associated with the 15A-DT sample date to the L-1 subphase. It is significant that almost all were the Type-A variety (see chapter 6). That is, the arrow points were finely made, lustrous white triangular specimens, not simply marginally retouched or functionally passable versions. This triangular shape first appears in the form of exotic points during the Edelhardt phase at Cahokia. One Edelhardt-phase example from the Merrell Tract derived from the upper fill of a building basin and was manufactured from Cobden chert (Kelly 1984). Another Edelhardt-phase example from below the East Palisade was made from Fort Payne chert and was serrated; its shape is not quite comparable to a Cahokia-notched triangular point, nor is the shape of its serrations (Koldehoff 1990a). Otherwise, the Type-A point style has no antecedents in the American Bottom region.

Given their abrupt appearance in the L-1 15A-DT refuse, it may not be unreasonable to view these projectile points not as a sign of increased hunting but as local symbols of the young paramountcy at Cahokia. That is, warfare or weapon symbolism might have been closely affiliated with the new regional chiefs of the American Bottom. The caches of over 1,000 finely made points in the Lohmann-phase Mound 72 provide an even more graphic illustration of the association between the paramountcy and warfare or weapon symbolism (Prentice 1990). The honored and dishonored males in Mound 72 provide further evidence of warfare (perhaps as an activity performed by young elite males, consistent with ethnohistoric accounts from around the world).

If the 15A-DT Type-A points were symbols of the new order, then we might expect that a few artisans—projectile-point makers—had produced the entire lot of finely chipped specimens under the aegis of Cahokian patrons. It might have been difficult for these patrons to control craft production if artisans and craft workers were dispersed across the landscape (see Welch 1991). Indeed the centralization of craft production and the attachment of artisans to the chiefly elite is an integral component of the prestige-goods economies of nonstate polities (Brumfiel and Earle 1987). Some of the 15A-DT Edelhardt- and Lohmann-phase residents manufactured axeheads, an activity at present unknown from any other late-prehistoric site in the American Bottom region. By the L-1 subphase, it seems that axehead manufacture was widespread across the excavated 15A-DT area. Knapped aphanitic rock is associated with 35 percent of the 15A-DT features. By the L-2 and L-3 subphases, the density of axehead-making waste had more than quadrupled, although the ubiquity of the rock waste was reduced to less than 15 percent of the features.

Like the projectile points, it is expected that centralized axehead production is indicative of elite support for a restricted number of craftspersons. Axeheads might have been a product made by a subcommunity or subgroup financed by Cahokian patrons for use in social exchanges. It is conceivable that, like the arrow points, axeheads might have been symbolic of the character of the Lohmann-phase paramountcy. Nonutilitarian axeheads or war clubs typically were used as badges of office in other Southeastern contexts (see Brown 1976a, 1976b; Conrad 1991). Of course, the 15A-DT unfinished or fragmentary specimens are the size characteristic of ordinary utilitarian celts; these were not the megalithic types found in caches elsewhere at the Cahokia, East St. Louis, and Lohmann sites (Esarey and Pauketat 1992). Hence, the Lohmann-phase Cahokian patrons may have been subsidizing the production of a (nominally) utilitarian item rather than a highly stylized war club or megalithic celt. Such utilitarian forms are found distributed throughout the American Bottom region, and it is plausible that the 15A-DT production was targeted for local consumption.

The central subsidization of a utilitarian item for local distribution would support the notion that, with a Lohmann-phase regional consolidation of political power, the reproduction of paramount authority and the new Cahokian order would have rested in part (and in the absence of a divine chiefship) on patron-client collaboration. Axeheads might have comprised a product by which low-ranking subgroups were compensated for their collaboration. The axe might still have symbolized the new Cahokian order and the low-ranking recipient's place within it. In fact, embedding such subtle symbolism in the form of a utilitarian object might have made it an effective tool in a dual sense!

The increased numbers of exotic adze blades in the L-1 material assemblage and in subsequent Lohmann-phase assemblages, while not locally manufactured, also may have had symbolic importance like the other hand-held axes or arrows. Unlike arrows, of course, adzes and axes are formal woodworking tools and might have been used to transform wood into elite symbols (e.g., canoes) or to transform physical landscapes (i.e., to clear trees). Assuming that their distribution was centrally controlled, then the nonlocal origin of the adze blades probably ensures that the tools were in some way symbolic of elite power. Adzes, axes, and arrows would have been components in the transformation of social and physical landscapes.

Perhaps this same argument should be extended to include the 15A-DT evidence of qualitative increases of local and exotic artifact densities at about A.D. 1050 (calibrated time). Without a doubt, increased densities of exotic cherts suggest the expansion of long-distance contacts by American-Bottom residents. However, since discarded primary debitage makes up the bulk of both local and exotic 15A-DT chert artifacts, it is equally clear that much chert had entered the Northern Bottom Expanse in raw form to be locally transformed into expedient or small bifacial tools. The L-1 density increase therefore is indicative of intensified tool manufacture. That is, the exotic cherts not only bespeak extensive long-distance relations (presumably by high-ranking Lohmann-phase subgroups) but also indicate the transformation of nonlocal exotica into local symbols (which in turn could have been employed to transform other materials or landscapes).

In conclusion, there is firm Lohmann-phase evidence that a considerable quantity and diversity of exotic raw material was imported to Cahokia and reworked into a variety of tools and symbols. These include finely made triangular projectile points, axeheads, and other chert tools. These locally made tools (along with nonlocal tools like adzes) may have connoted the power and structure of the consolidated Lohmann-phase political order. This indication is consistent with Welch's (1991) prestige-goods model of Moundville but places more significance on the local production and intraregional exchange of craft goods and transformation of social landscapes than do other prestige-goods constructs (Brown et. al 1990; Frankenstein and Rowlands 1978; Muller 1987; Peregrine 1992).

The Class Struggle at Cahokia

As discussed above, members of the Edelhardt- and Lohmann-phase subcommunities at 15A-DT were engaged in the production of axeheads. It is significant that axehead production, as alluded to above, is entirely absent from other analyzed Lohmann-phase community remains from Cahokia like the Interpretive Center Tract-II. Although large megalithic celts were found at three political-administrative centers, nowhere has there been identified the high density of igneous-rock refuse like that of the Lohmann-phase 15A-DT sample.

This axehead-production information is critical to our understanding of the articulation of subcommunities within the larger Cahokian community. Equally important, however, is the near absence of microlithic artifacts and marine-shell residues in 15A-DT Lohmann-phase refuse. This absence of shell-working artifacts stands in stark contrast to their prominence in the Lohmann- and Stirling-phase material assemblages from the Kunnemann Tract (see Holley 1990; Mason and Perino 1961; Pauketat 1993; Yerkes 1991). Whereas members of the 15A-DT subcommunity were engaged in the production of axeheads, they did not manufacture shell beads. Rural households did manufacture shell disk beads at least sporadically during the Lohmann phase (Milner et al. 1984:165; Pauketat 1991), and occupants of the Kunnemann Tract at Cahokia were manufacturing not only shell beads but entire bead-and-pendant necklaces and perhaps other ornaments. Given this axehead and shell-working evidence, we may tentatively conclude that the central subcommunities and rural homesteads were integrated into a Cahokian community that featured an as-yet poorly understood division of labor (Fowler 1989:201–202).

The Alienation of Lohmann-Phase Households

Given the ubiquity of EM-3 and L-1 aphanitic-rock debitage, it is unlikely that one or a few specialists had been scattering their garbage all over Tract 15A and the Dunham Tract. Instead, it would appear that numerous households had been making axeheads there for years. The density of the L-1 rock refuse represents only a slight and statistically insignificant increase over the EM-3 levels. The ubiquity of the L-1 refuse and, by inference, the number of people involved in celt manufacture might be an indicator of the continuation of Emergent Mississippian subcommunity or subgroup integrity immediately after the large-scale political, economic, and social changes that accompanied A.D. 1050 (calibrated time). However, a reduction in the number of people involved in axehead making appears indicated by a low ubiquity index in the L-2 and L-3 subphase remains at the same time that the density of axehead-making waste more than quadrupled (a pattern duplicated by galena). We may surmise from this pattern that, compared to the EM-3 and L-1 subphases, fewer households might have been making celts at much-intensified production levels.

We should recall at this point that the courtyard group of the Emergent Mississippi period appears to have been dissolved during the Lohmann phase. In the place of this traditional arrangement emerged a larger-scale community structure characterized by plazas and clusters of circular and large rectangular buildings segregated from clusters of smaller rectangular houses. The resulting Mississippian community may have been divisible into subcommunities at the scale of mound-and-plaza units rather than courtyard groups (Fowler 1989:201–205).

The significance of the dissolution of the traditional Emergent Mississippian courtyard group cannot be overstated. The courtyard, as the focal point of traditional social life, would have provided the spatial setting for the reproduction of traditional subgroup ideologies (see Kus 1983). It would have engendered social resistance to top-down change and would have been an impediment to the reproduction of a new regional-hierarchical order. Consequently, the young Cahokian paramountcy may have successfully promoted the need to reorder and reconstruct large subcommunity neighborhoods. Such reordering would have accorded with the new political-kin organizations. Such reconstruction could have occurred in conjunction with the same traditional ritual cycle that had witnessed the earlier rebuildings of single-post houses around courtyards. Of course, with the masses of folks moving into the paramount center, courtyard-group cohesion may have been difficult to maintain, regardless of the paramountcy's promotion.

Whether the elimination of Emergent Mississippian courtyards was a cause or consequence of the changing social foundations of the American Bottom, the net effect would have been to erase the means of reproducing traditional subgroup ideologies. The circular sweat lodges may represent a new ritual context for the negotiation of conflicting ideologies and thus reproduction of the new Cahokian order. The divergence of rectangular building size so obvious by the L-2 and L-3 subphases probably signals the degree to which the traditional ideologies of a rank hegemony had been or were becoming subordinated within an emerging nonstate class hegemony.

Under these Lohmann-phase circumstances and perhaps indicated by the diachronic igneous rock and galena density and ubiquity data, *households* may have replaced the traditional Emergent Mississippian subgroups as the basal units of articulation with the larger Cahokian community. Households, not courtyard groups, would have been articulated with powerful central patrons. Households, as clients, would have been supported by the new Lohmann-phase paramountcy rather than (suprahousehold) nonelite subgroups. Kin-based, nonstate classes would have been a result of the reconciliation of kinship and chiefly politics in the context of patron-client relations. This is not to say that the conical clans or kin-based hierarchies of simple chiefdoms would have been eliminated. Low- and high-ranking individuals still would have been genealogically linked in a structural sense (e.g., Knight 1990). However, in a quantitative sense fewer lower-ranking individuals might have been so connected to an elite stratum. Moreover, with class and hierarchical solidarity the low-ranking American Bottom households would have lost the means of advancing within a social hierarchy. The traditional horizontal linkages would have given way to a new political-kinship organization. The alienation of the masses and formation of hierarchical solidarity would have turned kinship on its head as it became the basis for justifying social distinctions rather than leveling those distinctions.

The horizontal social ties of subgroups and therefore the contact between subgroups would have been reduced in practical importance relative to vertical-hierarchical social relations. Perhaps the movement of subterranean storage into building interiors at central and rural locations (Mehrer 1988; Mehrer and Collins 1989; Collins 1990) was an attempt by producers or households to hide the stored goods from not only elite appropriators but also other producer households (see DeBoer 1988). The dissolution of subgroup solidarity and its replacement by what could be misconstrued as household autonomy (i.e., reliance upon centralized authority rather than decentralized community) at both rural and central locations in effect would have been tantamount to the alienation of nonelite or peripheral individuals from their traditional (Emergent Mississippian) ideologies. These same alienated primary producers, especially rural farmers, would have been the source of most of the staple goods available to and used by the patrons of the Central Political-Administrative Complex to support the entourages and attached producers of chiefly administrations.

Without the alienation of primary producers from traditional modes of thinking and acting, it is doubtful whether the increased tribute or labor requirements of an expanding paramountcy could have been met. As noted by Smith (1978), this settlement pattern was an energy-efficient adaptation to floodplain environments. It is interesting then that the dispersed pattern of rural homesteads has been recognized as the standard Mississippian pattern throughout the Mississippi River alluvial valley to the south. Smith (1978) correlated this pattern with chiefly political structure, and following his lead, we may infer that the alienation of primary producers (a prerequisite of this settlement pattern) also was a component of Mississippian culture. However, this conclusion necessitates locating Mississippian culture within the domain of elite social reproduction.

Mississippian Political Culture

Griffin (1985, 1990) and Smith (1984, 1990a) have firmly established that Mississippian was not a homogeneous entity that emanated from a single locus and spread out across the Southeast. Rather, "the Mississippian emergence represents a broad scale, extremely complex, and parallel set of paradoxically discrete yet interconnected historical developmental sequences" (Smith 1990a:1). As iterated by Knight (1986), Mississippian might be defined as "a prevalent variety of socio-religious organization cross-cutting other cultural and ecological boundaries" or a "ritual pattern" shared by interior Southeastern North American riverine polities. "Concerning . . . the much discussed 'sudden' expansion of Mississippianism, the problem might be revised as follows: How did such a system arise as a type, and what characteristics did it have that allowed it to dominate quickly the social geography of the southeastern United States during the late prehistoric period?" (Knight 1986:681).

Mississippian culture in the American Bottom was neither a concomitant of the simple social ranking of the Emergent Mississippi period nor the divine chiefship of Stirling-phase Cahokia. The 15A-DT data when viewed in concert with other archaeological evidence from the American Bottom region strongly supports the correspondence of certain cultural elements with political change. Wall-trench buildings, large plazas, circular buildings, triangular projectile points, the transformation of regional settlement patterns, and perhaps the upsurge in the use of shell temper in pots arrived on the heels of the regional political consolidation at Cahokia around A.D. 1050.

This observation in itself is not novel, but in the present theoretical light, the coincidence of political and cultural realms serves further to refine our conceptualization of the process of Mississippianization. A necessary concomitant of the consolidation of chiefly authority in the form of regional control would have been the rather immediate expansion of external alliances and claims to authority. We might just slightly adapt the statement by Wright (1984:50) as follows: once paramount office was achieved, the ritual prerogatives of the paramount were bolstered with claims to more esoteric knowledge.

Elements of Cahokia-Mississippian culture were components of a panregional cultural milieu in the central Mississippi valley and elsewhere to the south. Given that its development "took place relatively simultaneously over a wide geographic area" (Smith 1984:30), the Mississippian tradition may be seen to consist of an integrated set of symbols related (initially at least) to a particular consciousness—an elite consciousness—that appropriated to variable degrees of success the world(s) of nonelites. The cultural milieu was in essence a political-ideological milieu.

With the expansion of the American-Bottom political economy, the entrance of Mississippian culture into the Northern Bottom Expanse may be seen as nothing more than a byproduct of the claims of regional lords to distant sources of knowledge and power (*sensu* Helms 1979, 1988). This esoteric knowledge and the exotic styles and technologies find integration with the political ideology of a newly established paramountcy in the form of a *political culture*. The attributes of a Mississippian political culture might be seen as efficient technological innovations, but the agents of innovation were the high-ranking aspirants to and holders of chiefly office. Efficiency must be defined from an elite perspective.

Given that chiefly agents would have sought to reproduce their power, it can be expected that Mississippian political culture would have included specific technologies, ritual knowledge, and ways of organizing labor, particularly as these relate to agricultural production (to be appropriated by the elite). The centralization of agricultural and fertility rites would have gone a long way toward diffusing the high-ranking notions of the cosmos and its relationship to the masses. The ways of the new and prestigious (Lohmann-phase) lords of Cahokia may have been inherently powerful by virtue of their knowledge of and control over exotica and esoterica. The spread of Mississippian political culture need not have been coerced; collaborative political tactics might have been all that were needed to diffuse it. The consensual adoption of Cahokia-Mississippian political culture thus was also the spread of the ideas of the dominant subgroup(s) of the American Bottom social formation. Mississippian political culture hence appropriated the historically constituted traditional cultures of the hinterlands, merging with them and later becoming the Mississippian cultural tradition in the region.

Moreover, Cahokia-Mississippian would have had an expansionistic quality independent of direct political authority or perhaps even centralized ritual. A whole suite of agricultural and nonagricultural knowledge or ways of doing things may have been desirable to the people living along the margins of the American Bottom region beyond the direct control of Cahokia simply because of its association with the knowledgeable and powerful lords of Cahokia. This may have included the manufacture of pots using crushed shell temper or the construction of buildings using wall trenches. The expansionistic quality of Mississippian political culture was, in a sense, the playing out of a long-term cultural-hegemonic process discussed in chapter 2. The development and eventual disintegration of the Cahokian polity was also a consequence of this same process.

The Ascent of Chiefs

The cultural-hegemonic process, involving the diffusion of an elite ideology and the alienation of primary producers, goes a long way toward explaining the appearance of what might appropriately be labeled the divine chiefship of the Stirling phase. Manifestations of this chiefship include Ramey iconography; the redundant use of color and shape symbolism; the continual pursuit of mound, temple, and hearth construction and renewal; and the central constructions of the Post-Circle Monument, giant domiciles, rotundas, and compounds. It is noteworthy that the construction of the first Post-Circle Monument—an elite-controlled device for the ritual interaction with the cosmos (Smith 1992a)—corresponds to the earliest occurrence of Ramey iconography that also represents the order of the cosmos (Pauketat and Emerson 1991). Given this correspondence, one could speculate that the Cahokian elite found it desirable or necessary to promulgate their elite values and beliefs about the cosmos and the commoners in a series of coeval material expressions either visible to or ultimately received by commoners. This potentially abrupt arrival of the material trappings of divine chiefship at A.D. 1100 (calibrated time) might signal the inauguration, re-inauguration, or renewal of a paramount officeholder who employed a set of strategic efforts to lay claim to cosmic power (enabled by the political-economic development of the Lohmann phase).

However they were introduced, the symbols of this transformed paramountcy persisted for decades; Ramey iconography lasted for a century or more! The suspected temples and domiciles of the Stirling-phase Cahokian elite were big, perhaps indicative of their enlarged social prominence. The Stirling-phase elite ideology was not simply a short-lived political tactic; it was authority transformed. For the first time, representations of deities (e.g., sky-world thunderers) were associated with a medium presumably manufactured under the aegis of chiefly officeholders and intended for political underlings and the nonelite masses (Pauketat and Emerson 1991). Color and shape symbolism embued the important buildings of Cahokia; construction of elite monuments was a focal point of regular centralized rites.

Given this sort of sacral authority, it can be assumed that Stirling-phase officeholders would have been entitled to tribute and corvée simply by virtue of the sanctity of chiefly office. There might have been little incentive for the sort of collaborative tactics suspected to have characterized Lohmann-phase political arenas, and, in fact, the density and diversity of exotic goods in the refuse of 15A-DT and other Stirling-phase central and rural samples do appear to decrease (Pauketat 1992:39). At the same time, Stirling-phase rural locales seem to have witnessed greater population density and residential stability, increased building- and facility-form diversity, and decreased subterranean storage outside of domiciles (Emerson 1992; Mehrer 1988:149–155; Milner 1986; Pauketat 1992:40). At Cahokia's Interpretive Center Tract-II, the rigid orientation of buildings and use of external subterranean pits of the Lohmann phase gave way to more loosely arranged Stirling-phase houses with few external pits (Collins 1990:228–235).

For all intents and purposes, these household and community data point toward a sociopolitical *decentralization* already taking place during the Stirling phase at the same time that a divine chiefship appeared in its fullest American Bottom expression. Given the increased space required in the heart of Cahokia by the monumental constructions evident on Tract 15A and 15B, it is reasonable to attribute a certain degree of this physical movement of nonelite households out of Cahokia simply to the increased sanctity of Cahokia and the Central Political-Administrative Complex. That is, Cahokia increasingly was reserved for political-religious monuments and elite activities. The nonelite may have been increasingly pushed to the margins of the site. Perhaps Milner's (1986) observed increase in the rural population of a portion of the Northern Bottom Expanse is a consequence of emigration from Mississippian administrative centers.

The elevated religious status of the Stirling-phase elite might have removed them from certain political spheres and may be seen as an integral component of political decentralization. The Stirling-phase elite, their power symbolized in almost every medium available to them, would have been lording over a polity in which the foundations of decentralization were being laid. These powerful lords, ever-more secure in their religious positions, might have found it unnecessary to conduct themselves in a collaborative manner or to continue extensifying their long-distance alliances, perhaps leaving such collaboration and extensification for lesser elites. However, this falling rate of political expansion or crisis of hierarchization may have been the beginning of the end of the complex chiefly hierarchy of the American Bottom, promoting the consolidation of factions within Cahokia as aspirants to office vied for prestige and political control.

In this manner, Cahokia's downfall might have been stretched out over a lengthy period of time, perhaps even witnessing the periodic and short-lived reconsolidations of political power within the context of the class hegemony as it had developed over the preceding century and a half. By the early Moorehead phase, it is clear that the population of the site had already declined dramatically. If we can interpolate based on the 15A-DT, Tract-15B, and ICT-II evidence, then domiciles were widely scattered across the Cahokia site. The diversity of building sizes and shapes decreased. Building size modes became a feature within rather than between individual domestic zones.

Certain trappings of the divine chiefship remained. Ramey Incised pots, for instance, were still made during the M-1 subphase. Shell-bead production probably was subsidized by Moorehead-phase lords as well, given that Moorehead-phase shell-working debris and sandstone files are associated with the Ramey Tract near Monks Mound (John E. Kelly, personal communication, May 1991; see Moorehead 1929; Pauketat 1987c:82). Sandstone tablets and perhaps war clubs were prestigious symbols at Cahokia, but otherwise few exotic items are associated with the Moorehead phase. By the M-2 subphase at Tract 15A, the exotic artifacts commonly found in the refuse were largely restricted to Union County items, not unlike the EM-2 subphase exotics centuries earlier. Had all factors remained constant after the Stirling phase, the class hegemony might have enabled another complex polity to reemerge. As it was, however, the political structure of the American Bottom continued to disintegrate, and the population moved out of the Northern Bottom Expanse (see Milner 1986). The regional population rapidly dwindled. No Sand Prairie phase remains were found at Tract 15A and the Dunham Tract, and few are known from elsewhere at Cahokia (cf. Fowler and Hall 1975:7–9). The Cahokian Leviathan had fallen, never to recover.

Conclusions

Regional political centralization in the American Bottom was an outcome of the political actions of Emergent Mississippian agents set in the sociohistorical contexts that featured regional asymmetries, social ranking, and intensive intercommunity interaction. While the gradual emergence of local ranked hierarchies, formation of patron-client relations, centralization of localized entities, and extension of long-distance exchange relations are thought to have led up to A.D. 1050, political events punctuated the transformation of regional political order and integrated some portion of the region under Cahokian authority. This regional consolidation and elevation of political office preceded the materialization of sacral authority by half a century, or a full generation after the political events that mark the beginning of the Lohmann phase and the Mississippi period.

In fact, it might be proposed that divine chiefship necessarily evolved in the context of a regionally centralized polity. Perhaps only by alleviating the factional disputes of competing local subgroups by subjugating them or dethroning their leaders was the promotion of chiefly office possible. Perhaps only when the developmental constraints of a rank hegemony were breached by the regional consolidation of political power were the fetters of local kin-based social relations cast off. Only in such a context could the necessary funds of power have been amassed permitting the continued expansion of the political economy, the appropriation of subaltern ideologies within a cultural hegemony, and ultimately the political-religious promotion of high office.

This is not to say that a considerable degree of sanctity was not a component of legitimate Emergent Mississippian and Lohmann-phase authority. Such legitimate authority in some sense would have been a necessary precursor to Cahokian consolidation. For instance, it is doubtful that a regional polity could have emerged from the Patrick or Sponemann phase. Yet the legitimate Emergent Mississippian authority was probably not a sufficient condition of Cahokian consolidation. Rather, we should place considerable weight on the transformative significance of political events that occurred at the EM-3 and L-1 interface and, in general, throughout human history.

It is through the perspective of people thinking and acting according to their prescribed beliefs, values, and ethics that we may come to grasp how and why people who lived free of ascribed hierarchy submitted themselves to that great Leviathan. Surrender to an ascribed hierarchy and a class hegemony, from a practice-theory perspective, would have been no common desire. It can only be understood as the long-term process in which actors with distinct or conflicting interests reproduced their perceptions of the world. The Hobbesian *generation* of that great Cahokian Leviathan involved aspirations and resistance, ideology and tradition, class and community in a struggle that lasted for decades.

From a midcontinental perspective, Cahokia was a cultural core, not in the sense of World-Systems Theory and not in the sense of an age-area diffusionist scenario, but it did usher the historical trajectories of the peripheral cultures to the north and west of the American Bottom (*sensu* Griffin 1952:362). No thriving economic system integrated all elements of the American Bottom region (or beyond), but rather a loosely knit prestige-goods economy was operant as a means for the elite to retain authority in the face of local resistance. There is something yet to be said for the hegemonic relations between polities in terms of prestige-goods economics, but this may best be considered as it affected the local reproduction of power relations between elite and nonelite, rather than excising the nonelite from the dynamic process. The centripetal mobilization of tribute may prove to be the only direct economic core-periphery relationship, thus shrinking the effective size of the system to an intraregional level, not an interregional one, since tribute collection might be difficult beyond the bounds of the American Bottom region.

In terms of chiefly political-economic dynamics, Cahokia may not have been exceptional among Southeastern Native American polities. However, in terms of its unique sociohistory—the timing and scale of regional political consolidation and its possible relation to the peripheral social formations to the north and west of the American Bottom—the Cahokian

Leviathan was perhaps a historical exception. The actions of a handful of elite individuals around A.D. 1050, understood in the proper cultural context, may be seen in some measure to have altered indirectly the consciousness of midcontinental Native American individuals for centuries thereafter.

Bibliography

Abercrombie, Nicholas, Stephen Hill, and Bryan S. Turner
  1980 *The Dominant Ideology Thesis.* George Allen and Unwin, London.
Abrahams, R. G.
  1966 Succession to the Chiefship in Northern Unyamwezi. In *Succession to High Office*, edited by J. Goody, pp. 127–41. Cambridge University Press, Cambridge.
  1967 *The Political Organization of Unyamwezi.* Cambridge University Press, Cambridge.
Adams, Robert McCormick
  1949 Archaeological Investigations in Jefferson County, Missouri. *The Missouri Archaeologist* 11(3–4).
Ahler, Steven R., and Peter J. DePuydt
  1987 *A Report on the 1931 Powell Mound Excavations, Madison County, Illinois.* Illinois State Museum Reports of Investigations 43. Springfield.
Anderson, David G.
  1990 Stability and Change in Chiefdom-level Societies: An Examination of Mississippian Political Evolution on the South Atlantic Slope. In *Lamar Archaeology: Mississippian Chiefdoms in the Deep South*, edited by M. Williams and G. Shapiro, pp. 187–213. University of Alabama Press, Tuscaloosa.
Anderson, Duane C.
  1987 Toward a Processual Understanding of the Initial Variant of the Middle Missouri Tradition: The Case of the Mill Creek Culture of Iowa. *American Antiquity* 52:522–37.
Anderson, James
  1977 A Cahokia Palisade Sequence. In *Explorations into Cahokia Archaeology*, edited by M. Fowler, pp. 89–99. Illinois Archaeological Survey, Bulletin 7. Urbana.
Arnold, Dean E.
  1985 *Ceramic Theory and Cultural Process.* Cambridge University Press, Cambridge.
Bailey, Anne M.
  1981 The Renewed Discussions on the Concept of the Asiatic Mode of Produc-

tion. In *The Anthropology of Pre-Capitalist Societies,* edited by J. S. Kahn and J. R. Llobera, pp. 89–107. Macmillan, London.

Ball, Terence

1983 On Making History in Vico and Marx. In *Vico and Marx: Affinities and Contrasts,* edited by G. Tagliacozzo, pp. 78–93. Humanities, Atlantic Highlands, N.J.

Bareis, Charles J.

1963 University of Illinois projects. *Second Annual Report: American Bottoms Archaeology, July 1, 1962–June 30, 1963,* edited by M. L. Fowler, pp. 3–8. Illinois Archaeological Survey, Urbana.

1967 *Interim Report on Preliminary Site Examination Undertaken in Archaeological Section A of FAI 255 South of Business 40 in the Interstate Portion of Area S-34-4 of the Cahokia Site, St. Clair County, Illinois. Department of Anthropology Research Reports* 1. Urbana.

1972 Reports on Preliminary Site Examinations Undertaken at the Holliday No. 2 Site (S-68) and the Lienesch Site (S-67) on FAI 64, St. Clair County, Illinois. Unpublished report, Department of Anthropology, University of Illinois, Urbana.

1975a Report of 1971 University of Illinois–Urbana Excavations at the Cahokia Site. In *Cahokia Archaeology: Field Reports,* edited by M. L. Fowler, pp. 9–11. Illinois State Museum Research Series, Papers in Anthropology 3. Springfield.

1975b Report of 1972 University of Illinois–Urbana Excavations at the Cahokia Site. In *Cahokia Archaeology: Field Reports,* edited by M. L. Fowler, pp. 12–15. Illinois State Museum Research Series, Papers in Anthropology 3. Springfield.

1976 *The Knoebel Site, St. Clair County, Illinois.* Illinois Archaeological Survey Circular 7. Urbana.

Bareis, Charles J., and Donald Lathrap

1962 University of Illinois Projects. In *First Annual Report: American Bottoms Archaeology, July 1, 1961–June 30, 1962,* edited by M. L. Fowler, pp. 3–9. Illinois Archaeological Survey, Urbana.

Bareis, Charles J., and James W. Porter

1965 Megascopic and Petrographic Analyses of a Foreign Pottery Vessel from the Cahokia Site. *American Antiquity* 31:95–101.

Bareis, Charles J., and James W. Porter (editors)

1984 *American Bottom Archaeology.* University of Illinois Press, Urbana.

Bargatsky, Thomas

1988 Evolution, Sequential Hierarchy, and Areal Integration: The Case of Traditional Samoan Society. In *State and Society: The Emergence and Development of Social Hierarchy and Political Centralization,* edited by J. Gledhill, B. Bender, and M. T. Larsen, pp. 43–56. Unwin Hyman, London.

Barker, Alex

1992 Powhatan's Pursestrings: Uses of Surplus in a Seventeenth Century Virginia Chiefdom. In *Lords of the Southeast: Elites in Ethnohistorical and*

Archaeological Perspective, edited by A. Barker and T. R. Pauketat, pp. 61–80. American Anthropological Association, Archeological Papers 3. Washington, D.C.

Barrett, S. A.
1933   *Ancient Aztalan.* Bulletin of the Public Museum of the City of Milwaukee 13. Milwaukee, Wis.

Barth, Frederik
1959   *Political Leadership Among the Swat Pathans.* London School of Economics Monographs on Social Anthropology 19. London.
1975   *Ritual and Knowledge Among the Baktaman of New Guinea.* Yale University Press, New Haven, Conn.
1989   *Cosmologies in the Making: A Generative Approach to Cultural Variation in Inner New Guinea.* Cambridge University Press, Cambridge.

Beinart, William
1982   *The Political Economy of Pondoland 1860–1930.* Cambridge University Press, Cambridge.

Bell, Robert E.
1958   *Guide to the Identification of Certain American Indian Projectile Points.* Oklahoma Anthropological Society, Special Bulletin 1. Oklahoma City.

Benchley, Elizabeth
1975   Summary Field Report of Excavations on the Southwest Corner of the First Terrace of Monks Mound: 1968, 1969, 1971. In *Cahokia Archaeology: Field Reports*, edited by M. L. Fowler, pp. 16–24. Illinois State Museum Research Series, Papers in Anthropology 3. Springfield.

Bender, Barbara
1978   Gatherer-Hunter to Farmer: A Social Perspective. *World Archaeology* 10:204–22.

Bender, Margaret M., David A. Baerreis, and R. L. Steventon
1981   Further Light on Carbon Isotopes and Hopewell Agriculture. *American Antiquity* 46:346–54.

Bentz, Charles, Dale L. McElrath, Fred A. Finney, and Richard B. Lacampagne
1988   *Late Woodland Sites in the American Bottom Uplands.* FAI-270 Site Reports 18. University of Illinois Press, Urbana.

Berres, Thomas E.
1984   *A Formal Analysis of Ceramic Vessels from the Schlemmer Site (11-S-382): A Late Woodland/Mississippian Occupation in St. Clair County, Illinois.* Unpublished M.A. thesis, Department of Anthropology, Western Michigan University, Kalamazoo.

Bidet, Jacques
1979   Questions to Pierre Bourdieu. *Critique of Anthropology* 4:203–8.

Blanton, Robert E., Steven A. Kowalewski, Gary Feinman, and Jill Appel
1981   *Ancient Mesoamerica: A Comparison of Change in Three Regions.* Cambridge University Press, Cambridge.

194   *Bibliography*

Bloch, Maurice
  1989   From Cognition to Ideology. In *Ritual, History and Power: Selected Papers in Anthropology*, by M. Bloch, pp. 106–36. London School of Economics, Monographs on Social Anthropology 58.
Bourdieu, Pierre
  1977   *Outline of a Theory of Practice*. Cambridge University Press, Cambridge.
Brackenridge, Henry M.
  1814   *Views of Louisiana* (1962 edition). Quadrangle Books, Chicago.
Braun, David P., and Steven Plog
  1982   Evolution of "Tribal" Social Networks: Theory and North American Evidence. *American Antiquity* 47:504–25.
Brenner, Robert
  1977   The Origins of Capitalist Development: A Critique of Neo–Smithian Marxism. *New Left Review* 104:25–92.
Brown, D. J. J.
  1979   The Structuring of Polopa Feasting and Warfare. *Man* (n.s.) 14:712–33.
Brown, James A.
  1971   The Dimensions of Status in the Burials at Spiro. In *Approaches to the Social Dimensions of Mortuary Practices*, edited by J. A. Brown, pp. 92–112. Memoirs of the Society for American Archaeology 25.
  1976a The Southern Cult Reconsidered. *Midcontinental Journal of Archaeology* 1:115–35.
  1976b *Spiro Studies*. Vol. 4. *The Artifacts*. Third Annual Report of Caddoan Archaeology–Spiro Focus Research, Part 2. University of Oklahoma Research Institute, Norman.
  1985   The Mississippian Period. In *Ancient Art of the American Woodland Indians*, pp. 92–145. Harry N. Abrams, New York.
  1989   On Style Divisions of the Southeastern Ceremonial Complex: A Revisionist Perspective. In *The Southeastern Ceremonial Complex: Artifacts and Analysis*, edited by P. Galloway, pp. 183–204. University of Nebraska, Lincoln.
Brown, James A., Richard A. Kerber, and Howard D. Winters
  1990   Trade and the Evolution of Exchange Relations at the Beginning of the Mississippian Period. In *The Mississippian Emergence*, edited by B. D. Smith, pp. 251–80. Smithsonian Institution Press, Washington, D.C.
Brumfiel, Elizabeth M.
  1989   Factional Competition in Complex Society. In *Domination and Resistance*, edited by D. Miller, M. Rowlands, and C. Tilley, pp. 127–39. Unwin Hyman, London.
Brumfiel, Elizabeth M., and Timothy K. Earle
  1987   Specialization, Exchange, and Complex Societies: An Introduction. In *Specialization, Exchange, and Complex Societies*, edited by E. M. Brumfiel and T. K. Earle, pp. 1–9. Cambridge University Press, Cambridge.
Buck, P. H. (Te Rangi Hiroa)
  1934   *Mangaian Society*. Bernice P. Bishop Museum Bulletin 122. Honolulu.

1949   *The Coming of the Maori*. Whitcombe and Tombs, London.

Bushnell, David I., Jr.
1904   *The Cahokia and Surrounding Mound Groups*. Papers of the Peabody Museum of American Archaeology and Ethnology, Harvard University, 3(1). Cambridge, Mass.

Carneiro, Robert L.
1981   The Chiefdom: Precursor of the State. In *Transitions to Statehood in the New World*, edited by G. Jones and R. Kantz, pp. 37–79. Cambridge University Press, Cambridge.

Champion, Timothy C.
1989   Introduction. In *Centre and Periphery: Comparative Studies in Archaeology*, edited by T. C. Champion, pp. 1–21. Unwin Hyman, London.

Chapman, Carl H.
1980   *The Archaeology of Missouri, 2*. University of Missouri Press, Columbia.

Childe, V. Gordon
1954   *What Happened in History*. Penguin Books, Harmondsworth, England (originally published 1942).

Chilver, E. M., and P. M. Kaberry
1967   The Kingdom of Kom in West Cameroon. In *West African Kingdoms in the Nineteenth Century*, edited by D. Forde and P. M. Kaberry, pp. 123–51. Oxford University Press, London.

Chmurny, William W.
1973   *The Ecology of the Middle Mississippian Occupation of the American Bottom*. Unpublished Ph.D. dissertation, Department of Anthropology, University of Illinois at Urbana.

Cobb, Charles R.
1988   *Mill Creek Chert Biface Production: Mississippian Political Economy in Illinois*. Unpublished Ph.D. dissertation, Department of Anthropology, Southern Illinois University at Carbondale.

Collins, James M.
1990   *The Archaeology of the Cahokia Mounds ICT-II: Site Structure*. Illinois Cultural Resources Study 10. Illinois Historic Preservation Agency, Springfield.

Comaroff, Jean, and John Comaroff
1986   Christianity and Colonialism in South Africa. *American Ethnologist* 13:1–20.
1991   *Of Revelation and Revolution: Christianity, Colonialism, and Consciousness in South Africa*. University of Chicago Press, Chicago.

Comaroff, John L.
1978   Rules and Rulers: Political Processes in a Tswana Chiefdom. *Man* (n.s.) 13:1–20.
1982   Dialectical Systems, History and Anthropology: Units of Study and Questions of Theory. *Journal of Southern African Studies* 8:143–72.

Conant, A. J.
1877   The Mounds and Their Builders or Traces of Prehistoric Man in Missouri.

In *The Commonwealth of Missouri*, edited by C. R. Barns, pp. 1–122. St. Louis.

Conrad, Lawrence
1989   The Southeastern Ceremonial Complex on the Northern Middle Mississippian Frontier: Late Prehistoric Politico-Religious Systems in the Central Illinois River Valley. In *The Southeastern Ceremonial Complex: Artifacts and Analysis*, edited by P. Galloway, pp. 93–113. University of Nebraska Press, Lincoln.
1991   The Middle Mississippian Cultures of the Central Illinois Valley. In *Cahokia and the Hinterlands: Middle Mississippian Cultures of the Midwest*, edited by T. E. Emerson and R. B. Lewis, pp. 119–63. University of Illinois Press, Urbana.

Coquery-Vidrovitch, Catherine
1977   Research on an African Mode of Production. In *African Social Studies: A Radical Reader*, edited by P. C. W. Gutkind and P. Waterman, pp. 77–92. Monthly Review Press, New York.

Cordy, Ross H.
1981   *A Study of Prehistoric Social Change: The Development of Complex Societies in the Hawaiian Islands*. Academic Press, New York.

Costin, Cathy Lynne
1991   Craft Specialization: Issues in Defining, Documenting, and Explaining the Organization of Production. In *Archaeological Method and Theory 3*, edited by M. B. Schiffer, pp. 1–56. University of Arizona Press, Tucson.

Crane, H. R., and J. B. Griffin
1964   University of Michigan Radiocarbon Dates IX. *Radiocarbon* 6:1–24.

Cross, Paula G.
1983   Vertebrate Faunal Remains from the Turner and DeMange Sites. In *The Turner and DeMange Sites*, by G. R. Milner, pp. 201–12. FAI-270 Site Reports 4. University of Illinois Press, Urbana.
1991   Animal Remains. In *The Lohmann Site: An Early Mississippian Center in the American Bottom*, by D. Esarey and T. R. Pauketat, pp. 145–52. FAI-270 Site Reports 25. University of Illinois Press, Urbana.

Dalan, Rinita A.
1989   *Geophysical Investigations of the Prehistoric Cahokia Palisade Sequence*. Illinois Cultural Resources Study 8. Illinois Historic Preservation Agency, Springfield.

DeBoer, Warren R.
1988   Subterranean Storage and the Organization of Surplus: The View from Eastern North America. *Southeastern Archaeology* 7:1–20.

Dincauze, Dena F., and Robert J. Hasenstab
1989   Explaining the Iroquois: Tribalization on a Prehistoric Periphery. In *Centre and Periphery: Comparative Studies in Archaeology*, edited by T. C. Champion, pp. 67–87. Unwin Hyman, London.

Dorothy, Lawrence G.
1980   The Ceramics of the Sand Point Site (20BG14), Baraga County, Michigan: A Preliminary Description. *The Michigan Archaeologist* 26(3–4):39–90.

Drennan, Robert D.
1987   Regional Demography in Chiefdoms. In *Chiefdoms in the Americas*, edited by R. Drennan and C. A. Uribe, pp. 307–23. University Press of America, Lanham, Md.

Drennan, Robert D., and C. A. Uribe (editors)
1987   *Chiefdoms in the Americas*. University Press of America, Lanham, Md.

Dunavan, Sandra L.
1990   Floral Remains. In *Selected Early Mississippian Household Sites in the American Bottom*, by D. K. Jackson and N. H. Hanenberger, pp. 389–403. FAI-270 Site Reports 22. University of Illinois Press, Urbana.

Dunnell, Robert C.
1980   Evolutionary Theory and Archaeology. In *Advancements in Archaeological Method and Theory* 3, edited by M. B. Schiffer, pp. 35–99. Academic Press, New York.

Durkheim, Emile
1933   *On the Division of Labor in Society*. Free Press, New York (originally published 1893).

Dye, David H., and Cheryl A. Cox (editors)
1990   *Towns and Temples Along the Mississippi*. University of Alabama Press, Tuscaloosa.

Earle, Timothy K.
1977   A Reappraisal of Redistribution: Complex Hawaiian Chiefdoms. In *Exchange Systems in Prehistory*, edited by T. K. Earle and J. E. Ericson, pp. 213–29. Academic Press, New York.
1978   *Economic and Social Organization of a Complex Chiefdom: The Halelea District, Kaua'i, Hawaii*. Museum of Anthropology, Anthropological Papers 63. University of Michigan, Ann Arbor.
1987a Chiefdoms in Archaeological and Ethnohistorical Perspective. *Annual Review of Anthropology* 16:279–308.
1987b Specialization and the Production of Wealth: The Hawaiian Chiefdom and the Inka Empire. In *Specialization, Exchange, and Complex Societies*, edited by E. Brumfiel and T. Earle, pp. 64–75. Cambridge University Press, Cambridge.
1989   The Evolution of Chiefdoms. *Current Anthropology* 30:84–88.
1991a The Evolution of Chiefdoms. In *Chiefdoms: Power, Economy, and Ideology*, edited by T. Earle, pp. 1–15. Cambridge University Press, Cambridge.

Earle, Timothy (editor)
1991b *Chiefdoms: Power, Economy, and Ideology*. Cambridge University Press, Cambridge.

Earle, Timothy K., and Jonathon E. Ericson (editors)
1977   *Exchange Systems in Prehistory*. Academic Press, New York.

Eisenstadt, S. N.
   1959   Primitive Political Systems: A Preliminary Comparative Analysis. *American Anthropologist* 61:200–222.
Ekholm, Kajsa
   1972   *Power and Prestige: The Rise and Fall of the Kongo Kingdom.* Uppsala.
Ekholm, Kajsa, and Jonathan Friedman
   1979   "Capital" Imperialism and Exploitation in Ancient World Systems. In *Power and Propaganda: A Symposium on Ancient Empires*, edited by M. T. Larsen, pp. 41–58. Copenhagan Studies in Assyriology 7.
   1985   Towards a Global Anthropology. *Critique of Anthropology* 5(1):97–119.
Emerson, Thomas E.
   1982   *Mississippian Stone Images in Illinois.* Illinois Archaeological Survey, Circular 6. Urbana.
   1983   The Bostrom Figure Pipe and the Cahokia Effigy Style in the American Bottom. *Midcontinental Journal of Archaeology* 8:257–67.
   1989   Water, Serpents, and the Underworld: An Exploration into Cahokia Symbolism. In *The Southeastern Ceremonial Complex: Artifacts and Analysis*, edited by P. Galloway, pp. 45–92. University of Nebraska Press, Lincoln.
   1991   Some Perspectives on Cahokia and the Northern Mississippian Expansion. In *Cahokia and the Hinterlands: Middle Mississippian Cultures of the Midwest*, edited by T. E. Emerson and R. B. Lewis, pp. 221–36. University of Illinois Press, Urbana.
   1992   The Mississippian Dispersed Village as a Social and Environmental Strategy. In *Late Prehistoric Agriculture: Observations from the Midwest*, edited by W. I. Woods, pp. 198–216. Studies in Illinois Archaeology 8. Illinois Historic Preservation Agency, Springfield.
Emerson, Thomas E., and Douglas K. Jackson
   1984   *The BBB Motor Site.* FAI-270 Site Reports 6. University of Illinois Press, Urbana.
   1987   *The Marcus Site.* FAI-270 Site Reports 17, part 2. University of Illinois Press, Urbana.
Emerson, Thomas E., and R. Barry Lewis (editors)
   1991   *Cahokia and the Hinterlands: Middle Mississippian Cultures of the Midwest.* University of Illinois Press, Urbana.
Ericson, Jonathon E., and Timothy K. Earle (editors)
   1982   *Contexts for Prehistoric Exchange.* Academic Press, New York.
Esarey, Duane, and Timothy R. Pauketat
   1992   *The Lohmann Site: An Early Mississippian Center in the American Bottom.* FAI-270 Site Reports 25. University of Illinois Press, Urbana.
Farnsworth, Kenneth B., and Thomas E. Emerson
   1989   The Macoupin Creek Figure Pipe and Its Archaeological Context: Evidence for Late Woodland-Mississippian Interaction Beyond the Northern Border of Cahokia Settlement. *Midcontinental Journal of Archaeology* 14:18–37.

Feinman, Gary M.
  1991 Demography, Surplus, and Inequality: Early Political Formations in Highland Mesoamerica. In *Chiefdoms: Power, Economy, and Ideology*, edited by T. Earle, pp. 229–62. Cambridge University Press, Cambridge.

Feinman, Gary M., Stephen A. Kowalewski, Laura Finsten, Richard E. Blanton, and Linda Nicholas
  1985 Long-term Demographic Change: A Perspective from the Valley of Oaxaca, Mexico. *Journal of Field Archaeology* 12:333–62.

Feinman, Gary, and Jill Neitzel
  1984 Too Many Types: An Overview of Sedentary Prestate Societies in the Americas. *Advances in Archaeological Method and Theory* 7:39–102. Academic Press, New York.

Feinman, Gary M., and Linda M. Nicholas
  1987 Labor, Surplus, and Production: A Regional Analysis of Formative Oaxacan Socio-economic Change. In *Coasts, Plains and Deserts: Essays in Honor of Reynold J. Ruppé*, edited by S. W. Gaines, pp. 27–50. Arizona State University, Anthropological Research Papers 38. Tempe.

Femia, Joseph V.
  1981 *Gramsci's Political Thought: Hegemony, Consciousness, and the Revolutionary Process*. Oxford University Press.

Ferdon, Edwin, J., Jr.
  1987 *Early Tonga as the Explorers Saw It, 1616–1810*. The University of Arizona Press, Tucson.

Finney, B.
  1966 Resource Distribution and Social Structure in Tahiti. *Ethnology* 5:80–86.

Finney, Fred A.
  1985 *The Carbon Dioxide Site*. FAI-270 Site Reports 11, part 1. University of Illinois Press, Urbana.
  1987 Ceramics. In *The George Reeves Site*, by D. L. McElrath and F. A. Finney, pp. 222–59, 276–81, 340–46. FAI-270 Site Reports 15. University of Illinois Press, Urbana.

Firth, Raymond
  1979 The Sacredness of Tikopian Chiefs. In *Politics in Leadership: A Comparative Perspective*, edited by W. A. Shack and P. S. Cohen, pp. 139–66. Clarendon Press, Oxford.
  1983 *We, the Tikopia*. Stanford University Press, Stanford, Calif. (originally published 1936).

Flannery, Kent V.
  1983 Divergent Evolution. In *The Cloud People*, edited by K. V. Flannery and J. Marcus, pp. 1–4. Academic Press, New York.

Flint, Timothy
  1826 *Recollections of the Last Ten Years, Passed in Occasional Residences and Journeyings in the Valley of the Mississippi, From Pittsburg and the Missouri to the Gulf of Mexico, and From Florida to the Spanish Frontier; in a Series of*

Letters to the Rev. James Flint, of Salem, Massachusetts. Cummings, Illiard, and Company, Boston.

Ford, Richard I.

1974 Northeastern Archaeology: Past and Future Directions. *Annual Review of Anthropology* 3:385–413.

1977 Evolutionary Ecology and the Evolution of Human Ecosystems: A Case Study From the Midwestern U.S.A. In *Explanation of Prehistoric Change*, edited by J. N. Hill, pp.153–84. University of New Mexico Press, Albuquerque.

1979 Gathering and Gardening: Trends and Consequences of Hopewell Subsistence Strategies. In *Hopewell Archaeology: The Chillicothe Conference*, edited by D. S. Brose and N. Greber, pp. 234–38. Kent State University Press, Kent, Ohio.

1985 The Processes of Plant Food Production in Prehistoric North America. In *Prehistoric Food Production in North America*, edited by R. I. Ford, pp. 1–18. University of Michigan Museum of Anthropology, Anthropological Papers 75. Ann Arbor.

Fortier, Andrew C.

1985 *The Robert Schneider Site.* FAI-270 Site Reports 11, part 2. University of Illinois Press, Urbana.

Fortier, Andrew C., Richard B. Lacampagne, and Fred A. Finney

1984 *The Fish Lake Site.* FAI-270 Site Reports 8. University of Illinois Press, Urbana.

Fortier, Andrew C., Thomas O. Maher, and Joyce A. Williams

1991 *The Sponemann Site: The Formative Emergent Mississippian Sponemann Phase Occupations.* FAI-270 Site Reports 23. University of Illinois Press, Urbana.

Fowke, Gerard

1913 *Prehistoric Objects Classified and Described.* Missouri Historical Society, Department of Archaeology, Bulletin 1. Jefferson Memorial, St. Louis.

Fowler, Melvin L.

1974 Cahokia: Ancient Capital of the Midwest. *Addison-Wesley Module in Anthropology* 48:3–38.

1975a A Pre-Columbian Urban Center on the Mississippi. *Scientific American* 233(2):92–101.

1977 The Cahokia Site. In *Explorations into Cahokia Archaeology*, edited by M. L. Fowler, pp. 1–42. Illinois Archaeological Survey Bulletin 7. Urbana.

1978 Cahokia and the American Bottom: Settlement Archaeology. In *Mississippian Settlement Patterns*, edited by B. D. Smith, pp. 455–78. Academic Press, New York.

1989 *The Cahokia Atlas: A Historical Atlas of Cahokia Archaeology.* Studies in Illinois Archaeology 6. Illinois Historic Preservation Agency, Springfield.

1991 Mound 72 and Early Mississippian at Cahokia. In *New Perspectives on*

Cahokia: Views from the Periphery, edited by J. B. Stoltman, pp. 1–28. Prehistory Press, Madison, Wis.

Fowler, Melvin L. (editor)
1975b *Cahokia Archaeology: Field Reports*. Illinois State Museum Research Series, Papers in Anthropology 3. Springfield.

Fowler, Melvin L., and James Anderson
1975 Report of 1971 excavations at Mound 72, Cahokia Mounds State Park. In *Cahokia Archaeology: Field Reports*, edited by M. L. Fowler, pp. 25–27. Illinois State Museum Papers in Anthropology 3. Springfield.

Fowler, Melvin L., and Robert L. Hall
1975 Archaeological Phases at Cahokia. In *Perspectives in Cahokia Archaeology*, pp. 1–14. *Illinois Archaeological Survey, Bulletin 10*. Urbana.
1978 Late Prehistory of the Illinois Area. In *Handbook of North American Indians* 15:560–68. Smithsonian Institution, Washington, D.C.

Frankenstein, Susan, and Michael Rowlands
1978 The Internal Structure and Regional Context of Early Iron Age Society in Southwestern Germany. *Bulletin of the Institute of Archaeology of London* 15:73–112.

Frazer, Sir James George
1947 *The Golden Bough: A Study in Magic and Religion*. Macmillan, New York (originally published 1922).

Fried, Morton H.
1967 *The Evolution of Political Society*. Random House, New York.

Friedman, Jonathan A.
1982 Catastrophe and Continuity in Social Evolution. In *Theory and Explanation in Archaeology: The Southampton Conference*, edited by C. Renfrew, M. J. Rowlands, and B. A. Seagraves, pp. 175–96. Academic Press, New York.

Friedman, Jonathan A., and Michael Rowlands
1978 Notes Towards an Epigenetic Model of the Evolution of "Civilisation." In *The Evolution of Social Systems*, edited by J. Friedman and M. Rowlands, pp. 201–76. University of Pittsburgh Press, Pittsburgh.

Friemuth, Glen A.
1974 The Lunsford-Pulcher Site: An Examination of Selected Traits and Their Social Implications in American Bottom Prehistory. Predissertation paper, Department of Anthropology, University of Illinois at Urbana.

Fugle, Eugene
1962 Test Excavations of the McCain site, 20B4-26, Caseyville, Illinois. Unpublished manuscript and field notes on file, Center for Archaeological Investigations, Southern Illinois University, Carbondale.

Fuller, Michael, and Neathery Fuller
1987 Two Effigy Pipes from the Davis Site, St. Louis County. *Missouri Archaeological Society Quarterly* (January–March):6–8.

Gailey, Christine W.
   1987   *Kinship to Kingship: Gender Hierarchy and State Formation in the Tongan Islands*. University of Texas Press, Austin.
Galloway, Patricia (editor)
   1989   *The Southeastern Ceremonial Complex: Artifacts and Analysis*. University of Nebraska Press, Lincoln.
Gibbon, Guy E.
   1974   A Model of Mississippian Development and Its Implications for the Red Wing Area. In *Aspects of Upper Great Lakes Anthropology*, edited by E. Johnson, pp. 129–37. Minnesota Prehistoric Archaeology Series 11.
Gibson, Jon L.
   1974   Aboriginal Warfare in the Southeast: An Alternative Perspective. *American Antiquity* 39:130–33.
Giddens, Anthony
   1979   *Central Problems in Social Theory*. Macmillan, London.
   1982   *Profiles and Critiques in Social Theory*. Macmillan, London.
Gledhill, John
   1984   The Transformation of Asiatic Formations: The Case of Late Prehispanic Mesoamerica. In *Marxist Perspectives in Archaeology*, edited by M. Spriggs, pp. 135–48. Cambridge University Press, Cambridge.
   1988   Introduction: The Comparative Analysis of Social and Political Transitions. In *State and Society: The Emergence and Development of Social Hierarchy and Political Centralization*, edited by J. Gledhill, B. Bender, and M. T. Larsen, pp. 1–29. Unwin Hyman, London.
Gledhill, John, and Michael J. Rowlands
   1982   Materialism and Socio-economic Process in Multi-linear Evolution. In *Ranking, Resource and Exchange*, edited by C. Renfrew and S. Shennan, pp. 144–49. Cambridge University Press, Cambridge.
Goad, Sharon I.
   1980   Chemical Analysis of Native Copper Artifacts from the Southeastern United States. *Current Anthropology* 21:270–71.
Godelier, Maurice
   1977   *Perspectives in Marxist Anthropology*. Cambridge University Press, Cambridge.
   1978   Economy and Religion: An Evolutionary Optical Illusion. In *Evolution of Social Systems*, edited by J. Friedman and M. J. Rowlands, pp. 3–11. University of Pittsburgh Press, Pittsburgh.
Goldman, Irving
   1967   Status Rivalry and Cultural Evolution in Polynesia. In *Comparative Political Systems*, edited by R. Cohen and J. Middleton, pp. 375–95. The Natural History Press, Garden City, N.Y. (original published 1955 in *American Anthropologist*).
   1970   *Ancient Polynesian Society*. University of Chicago Press, Chicago.
Goodman, Claire G.
   1984   *Copper Artifacts in Late Eastern Woodlands Prehistory*, edited by A.-M. Cantwell. Center for American Archaeology, Kampsville, Ill.

Goody, Jack
1982 *Cooking, Cuisine and Class: A Study in Comparative Sociology.* Cambridge University Press, Cambridge.

Gramsci, Antonio
1971 *Selections from the Prison Notebooks of Antonio Gramsci* (translated by Q. Hoare and G. N. Smith). International Publishers, New York.

Gregg, Michael L.
1975a A Population Estimate for Cahokia. In *Perspectives in Cahokia Archaeology*, pp. 126–36. Illinois Archaeological Survey, Bulletin 10. Urbana.
1975b *Settlement Morphology and Production Specialization: The Horseshoe Lake Site, A Case Study.* Unpublished Ph.D. dissertation, Department of Anthropology, University of Wisconsin, Milwaukee.

Griffin, James B.
1949 The Cahokia Ceramic Complexes. In *Proceedings of the Fifth Plains Conference for Archaeology*, edited by J. L. Champe, pp. 44–58. University of Nebraska, Lincoln.
1951 *A Preliminary Statement on the Collection from the Grassy Lake Site (Ms 4), Madison County, Illinois.* Greater St. Louis Archaeological Society Bulletin 6.
1952 Culture Periods in Eastern United States Archeology. In *Archeology of Eastern United States*, edited by J. B. Griffin, pp. 352–64. University of Chicago Press, Chicago.
1967 Eastern North American Archaeology: A Summary. *Science* 156:175–91.
1977 The University of Michigan Excavations at the Pulcher Site in 1950. *American Antiquity* 42:462–90.
1984 A Historical Perspective. In *American Bottom Archaeology*, edited by C. J. Bareis and J. W. Porter, pp. xv–xvii. University of Illinois Press, Urbana.
1985 Changing Concepts of the Prehistoric Mississippian Cultures of the Eastern United States. In *Alabama and the Borderlands: From Prehistory to Statehood*, edited by R. Reid Badger and L. A. Clayton, pp. 40–63. University of Alabama Press, Tuscaloosa.
1990 Comments on the Late Prehistoric Societies of the Southeast. In *Towns and Temples Along the Mississippi*, edited by D. H. Dye and C. A. Cox, pp. 1–15. University of Alabama Press, Tuscaloosa.
1992 Fort Ancient Has No Class: The Absence of an Elite Group in Mississippian Societies in the Central Ohio Valley. In *Lords of the Southeast: Elites in Ethnohistorical and Archaeological Perspective*, edited by A. Barker and T. R. Pauketat, pp. 53–59. American Anthropological Association, Archeological Papers 3. Washington, D.C.

Griffin, James B., and Albert C. Spaulding
1951 The Central Mississippi Valley Archaeological Survey, Season 1950—A Preliminary Report. *Journal of the Illinois State Archaeological Society* 1(3):74–81.

Griffith, Roberta Jean
1981 *Ramey Incised Pottery.* Illinois Archaeological Survey, Circular 5. Urbana.

Grimm, Robert E.
  1980   *Cahokia Brought to Life* (second printing). Greater St. Louis Archaeological Society, St. Louis.
Godelier, Maurice
  1978   Economy and Religion: An Evolutionary Optical Illusion. In *The Evolution of Social Systems*, edited by J. Friedman and M. J. Rowlands, pp. 3–11. University of Pittsburgh Press.
Haas, Jonathan
  1982   *The Evolution of the Prehistoric State.* Columbia University Press, New York.
Hadfield, Emma
  1920   *Among the Natives of the Loyalty Group.* Macmillan, London.
Hall, Robert L.
  1964a Illinois State Museum Projects. In *Third Annual Report: American Bottoms Archaeology, July 1, 1963-June 30, 1964,* edited by M. L. Fowler, pp. 11–15. Illinois Archaeological Survey, Urbana.
  1964b Report of Phase 3 Archaeological Salvage Project: FAI Route 70, Section 60-6, Tract 15A. Unpublished report. Illinois State Museum, Springfield.
  1966   Cahokia Chronology. Paper presented at the annual meeting of the Central States Anthropological Society, St. Louis.
  1967   The Mississippian Heartland and its Plains Relationship. *Plains Anthropologist* 12:175–83.
  1973   The Cahokia Presence Outside of the American Bottom. Paper presented at the annual meeting of the Central States Anthropological Society, St. Louis.
  1975   Chronology and Phases at Cahokia. In *Perspectives in Cahokia Archaeology,* pp. 15–31. Illinois Archaeological Survey, Bulletin 10. Urbana.
  1977   An Anthropocentric Perspective for Eastern United States Prehistory. *American Antiquity* 42:499–518.
  1980   An Interpretation of the Two-climax Model of Illinois Prehistory. In *Early Native America: Prehistoric Demography, Economy, and Technology,* edited by D. L. Browman, pp. 401–62. Mouton, The Hague.
  1985   Medicine Wheels, Sun Circles, and the Magic of World Center Shrines. *Plains Anthropologist* 30:181–93.
  1991   Cahokia Identity and Interaction Models of Cahokia Mississippian. In *Cahokia and the Hinterlands: Middle Mississippian Cultures of the Midwest,* edited by T. E. Emerson and R. B. Lewis, pp. 3–34. University of Illinois Press, Urbana.
Hall, Robert L., and Joseph O. Vogel
  1963   Illinois State Museum Projects. In *Second Annual Report: American Bottoms Archaeology, July 1, 1962-June 30, 1963,* edited by M. L. Fowler, pp. 24–27. Illinois Archaeological Survey, Urbana.
Hall, Robert L., and Warren L. Wittry
  1980   Summary Report on 1978 Investigations of Circle No. 2 of the Woodhenge: Cahokia Mounds State Historic Site. Unpublished report

submitted to the Illinois Department of Conservation. University of Illinois at Chicago Circle.

Halstead, Paul, and John O'Shea
  1982 A Friend in Need is a Friend Indeed: Social Storage and the Origins of Social Ranking. In *Ranking, Resource and Exchange*, edited by C. Renfrew, pp. 92–99. Cambridge University Press, Cambridge.

Hanenberger, Ned H.
  1990a The Karol Rekas Site (11-Ms-1255). In *Selected Early Mississippian Household Sites in the American Bottom*, by D. K. Jackson and N. H. Hanenberger, pp. 425–509. FAI-270 Site Reports 22. University of Illinois Press, Urbana.
  1990b The Olszewski Site (11-S-465). In *Selected Early Mississippian Household Sites in the American Bottom*, by D. K. Jackson and N. H. Hanenberger, pp. 253–423. FAI-270 Site Reports 22. University of Illinois Press, Urbana.

Hann, John H.
  1988 *Apalachee: The Land Between the Rivers*. University of Florida Press, Gainesville.

Hardin, Margaret A.
  1981 The Identification of Individual Style on Moundville Engraved Vessels: A Preliminary Note. *Southeastern Archaeological Conference Bulletin* 24:108–10.

Hargrave, Michael L.
  1982 *Archaeological Investigations at the Bluff Shadow Site, Monroe County, Illinois*. Center for Archaeological Investigations, Research Paper 31. Southern Illinois University, Carbondale.

Harn, Alan D.
  1971 *An Archaeological Survey of the American Bottoms in Madison and St. Clair Counties, Illinois*. Illinois State Museum Reports of Investigations 21 (part 2). Springfield.
  1980 Comments on the Spatial Distribution of Late Woodland and Mississippian Ceramics in the General Cahokia Sphere. *Rediscovery* 1:17–26 (journal of the Illinois Association for the Advancement of Archaeology).

Hayden, Brian, and Aubrey Cannon
  1983 Where the Garbage Goes: Refuse Disposal in the Maya Highlands. *Journal of Anthropological Archaeology* 2:117–63.

Helms, Mary W.
  1979 *Ancient Panama: Chiefs in Search of Power*. University of Texas Press, Austin.
  1980 Succession to High Office in Pre-Columbian Circum-Caribbean Chiefdoms. *Man* (n.s.) 15:718–31.
  1987 Art Styles and Interaction Spheres in Central America and the Caribbean: Polished Black Wood in the Greater Antilles. In *Chiefdoms in the Americas*, edited by R. Drennan and C. A. Uribe, pp. 67–83. University Press of America, Lanham, Md.
  1988 *Ulysses' Sail: An Ethnographic Odyssey of Power, Knowledge, and Geographical Distance*. Princeton University Press, Princeton, N.J.

1992 Political Lords and Political Ideology in Southeastern Chiefdoms: Comments and Observations. In *Lords of the Southeast: Social Inequality and the Native Elites of Southeastern North America*, edited by A. W. Barker and T. R. Pauketat, pp. 185–94. American Anthropological Association, Archeological Papers 3. Washington, D.C.

Henning, Dale R.
1967 Mississippian Influences on the Eastern Plains Border: An Evaluation. *Plains Anthropologist* 12:184–94.

Hickey, Gerald C.
1982 *Sons of the Mountains: Ethnohistory of the Vietnamese Central Highlands to 1954.* Yale University Press, New Haven.

Hines, P.
1977 On Social Organization in the Middle Mississippian: States or Chiefdoms? *Current Anthropology* 18:337–38.

Hobbes, Thomas
1985 *Leviathan*, edited by C. B. Macpherson. Penguin Books, London (originally published 1651).

Hodder, Ian
1977 The Distribution of Material Culture Items in the Baringo District, Western Kenya. *Man* 12:239–69.
1986 *Reading the Past.* Cambridge University Press, Cambridge.
1989 This Is Not an Article about Material Culture as Text. *Journal of Anthropological Archaeology* 8:250–69.

Hoehr, Peter
1980 Utilitarian Artifacts from the Cahokia Site. In *Cahokia Brought to Life* (second printing), edited by R. E. Grimm, pp. 41–45. The Greater St. Louis Archaeological Society, St. Louis.

Holder, Preston
1958 Archaeological Study of Kunnemann Mound, Central Cahokia Group of Illinois, Threatened by Destruction. *Year Book of the American Philosophical Society, 1957*:384–85.
1968 Comment in "Brief of Symposium on the 'Southern Cult.'" In *The Waring Papers: The Collected Works of Antonio J. Waring*, edited by S. Williams, pp. 72–77. Peabody Museum, Cambridge, Mass.

Holley, George R.
1989 *The Archaeology of the Cahokia Mounds ICT-II: Ceramics.* Illinois Cultural Resources Study 11. Illinois Historic Preservation Agency, Springfield.
1990 Investigations at the Kunnemann Tract, Cahokia Mounds Historic Site, Madison County, Illinois. Unpublished report submitted to the Illinois Historic Preservation Agency, Springfield.

Holley, George R., Rinita A. Dalan, Neal H. Lopinot, and Philip A. Smith
1990 Investigations in the Grand Plaza, Cahokia Mounds Historic Site, St. Clair County, Illinois. Unpublished report submitted to the Illinois Historic Preservation Agency, Springfield. Southern Illinois University at Edwardsville.

Holley, George R., Neal H. Lopinot, William I. Woods, and John E. Kelly
 1989 Dynamics of Community Organization at Prehistoric Cahokia. In *House-holds and Communities, Proceedings of the 21st Annual Chacmool Conference*, edited by S. MacEachern, D. J. W. Archer, and R. D. Garvin, pp. 339–49. University of Calgary.
Holley, George R., Neal H. Lopinot, Rinita A. Dalan, and William I. Woods
 1990 *The Archaeology of the Cahokia Palisade: The South Palisade Investigations.* Illinois Cultural Resources Study 14. Illinois Historic Preservation Agency, Springfield.
House, John H.
 1975 Prehistoric Lithic Resource Utilization in the Cache Basin: Crowley's Ridge Chert and Quartzite and Pitkin Chert. In *The Cache River Archeological Project*, assembled by M. B. Schiffer and J. H. House, pp. 81–91. Arkansas Archeological Survey, Research Series 8. Fayetteville.
Howland, Henry R.
 1877 Recent Archaeological Discoveries in the American Bottom. *Buffalo Society of Natural Sciences, Bulletin* 3(5):204–11.
Hudson, Charles
 1984 Elements of Southeastern Indian Religion. *Iconography of Religions* 10(1). Institute of Religious Iconography, State University of Groningen, Leiden, The Netherlands.
Hunt, William J., Jr.
 1974 *Late Woodland–Mississippian Relationships at the River Bend East Site (23SL79), St. Louis County, Missouri.* Unpublished M.A. thesis, Department of Anthropology, University of Nebraska, Lincoln.
Hus, Henry
 1908 An Ecological Cross Section of the Mississippi River in the Vicinity of St. Louis, Missouri. *Report of the Missouri Botanical Garden* 34:125–268.
Iseminger, William R.
 1980 Cahokia: A Mississippian Metropolis. *Historic Illinois* 2(6):1–4.
 1985 Cahokia Mounds Museum Society Archaeological Field School: 1985 Woodhenge Excavations at Cahokia Mounds State Historic Site Summary Report. Unpublished report submitted to the Illinois Historic Preservation Agency, Springfield.
 1990 Features. In *The Archaeology of the Cahokia Palisade: The East Palisade Investigations*, by W. R. Iseminger et al., pp. 18–38. Illinois Cultural Resources Study 14. Illinois Historic Preservation Agency, Springfield.
Iseminger, William R., Timothy R. Pauketat, Brad Koldehoff, Lucretia S. Kelly, and Leonard Blake
 1990 *The Archaeology of the Cahokia Palisade: The East Palisade Investigations.* Illinois Cultural Resources Study 14. Illinois Historic Preservation Agency, Springfield.
Ives, David J.
 1984 The Crescent Hills Prehistoric Quarrying Area: More than Just Rocks. In *Prehistoric Chert Exploitation: Studies from the Midcontinent*, edited by

B. M. Butler and E. E. May, pp. 187–95. Center for Archaeological Investigations, Occasional Paper 2. Carbondale.

Ives, John C.
1962   Mill Creek Pottery. *Journal of the Iowa Archaeological Society* 11(3). Iowa City.

Izikowitz, Karl Gustav
1979   *Lamet: Hill Peasants in French Indonesia.* AMS Press, New York.

Jackson, Douglas K.
1984   *The Determann Borrow Site, Madison County, Illinois.* Resource Investigation Program, Research Reports 14. University of Illinois, Urbana.
1990a   The Esterlein Site (11-Ms-598). In *Selected Early Mississippian Household Sites in the American Bottom,* by D. K. Jackson and N. H. Hanenberger, pp. 91–216. FAI-270 Site Reports 22. University of Illinois Press, Urbana.
1990b   The Sandy Ridge Farm Site (11-S-660). In *Selected Early Mississippian Household Sites in the American Bottom,* by D. K. Jackson and N. H. Hanenberger, pp. 217–52. FAI-270 Site Reports 22. University of Illinois Press, Urbana.

Jackson, Douglas K., and Ned H. Hanenberger
1990   *Selected Early Mississippian Household Sites in the American Bottom.* FAI-270 Site Reports 22. University of Illinois Press, Urbana.

Jackson, Douglas K., Andrew C. Fortier, and Joyce A. Williams
1992   *The Sponemann Site 2: The Mississippian and Oneota Occupations.* FAI-270 Site Reports 24. University of Illinois Press, Urbana.

Jacobitti, Edmund E.
1983   From Vico's Common Sense to Gramsci's Hegemony. In *Vico and Marx: Affinities and Contrasts,* edited by G. Tagliacozzo, pp. 367–87. Humanities, New Jersey.
1986   Political Thought and Rhetoric in Vico. In *New Vico Studies, Vol. 4,* edited by G. Tagliacozzo and D. P. Verene, pp. 73–88. Institute for Vico Studies, New York.

Johannessen, Sissel
1984a   Paleoethnobotany. In *American Bottom Archaeology,* edited by C. J. Bareis and J. W. Porter, pp. 197–214. University of Illinois Press, Urbana.
1984b   Plant Remains. In *The Robinson's Lake Site,* by G. R. Milner, pp. 124–32. FAI-270 Site Reports 10. University of Illinois Press, Urbana.
1984c   Plant Remains from the Edelhardt Phase. In *The BBB Motor Site,* by T. E. Emerson and D. K. Jackson, pp. 169–89. FAI-270 Site Reports 6. University of Illinois Press, Urbana.
1985a   Emergent Mississippian Plant Remains. In *The Robert Schneider Site,* by A. C. Fortier, pp. 284–88. FAI-270 Site Reports 11, part 2. University of Illinois Press, Urbana.
1985b   Plant Remains. In *The Carbon Dioxide Site,* by F. A. Finney, pp. 97–108. FAI-270 Site Reports 11, part 1. University of Illinois Press, Urbana.
1985c   Mississippian Plant Remains. In *The Robert Schneider Site,* by A. C. Fortier,

pp. 259–63. FAI-270 Site Reports 11, part 2. University of Illinois Press, Urbana.

1987   Patrick Phase Plant Remains. In *The Range Site: Archaic through Late Woodland Occupations*, by J. E. Kelly, A. C. Fortier, S. J. Ozuk, and J. A. Williams, pp. 404–16. FAI-270 Site Reports 16. University of Illinois Press, Urbana.

1991   Plant Remains. In *The Lohmann Site: An Early Mississippian Center in the American Bottom*, by D. Esarey and T. R. Pauketat. FAI-270 Site Reports 25. University of Illinois Press, Urbana.

Johannessen, Sissel, and Lucy A. Whalley

1988   Floral Analysis. In *Late Woodland Sites in the American Bottom Uplands*, by C. Bentz, D. L. McElrath, F. A. Finney, and R. B. Lacampagne, pp. 265–88. FAI-270 Site Reports 18. University of Illinois Press, Urbana.

Jones, G. I.

1966   Chiefly Succession in Basutoland. In *Succession to High Office*, edited by J. Goody, pp. 57–81. Cambridge University Press, Cambridge.

Justice, Noel D.

1987   *Stone Age Spear and Arrow Points of the Midcontinental and Eastern United States: A Modern Survey and Reference.* Indiana University Press, Bloomington.

Kelly, Arthur R.

1931   Letter of 6 January 1931 to Warren K. Moorehead, on file at the University of Michigan, Museum of Anthropology, Ann Arbor.

1932   Reports: Archaeological Field Work in North America during 1931. *American Anthropologist* (n.s.) 34:476–515.

1933   Some Problems of Recent Cahokia Archaeology. *Transactions of the Illinois State Academy of Science* 25(4):101–3.

Kelly, John E.

1980   *Formative Developments at Cahokia and the Adjacent American Bottom: A Merrell Tract Perspective.* Unpublished Ph.D. dissertation, Department of Anthropology, University of Wisconsin at Madison.

1984a   Late Bluff Chert Utilization on the Merrell Tract, Cahokia. In *Prehistoric Chert Exploitation: Studies from the Midcontinent*, edited by B. M. Butler and E. E. May, pp. 23–44. Center for Archaeological Investigations, Occasional Paper 2. Carbondale.

1984b   Wells Incised Plates: Their Context and Affinities with O'Byam Incised. Paper presented at the Paducah Ceramics Conference, Paducah.

1990a   The Emergence of Mississippian Culture in the American Bottom Region. In *The Mississippian Emergence*, edited by B. Smith, pp. 113–52. Smithsonian Institution Press, Washington, D.C.

1990b   Range Site Community Patterns and the Mississippian Emergence. In *The Mississippian Emergence*, edited by B. Smith, pp. 67–112. Smithsonian Institution Press, Washington, D.C.

1990c   The Realm of Public Architecture at Cahokia. Paper presented at the 47th annual meeting of the Southeastern Archaeological Conference, Mobile, Ala.

1991a Cahokia and its Role as a Gateway Center in Interregional Exchange. In *Cahokia and the Hinterlands: Middle Mississippian Cultures of the Midwest,* edited by T. E. Emerson and R. B. Lewis, pp. 61–80. University of Illinois Press, Urbana.

1991b The Evidence for Prehistoric Exchange and its Implications for the Development of Cahokia. In *New Perspectives on Cahokia: Views from the Periphery,* edited by J. B. Stoltman, pp. 65–92. Prehistory Press, Madison, Wis.

1991c Myth-conceptions about Cahokia's Urbane Character. Paper presented in the symposium "Exploring and Exploding Myths About Cahokia," 56th annual meeting of the Society for American Archaeology, New Orleans.

n.d.   Archaeological Investigations of the East St. Louis Mound Center: Past and Present. Draft manuscript on file, Contract Archaeology Program, Southern Illinois University at Edwardsville.

Kelly, John E., and Bonnie L. Gums
1987   Phase I Cultural Resource Investigations of the I-55/70 Expressway, East St. Louis, St. Clair County, Illinois. Unpublished report submitted to the Illinois Department of Transportation. Southern Illinois University at Edwardsville.

Kelly, John E., James Mertz, and Larry Kinsella
1989   Recent Salvage Investigations in the American Bottom. *Illinois Archaeological Survey Newsletter* 4(2).

Kelly, John E., Steven J. Ozuk, Douglas K. Jackson, Dale L. McElrath, Fred A. Finney, and Duane Esarey
1984a Emergent Mississippian Period. In *American Bottom Archaeology,* edited by C. J. Bareis and J. W. Porter, pp. 128–57. University of Illinois Press, Urbana.

Kelly, John E., Fred A. Finney, Dale L. McElrath, and Steven J. Ozuk
1984b Late Woodland Period. In *American Bottom Archaeology,* edited by C. J. Bareis and J. W. Porter, pp. 104–27. University of Illinois Press, Urbana.

Kelly, John E., Andrew C. Fortier, Steven J. Ozuk, and Joyce A. Williams
1987   *The Range Site: Archaic through Late Woodland Occupations.* FAI-270 Site Reports 16. University of Illinois Press, Urbana.

Kelly, John E., Steven J. Ozuk, and Joyce Williams
1990   *The Range Site 2: The Emergent Mississippian Dohack and Range Phase Occupations.* FAI-270 Site Reports 20. University of Illinois Press, Urbana.

Kelly, Lucretia S.
1979   *Animal Resource Exploitation by Early Cahokia Populations on the Merrell Tract.* Illinois Archaeological Survey, Circular 4. Urbana.

1987   Patrick Phase Faunal Remains. In *The Range Site: Archaic through Late Woodland Occupations,* by J. E. Kelly, A. C. Fortier, S. J. Ozuk, and J. A. Williams, pp. 350–403. FAI-270 Site Reports 16. University of Illinois Press, Urbana.

1990a Faunal Remains. In *The Archaeology of the Cahokia Palisade, East Palisade Investigations*, by W. R. Iseminger et al., pp. 109–34. Illinois Cultural Resources Study 14. Illinois Historic Preservation Agency, Springfield.

1990b Range Phase Faunal Analysis. In *The Range Site 2: The Emergent Mississippian Dohack and Range Phase Occupations*, by J. E. Kelly, S. J. Ozuk, and J. A. Williams, pp. 487–511. FAI-270 Site Reports 20. University of Illinois Press, Urbana.

Kelly, Lucretia S., and Paula G. Cross

1984 Zooarchaeology. In *American Bottom Archaeology*, edited by C. J. Bareis and J. W. Porter, pp. 215–32. University of Illinois Press, Urbana.

1988 Faunal Analysis. In *Late Woodland Sites in the American Bottom Uplands*, by C. Bentz, D. L. McElrath, F. A. Finney, and R. B. Lacampagne, pp. 289–313. FAI-270 Site Reports 18. University of Illinois Press, Urbana.

Kirch, Patrick V.

1984 *The Evolution of Polynesian Chiefdoms*. Cambridge University Press, Cambridge.

Kirsch, A. Thomas

1973 Feasting and Social Oscillation: A Working Paper on Religion and Society in Upland Southeast Asia. Cornell University, Southeast Asia Program, Data Paper 92. Ithaca, N.Y.

Knight, Vernon James, Jr.

1981 *Mississippian Ritual*. Ph.D. dissertation, Department of Anthropology, University of Florida. University Microfilms, Ann Arbor, Mich.

1986 The Institutional Organization of Mississippian Religion. American Antiquity 51:675–87.

1990 Social Organization and the Evolution of Hierarchy in Southeastern Chiefdoms. *Journal of Anthropological Research* 46:1–23.

Kohl, Phil

1984 Force, History and the Evolutionist Paradigm. In *Marxist Perspectives in Archaeology*, edited by M. Spriggs, pp. 127–34. Cambridge University Press, Cambridge.

1987 The Use and Abuse of World Systems Theory: The Case of the Pristine West Asian State. *Advances in Archaeological Method and Theory* 11:1–35. Academic Press, New York.

Koldehoff, Brad

1987 The Cahokia Flake Tool Industry: Socioeconomic Implications for Late Prehistory in the Central Mississippi Valley. In *The Organization of Core Technology*, edited by J. Johnson and C. Morrow, pp. 151–86. Westview Press, Boulder, Colo.

1989 Cahokia's Immediate Hinterland: The Mississippian Occupation of Douglas Creek. *Illinois Archaeology* 1:39–68.

1990a *Household Specialization: The Organization of Mississippian Chipped-Stone-Tool Production*. Unpublished M.A. thesis, Department of Anthropology, Southern Illinois University, Carbondale.

1990b Lithics. In *The Archaeology of the Cahokia Palisade: The East Palisade Investi-*

gations, by W. R. Iseminger et al., pp. 77–108. Illinois Cultural Resources Study 14. Illinois Historic Preservation Agency, Springfield.

Kozlovich, Gene
1953   Survey Report of the Present Condition of the Cahokia Mound Group. Unpublished report of the Central Mississippi Valley Archaeological Survey, on file, University of Michigan Museum of Anthropology, Ann Arbor.

Kristiansen, Kristian
1984   Ideology and Material Culture: An Archaeological Perspective. In *Marxist Perspectives in Archaeology*, edited by M. Spriggs, pp. 72–100. Cambridge University Press, Cambridge.

Kuper, Hilda
1965   *An African Aristocracy: Rank Among the Swazi*. (originally published 1947). Oxford University Press, London.

Kus, Susan M.
1983   The Social Representation of Space: Dimensioning the Cosmological and the Quotidian. In *Archaeological Hammers and Theories*, edited by J. A. Moore and A. S. Keene, pp. 277–98. Academic Press, New York.

Kuttruff, Carl
1974   *Late Woodland Settlement and Subsistence in the Lower Kaskaskia River Valley*. Unpublished Ph.D. dissertation, Department of Anthropology, Southern Illinois University at Carbondale.

LaDassor, Gray
1980   Cahokia Ornaments. In *Cahokia Brought to Life* (2d printing), edited by R. E. Grimm, pp. 32–41. Greater St. Louis Archaeological Society.

Laitin, David D.
1986   *Hegemony and Culture: Politics and Religious Change Among the Yoruba*. University of Chicago Press, Chicago.

Lambert, Bernd
1966   The Economic Activities of a Gilbertese Chief. In *Political Anthropology*, edited by M. J. Swartz, V. W. Turner, and A. Tuden. Aldine, Chicago.
1971   The Gilbert Islands: Micro-individualism. In *Land Tenure in the Pacific*, edited by R. Cracombe, pp. 146–71. Oxford University Press, Melbourne.

Leach, Edmund R.
1965   *Political Systems of Highland Burma: A Study of Kachin Social Structure* (originally published 1954). Beacon Press, Boston.

Lehman, F. K.
1963   *The Structure of Chin Society: A Tribal People of Burma Adapted to a Non-Western Civilization*. Illinois Studies in Anthropology 3. University of Illinois Press, Urbana.

Linares, Olga F.
1977   *Ecology and the Arts in Ancient Panama: On the Development of Social Rank and Symbolism in the Central Provinces*. Studies in Pre-Columbian Art and Archaeology 17. Dumbarton Oaks, Trustees for Harvard University, Washington, D.C.

Little, Elizabeth A.
1987   Inland Waterways in the Northeast. *Midcontinental Journal of Archaeology* 12:55–76.

Little, Kenneth
1967   The Mende Chiefdoms of Sierra Leone. In *West African Kingdoms in the Nineteenth Century*, edited by D. Forde and P. Kaberry, pp. 239–59. Oxford University Press, London.

Lloyd, Peter C.
1965   The Political Structure of African Kingdoms: An Exploratory Model. In *Political Systems and the Distribution of Power*, edited by M. Banton, pp. 63–112. Tavistock, London.

Lopinot, Neal H.
1991   Archaeobotanical Remains. In *The Archaeology of the Cahokia Mounds ICT-II: Biological Remains*, part 1. Illinois Cultural Resources Study 13. Illinois Historic Preservation Agency. Springfield.
1992   Spatial and Temporal Variability in Mississippian Subsistence: The Archaeobotanical Record. In *Late Prehistoric Agriculture*, edited by W. I. Woods, pp. 44–94. Studies in Illinois Archaeology 8. Illinois Historic Preservation Agency, Springfield.

Lynott, Mark J., Thomas W. Boutton, James E. Price, and Dwight E. Nelson
1986   Stable Carbon Isotopic Evidence for Maize Agriculture in Southeast Missouri and Northeast Arkansas. *American Antiquity* 51:51–65.

McElrath, Dale L., and Fred A. Finney
1987   *The George Reeves Site*. FAI-270 Site Reports 15. University of Illinois Press, Urbana.

McElrath, Dale L., Joyce A. Williams, Thomas O. Maher, and Michael C. Meinkoth
1987   *The Radic Site*. FAI-270 Site Reports 17, part 1. University of Illinois Press, Urbana.

McGuire, Randall H.
1991   *A Marxist Archaeology*. Academic Press, San Diego.

McKern, W. C.
1939   The Midwestern Taxonomic Method as an Aid to Archaeological Culture Study. *American Antiquity* 4:301–13.

McNutt, Charles H.
1973   On the Methodological Validity of Frequency Seriation. *American Antiquity* 38:45–60.

McQueen, Henry S.
1943   Geology of the Fire Clay Districts of East Central Missouri. *Missouri Geological Survey and Water Resources, Second Series* 28. Rolla.

Maher, Thomas O.
1987   Merrell Phase Ceramics. In *The Radic Site*, by D. L. McElrath, J. A. Williams, T. O. Maher, and M. C. Meinkoth, pp. 94–137. FAI-270 Site Reports 17, part 1. University of Illinois Press, Urbana.

Mair, Lucy
1964   *Primitive Government*. Penguin Books, Baltimore, Md.

Malinowski, Bronislaw
   1961   *Argonauts of the Western Pacific* (originally published 1922). Dutton, New York.
Marcus, George E.
   1977   Succession Disputes and the Position of the Nobility in Modern Tonga. *Oceania* 47(3):220–41, 47(4):284–99.
   1980   *The Nobility and the Chiefly Tradition in Modern Tonga.* University of Hawaii Press, Honolulu.
   1989   Chieftainship. In *Developments in Polynesian Ethnology,* edited by A. Howard and R. Borofsky, pp. 175–209. University of Hawaii Press, Honolulu.
Marcus, George E., and Michael M. J. Fischer
   1986   *Anthropology as Cultural Critique: An Experimental Moment in the Human Sciences.* University of Chicago Press, Chicago.
Marquardt, William H.
   1985   Complexity and Scale in the Study of Fisher-Gatherer-Hunters: An Example from the Eastern United States. In *Prehistoric Hunter-Gatherers: The Emergence of Cultural Complexity,* edited by T. D. Price and J. A. Brown, pp. 59–98. Academic Press, Orlando.
   1986   The Development of Cultural Complexity in Southwest Florida: Elements of a Critique. *Southeastern Archaeology* 5:63–70.
Marx, Karl
   1968   The Eighteenth Brumaire of Louis Bonaparte. In *Karl Marx and Frederick Engels: Selected Works,* pp. 95–180. Progress Publishers, Moscow.
   1978   Economic and Philosophic Manuscripts of 1844. In *The Marx-Engels Reader,* edited by R. C. Tucker, pp. 66–132. W. W. Norton, New York.
Marx, Karl, and Frederick Engels
   1989   *The German Ideology,* edited by C. J. Arthur. International Publishers, New York.
Mason, Ronald J., and Gregory Perino
   1961   Microblades at Cahokia, Illinois. *American Antiquity* 26:553–57.
Mauss, Marcel
   1974   *The Gift.* Routledge and Kegan Paul, London (originally published 1923–24).
Mehrer, Mark W.
   1982   *A Mississippian Community at the Range Site (11-S-47), St. Clair County, Illinois.* Unpublished M.A. thesis, Department of Anthropology, University of Illinois, Urbana-Champaign.
   1988   *The Settlement Patterns and Social Power of Cahokia's Hinterland Households.* Unpublished Ph.D. dissertation, Department of Anthropology, University of Illinois, Urbana.
Mehrer, Mark W., and James M. Collins
   1989   Household Archaeology at Cahokia and its Hinterlands. Paper presented in the symposium "Households and Settlements in the Mississip-

pian Period" at the 54th annual meeting of the Society for American Archaeology, Atlanta, Georgia.

Melbye, Jerome C.
1963   *The Kane Burial Mounds.* Southern Illinois University Museum, Archaeological Salvage Report 15. Carbondale.

Metraux, A.
1971   *Ethnology of Easter Island.* Bernice P. Bishop Museum Bulletin 160. Honolulu.

Milner, George R.
1982   *The Palmer Creek Terrace Site (11-Mo-756).* FAI-270 Archaeological Mitigation Project Report 58. Department of Anthropology, University of Illinois, Urbana.
1983   *The Turner and DeMange Sites.* FAI-270 Site Reports 4. University of Illinois Press, Urbana.
1984a   *The Julien Site.* FAI-270 Site Reports 7. University of Illinois Press, Urbana.
1984b   *The Robinsons Lake Site.* FAI-270 Site Reports 10. University of Illinois Press, Urbana.
1984c   Social and Temporal Implications of Variation among American Bottom Mississippian Cemeteries. *American Antiquity* 49:468–88.
1986   Mississippian Period Population Density in a Segment of the Central Mississippi Valley. *American Antiquity* 51:227–38.
1990   The Late Prehistoric Cahokia Cultural System of the Mississippi River Valley: Foundations, Florescence, and Fragmentation. *Journal of World Prehistory* 4 (1):1–43.

Milner, George R., Thomas E. Emerson, Mark W. Mehrer, Joyce A. Williams, and Duane Esarey
1984   Mississippian and Oneota Period. In *American Bottom Archaeology*, edited by C. J. Bareis and J. W. Porter, pp. 158–86. University of Illinois Press, Urbana.

Mitchell, J. Clyde
1956   *The Yao Village: A Study in the Social Structure of a Nyasaland Tribe.* Manchester University Press, Manchester.

Moorehead, Warren K.
1922   *The Cahokia Mounds: A Preliminary Paper.* University of Illinois, Urbana.
1923   *The Cahokia Mounds: A Report of Progress on the Exploration of the Cahokia Group.* University of Illinois, Urbana.
1929   *The Cahokia Mounds.* University of Illinois, Bulletin 26(4).

Morey, Nancy K. C.
1975   *Ethnohistory of the Colombian and Venezuelan Llanos.* Unpublished Ph.D. dissertation, Department of Anthropology, University of Utah.

Morgan, Lewis Henry
1974   *Ancient Society.* Peter Smith, Gloucester, Mass. (originally published 1877).

Morrison, Kenneth M.
1985   Discourse and the Accommodation of Values: Toward a Revision of

Mission History. *Journal of the American Academy of Religion* LIII/3:365–82.

Morse, Dan F.
1974 The Penetration of Northeast Arkansas by Mississippian Culture. In *For the Director: Research Essays in Honor of James B. Griffin*, edited by C. E. Cleland, pp. 186–211. University of Michigan Museum of Anthropology, Anthropological Papers 61. Ann Arbor.

Morse, Dan F., and Phyllis A. Morse
1983 *Archaeology of the Central Mississippi Valley.* Academic Press, New York.
1990 Emergent Mississippian in the Central Mississippi Valley. In *The Mississippian Emergence*, edited by B. D. Smith, pp. 153–73. Smithsonian Institution Press, Washington, D.C.

Muller, Jon
1978 The Kincaid System: Mississippian Settlement in the Environs of a Large Site. In *Mississippian Settlement Patterns*, edited by B. D. Smith, pp. 269–92. Academic Press, New York.
1984 Mississippian Specialization and Salt. *American Antiquity* 49:489–507.
1986a *Archaeology of the Lower Ohio River Valley.* Academic Press, Orlando.
1986b Pans and a Grain of Salt: Mississippian Specialization Revisited. *American Antiquity* 51:405–9.
1987 Salt, Chert, and Shell: Mississippian Exchange and Economy. In *Specialization, Exchange, and Complex Societies*, edited by E. Brumfiel and T. Earle, pp. 10–21. Cambridge University Press, Cambridge.

Muller, Jon, and Jeanette E. Stephens
1990 Mississippian Sociocultural Adaptation. In *Cahokia and the Hinterlands: Middle Mississippian Cultures of the Midwest*, edited by T. E. Emerson and R. B. Lewis, pp. 297–310. University of Illinois Press, Urbana.

Munson, Patrick J.
1971 An *Archaeological Survey of the Wood River Terrace and Adjacent Bottoms and Bluffs in Madison County, Illinois.* Illinois State Museum, Reports of Investigations 21, part 1. Springfield.
1974 Terraces, Meander Loops, and Archaeology in the American Bottoms, Illinois. *Transactions of the Illinois State Academy of Science* 67(4):384–92.

Nance, Jack D.
1984 Lithic Exploitation Studies in the Lower Tennessee-Cumberland Valleys, Western Kentucky. In *Prehistoric Chert Exploitation: Studies from the Midcontinent*, edited by B. M. Butler and E. E. May, pp. 101–27. Center for Archaeological Investigations, Occasional Paper 2. Southern Illinois University, Carbondale.

Nicholas, Ralph W.
1965 Factions: A Comparative Analysis. In *Political Systems and the Distribution of Power*, edited by M. Banton, pp. 21–61. Tavistock, London.
1966 Segmentary Factional Political Systems. In *Political Anthropology*, edited by M. J. Swartz, V. W. Turner, and A. Tuden, pp. 49–59. Aldine, Chicago.

Norris, F. Terry
  1974 The Centerville Site. Unpublished report submitted to the National Park Service, Mid-Atlantic Region. Southern Illinois University at Edwardsville.
  1975 Horseshoe Lake State Park Archaeological Survey. Unpublished report submitted to the Illinois State Museum, Springfield.
  1978 *Excavation at the Lily Lake Site: 1975 Season.* Southern Illinois University at Edwardsville Reports in Contract Archaeology 4.
Oberg, Kalervo
  1955 Types of Social Structure among the Lowland Tribes of South and Central America. *American Anthropologist* 57:472–87.
O'Brien, Patricia J.
  1972a *A Formal Analysis of Cahokia Ceramic from the Powell Tract.* Illinois Archaeological Survey Monograph 3. Urbana.
  1972b Urbanism, Cahokia and Middle Mississippian. *Archaeology* 25:189–97.
  1977 Some Ceramic Periods and Their Implications at Cahokia. In *Explorations into Cahokia Archaeology*, edited by M. L. Fowler, pp. 100–120. Illinois Archaeological Survey, Bulletin 7. Urbana.
  1989 Cahokia: The Political Capital of the "Ramey" State? *North American Archaeologist* 10:275–92.
Oliver, Douglas L.
  1974 *Ancient Tahitian Society.* University Press of Hawaii, Honolulu.
Ortner, Sherry B.
  1984 Theory in Anthropology Since the Sixties. *Comparative Studies in Society and History* 26:126–66.
O'Shea, John, and Paul Halstead
  1989 Conclusion: Bad Year Economics. In *Bad Year Economics: Cultural Responses to Risk and Uncertainty*, edited by P. Halstead and J. O'Shea, pp. 123–26. Cambridge University Press, Cambridge.
Ozuk, Steven J.
  1990 Range Phase Ceramics. In *The Range Site 2: The Emergent Mississippian Dohack and Range Phase Occupations*, by J. E. Kelly, S. J. Ozuk, and J. A. Williams, pp. 387–448. FAI-270 Site Reports 20. University of Illinois Press, Urbana.
Parker, Kathryn E.
  1992 Archaeobotany. In *The Sponemann Site 2: The Mississippian and Oneota Occupations*, by D. K. Jackson, A. C. Fortier, and J. A. Williams, pp. 305–24. FAI-270 Site Reports 24. University of Illinois Press, Urbana.
Parry, William
  1987 *Chipped Stone Tools in Formative Oaxaca, Mexico: Their Procurement, Production and Use.* University of Michigan, Museum of Anthropology, Memoir 20. Ann Arbor.
Patterson, Thomas C.
  1986 Ideology, Class Formation, and Resistance in the Inca State. *Critique of Anthropology* 6(1):75–85.

Pauketat, Timothy R.
1983   A Long-stemmed Spud from the American Bottom. *Midcontinental Journal of Archaeology* 8:1–15.
1984   Notes on Some Non-local Ceramics from an American Bottom Collection. *Illinois Antiquity* 16 (1):4–6 (newsletter of the Illinois Association for Advancement of Archaeology).
1986   *Predicting Occupation Span from Ceramic Refuse: A Case Study from the American Bottom.* Unpublished M.A. thesis, Department of Anthropology, Southern Illinois University, Carbondale.
1987a A Burned Domestic Dwelling at Cahokia. *Wisconsin Archeologist* 68(3): 212–37.
1987b A Functional Consideration of a Mississippian Domestic Vessel Assemblage. *Southeastern Archaeology* 6:1–15.
1987c Mississippian Domestic Economy and Formation Processes: A Response to Prentice. *Midcontinental Journal of Archaeology* 12(1):77–88.
1989   Monitoring Mississippian Homestead Occupation Span and Economy Using Ceramic Refuse. *American Antiquity* 54:288–310.
1990   Ceramics. In *The Archaeology of the Cahokia Palisade: The East Palisade Investigations,* by W. R. Iseminger, T. R. Pauketat, B. Koldehoff, L. S. Kelly, and L. Blake. Illinois Cultural Resources Study 14. Illinois Historic Preservation Agency, Springfield.
1991a The Crafty Elite of Cahokia: Redefining Mississippian "Specialization." Paper presented in the symposium "Exploring and Exploding Myths About Cahokia," 56th annual meeting of the Society for American Archaeology, New Orleans.
1991b *The Dynamics of Pre-State Political Centralization in the North American Midcontinent.* Unpublished Ph.D. dissertation, Department of Anthropology, University of Michigan, Ann Arbor.
1992   The Reign and Ruin of the Lords of Cahokia: A Dialectic of Dominance. In *Lords of the Southeast: Social Inequality and the Native Elites of Southeastern North America,* edited by A. W. Barker and T. R. Pauketat, pp. 31–52. American Anthropological Association, Archeological Papers 3. Washington, D.C.
1993   *Temples for Cahokia Lords: Preston Holder's 1955–1956 Excavation of Kunnemann Mound.* University of Michigan, Museum of Anthropology, Memoir 26.
Pauketat, Timothy R., and Thomas E. Emerson
1991   The Ideology of Authority and the Power of the Pot. *American Anthropologist* 93:919–41.
Pauketat, Timothy R., and Brad Koldehoff
1983   Emerald Mound and the Mississippian Occupation of the Central Silver Creek Valley. Paper presented at the 1983 Midwest Archaeological Conference, Iowa City.
1988   Salvage Data Recovery at the Olszewski Site: A Small Mississippian

Community in the American Bottom. *Rediscovery* 3:31–50. (journal of the Illinois Association for Advancement of Archaeology).

Pauketat, Timothy R., and William I. Woods
1986 Middle Mississippian Structure Analysis: The Lawrence Primas Site (11-Ms-895) in the American Bottom. *Wisconsin Archeologist* 67(2):104–27.

Peale, T. R.
1862 Ancient Mounds at St. Louis, Missouri, in 1819. In *Annual Report of the Smithsonian Institution for the Year 1861*, pp. 386–91. Washington, D.C.

Pearce, Frank
1989 *The Radical Durkheim*. Unwin Hyman, London.

Pearson, Delmont
1979 Untitled photo with caption. *Central States Archaeological Journal* 26(3): 160.

Peebles, Christopher S.
1971 Moundville and Surrounding Sites: Some Structural Considerations of Mortuary Practices II. In *Approaches to the Social Dimensions of Mortuary Practices*, edited by J. A. Brown. *Memoirs of the Society for American Archaeology* 25:68–91.
1990 From History to Hermeneutics: The Place of Theory in the Later Prehistory of the Southeast. *Southeastern Archaeology* 9:23–34.

Peebles, Christopher S., and Susan M. Kus
1977 Some Archaeological Correlates of Ranked Societies. *American Antiquity* 42:421–48.

Peregrine, Peter
1991 A Graph-theoretic Approach to the Evolution of Cahokia. *American Antiquity* 56:66–75.
1992 *Mississippian Evolution: A World-System Perspective*. Prehistory Press, Madison, Wis.

Perino, Gregory
1968 *Guide to the Identification of Certain American Indian Projectile Points*. Oklahoma Anthropological Society, Special Bulletin 3. Oklahoma City.
1971 The Mississippian Component at the Schild Site (No. 4), Greene County, Illinois. In *Mississippian Site Archaeology in Illinois*: 1. Illinois Archaeological Survey, Bulletin 8. Urbana.
1980 Cahokia notes. In *Cahokia Brought to Life*, edited by R. E. Grimm, pp. 61–67. Greater St. Louis Archaeological Society, St. Louis.
1985 *Selected Preforms, Points and Knives of the North American Indians*, Vol. 1. Points and Barbs Press, Idabel, Okla.

Phillips, Philip, and James A. Brown
1978 *Pre-Columbian Shell Engravings from the Craig Mound at Spiro, Oklahoma*, Part 1. Peabody Museum Press, Cambridge, Mass.
1984 *Pre-Columbian Shell Engravings from the Craig Mound at Spiro, Oklahoma*, Part 2. Peabody Museum Press, Cambridge, Mass.

Plog, Fred T.
1973   Diachronic anthropology. In *Research and Theory in Current Archaeology,* edited by C. L. Redman, pp. 181–98. Wiley, New York.
1977   Explaining Change. In *Explanation of Prehistoric Change,* edited by J. N. Hill, pp. 17–57. University of New Mexico, Albuquerque.

Pompa, Leon
1975   *Vico: A Study of the "New Science."* Cambridge University Press, Cambridge.

Porter, James W.
1963a *Bluff Pottery Analysis—Thin Section Experiment No. 1: Thin Sectioning All Sherds from One Trash Pit.* Southern Illinois University Museum Lithic Laboratory, Research Report 3. Carbondale.
1963b *Bluff Pottery Analysis—Thin Section Experiment No. 2: Analysis of Bluff Pottery from the Mitchell Site, Madison County, Illinois.* Southern Illinois University Museum Lithic Laboratory, Research Report 4. Carbondale.
1963c *Bluff Pottery Analysis—Thin Section Experiment No. 3: Paste and Temper Variations in One Bluff Pottery Variety.* Southern Illinois University Museum Lithic Laboratory, Research Report 5. Carbondale.
1963d Southern Illinois University Museum projects. In *Second Annual Report: American Bottoms Archaeology, July 1, 1962–June 30, 1963,* edited by M. L. Fowler, pp. 31–39. Illinois Archaeological Survey, Urbana.
1964   *Thin Section Descriptions of Some Shell Tempered Prehistoric Ceramics from the American Bottoms.* Southern Illinois University Museum Lithic Laboratory, Research Report 7. Carbondale.
1974   *Cahokia Archaeology as Viewed from the Mitchell Site: A Satellite Community at A.D. 1150–1200.* Ph.D. dissertation, Department of Anthropology, University of Wisconsin at Milwaukee. University Microfilms, Ann Arbor.
1977   The Mitchell Site and Prehistoric Exchange Systems at Cahokia: A.D. 1000±300. In *Explorations into Cahokia Archaeology,* edited by M. Fowler, pp. 137–64. Illinois Archaeological Survey Bulletin 7. Urbana.
1983   *Thin Section Analysis of Ceramics from the Robinsons Lake Site.* FAI-270 Archaeological Mitigation Project, Petrographic Report 1. Urbana.

Powell, H. A.
1967   Competitive Leadership in Trobriand Political Organization. In *Comparative Political Systems,* pp. 155–92. The Natural History Press, Garden City, N.Y. (originally published 1960 in *Journal of the Royal Anthropological Institute*).

Prentice, Guy
1983   Cottage Industries: Concepts and Implications. *Midcontinental Journal of Archaeology* 8:17–48.
1985   Economic Differentiation among Mississippian Farmsteads. *Midcontinental Journal of Archaeology* 10:77–122.
1986   An Analysis of the Symbolism Expressed by the Birger Figurine. *American Antiquity* 51:239–66.

1987   Marine Shells as Wealth Items in Mississippian Societies. *Midcontinental Journal of Archaeology* 12:193–223.
1990   Review Article: The Southeastern Ceremonial Complex. *Southeastern Archaeology* 9:69–75.
Prentice, Guy, and Mark Mehrer
1981   The Lab Woofie Site (11-S-346): An Unplowed Mississippian Site in the American Bottom Region of Illinois. *Midcontinental Journal of Archaeology* 6:33–53.
Rappaport, Roy
1979   *Ecology, Meaning, and Ritual.* North Atlantic Books, Richmond, Calif.
Rau, Charles
1869   A Deposit of Agricultural Flint Implements in Southern Illinois. In *Annual Report of the Board of Regents of the Smithsonian Institution for the Year 1868*, pp. 401–7. Washington, D.C.
Read, Margaret
1970   *The Ngoni of Nyasaland.* Frank Cass and Co., London.
Reed, Nelson A.
1977   Monks and Other Mississippian Mounds. In *Explorations in Cahokia Archaeology*, edited by M. L. Fowler, pp. 31–42. Illinois Archaeological Survey, Bulletin 7. Urbana.
Reed, Nelson A., James W. Bennett, and James W. Porter
1968   Solid Core Drilling of Monks Mound: Technique and Findings. *American Antiquity* 33:137–48.
Renfrew, Colin
1982   Socioeconomic Change in Ranked Societies. In *Ranking, Resource, and Exchange*, edited by C. Renfrew and S. Shennan, pp. 1–8. Cambridge University Press, Cambridge.
1987   Introduction: Peer Polity Interaction and Socio-political Change. In *Peer Polity Interaction and Socio-Political Change*, edited by C. Renfrew and J. F. Cherry, pp. 1–18. Cambridge University Press, Cambridge.
Rey, P. P.
1975   The Lineage Mode of Production. *Critique of Anthropology* 3:27–79.
Richards, Audrey I.
1940   The Political System of the Bemba Tribe—North-eastern Rhodesia. In *African Political Systems*, edited by M. Fortes and E. E. Evans-Pritchard, pp. 83–120. Oxford University Press, London.
1961   *Land, Labour, and Diet in Northern Rhodesia.* Oxford University Press, Oxford.
Riesenberg, Saul H.
1968   The Native Polity of Ponape. *Smithsonian Contributions to Anthropology* 10. Washington, D.C.
Roosevelt, Anna C.
1987   Chiefdoms in the Amazon and Orinoco. In *Chiefdoms in the Americas*, edited by R. Drennan and C. A. Uribe, pp. 153–85. University Press of America, Lanham, Md.

Roseberry, William
1989   *Anthropologies and Histories: Essays in Culture, History, and Political Economy.* Rutgers University Press, New Brunswick, N.J.
Rosenberg, Shawn W.
1988   *Reason, Ideology, and Politics.* Princeton University Press, Princeton, N.J.
Rountree, Helen C.
1989   *The Powhatan Indians of Virginia: Their Traditional Culture.* University of Oklahoma Press, Norman.
Rousseau, Jérome
1979   Kayan Stratification. *Man* (n.s.) 14:215–35.
Rowlands, Michael
1987   Centre and Periphery: A Review of a Concept. In *Centre and Periphery in the Ancient World,* edited by M. Rowlands, M. Larsen, and K. Kristiansen, pp. 1–11. Cambridge University Press, Cambridge.
Sackett, James R.
1985   Style and Ethnicity in the Kalahari: A Reply to Wiessner. *American Antiquity* 50:154–59.
Sahlins, Marshall A.
1958   *Social Stratification in Polynesia.* University of Washington Press, Seattle.
1963   Poor Man, Rich Man, Big-man, Chief: Political Types in Melanesia and Polynesia. *Comparative Studies in Society and History* 5:285–303.
1968   *Tribesmen.* Prentice-Hall, Englewood Cliffs, N.J.
1972   *Stone Age Economics.* Aldine-Atherton, Chicago.
1976   *Culture and Practical Reason.* University of Chicago Press, Chicago.
1981   *Historical Metaphors and Mythical Realities.* University of Michigan Press, Ann Arbor.
1985   *Islands of History.* University of Chicago Press, Chicago.
Salomon, Frank
1986   *Native Lords of Quito in the Age of the Incas.* Cambridge University Press, Cambridge.
Salzer, Robert J.
1975   Excavations at the Merrell Tract of the Cahokia Site: Summary Field Report, 1973. In *Cahokia Archaeology: Field Reports,* edited by M. L. Fowler. Illinois State Museum Research Series, Papers in Anthropology 3:1–8. Springfield.
Sanders, William T., and Barbara J. Price
1968   *Mesoamerica: The Evolution of a Civilization.* Random House, New York.
Scarry, John
1990   Mississippian Emergence in the Fort Walton Area: The Evolution of the Cayson and Lake Jackson Phases. In *The Mississippian Emergence,* edited by B. Smith, pp. 227–50. Smithsonian Institution Press, Washington, D.C.
Schapera, I.
1940   The Political Organization of the Ngwato of Bechuanaland Protectorate. In *African Political Systems,* edited by M. Fortes and E. E. Evans-Pritchard, pp. 56–82. Oxford University Press, London.

Service, Elman R.
1962 *Primitive Social Organization.* Random House, New York.
1975 *Origins of the State and Civilization.* Norton, New York.

Shennan, Stephen J.
1982 Exchange and Ranking: The Role of Amber in the Earlier Bronze Age of Europe. In *Ranking, Resource and Exchange,* edited by C. Renfrew, pp. 33–45, Cambridge University Press, Cambridge.
1987 Trends in the Study of Later European Prehistory. *Annual Review of Anthropology* 16:365–82.

Shils, Edward
1972 *The Intellectuals and the Powers and Other Essays.* University of Chicago Press, Chicago.
1975 *Center and Periphery: Essays in Macrosociology.* University of Chicago Press, Chicago.

Silverblatt, Irene
1988 Imperial Dilemmas, the Politics of Kinship, and Inca Reconstructions of History. *Comparative Studies in Society and History* 30:83–102.

Simmons, William S.
1983 Red Yankees: Narragansett Conversion in the Great Awakening. *American Ethnologist* 10:253–71.

Smith, Bruce D.
1978a Variation in Mississippian Settlement Patterns. In *Mississippian Settlement Patterns,* edited by B. D. Smith, pp. 479–503. Academic Press, New York.
1984 Mississippian Expansion: Tracing the Historical Development of an Explanatory Model. *Southeastern Archaeology* 3(1):13–32.
1986 The Archaeology of the Southeastern United States: From Dalton to deSoto, 10,500–500 B.P. In *Advances in World Archaeology,* vol. 5, edited by F. Wendorf and A. E. Close, pp. 1–92. Academic Press, New York.
1990a Introduction: Research on the Origins of Mississippian Chiefdoms in Eastern North America. In *The Mississippian Emergence,* edited by B. D. Smith, pp. 1–8. Smithsonian Institution Press, Washington, D.C.
1992a Mississippian Elites and Solar Alignments: A Reflection of Managerial Necessity, or Levers of Social Inequality? In *Lords of the Southeast: Social Inequality and the Native Elites of Southeastern North America,* edited by A. W. Barker and T. R. Pauketat, pp. 11–30. American Anthropological Association, Archeological Papers 3. Washington, D.C.
1992b Prehistoric Plant Husbandry in Eastern North America. In *The Origins of Agriculture: An International Perspective,* edited by C. W. Cowan and P. J. Watson, pp. 101–19. Smithsonian Institution Press, Washington D.C.

Smith, Bruce D. (editor)
1978b *Mississippian Settlement Patterns.* Academic Press, New York.
1990b *The Mississippian Emergence.* Smithsonian Institution Press, Washington, D.C.

Smith, Harriet M.
1977   The Murdock Mound: Cahokia Site. In *Explorations into Cahokia Archaeology*, edited by M. L. Fowler, pp. 49–88. Illinois Archaeological Survey, Bulletin 7. Urbana.
Smith, Marvin T., and David J. Hally
1992   Chiefly Behavior: Evidence from Sixteenth Century Spanish Accounts. In *Lords of the Southeast: Social Inequality and the Native Elites of Southeastern North America*, edited by A. W. Barker and T. R. Pauketat, pp. 99–109. American Anthropological Association, Archeological Papers 3. Washington, D.C.
Southall, Aidan
1956   *Alur Society: A Study in Process and Types of Domination*. W. Heffer and Sons, Cambridge, U.K.
Spencer, Charles
1982   *The Cuicatlán Cañada and Monte Albán*. Academic Press, New York.
1987   Rethinking the Chiefdom. In *Chiefdoms of the Americas*, edited by R. Drennan and C. A. Uribe, pp. 369–89. University Press of America, Lanham, Md.
1990   On the Tempo and Mode of State Formation: Neoevolutionism Reconsidered. *Journal of Anthropological Archaeology* 9:1–30.
Spriggs, Matthew
1988   The Hawaiian Transformation of Ancestral Society: Conceptualizing Chiefly States. In *States and Society: The Emergence and Development of Social Hierarchy and Political Centralization*, edited by J. Gledhill, B. Bender, and M. T. Larsen, pp. 57–73. Unwin Hyman, London.
Steponaitis, Vincas P.
1978   Location Theory and Complex Chiefdoms: A Mississippian Example. In *Mississippian Settlement Patterns*, edited by B. D. Smith, pp. 417–53. Academic Press, New York.
1981   Settlement Hierarchies and Political Complexity in Nonmarket Societies: The Formative Period of the Valley of Mexico. *American Anthropologist* 83:320–63.
1983a   *Ceramics, Chronology, and Community Patterns: An Archaeological Study at Moundville*. Academic Press, New York.
1983b   The Smithsonian Insititution's Investigations at Moundville in 1869 and 1882. *Midcontinental Journal of Archaeology* 8:127–60.
1986   Prehistoric Archaeology in the Southeastern United States, 1970–1985. *Annual Review of Anthropology* 15:363–404.
Steward, Julian H., and Louis C. Faron
1959   *Native Peoples of South America*. McGraw-Hill, New York.
Stocking, George W., Jr.
1982   *Race, Culture, and Evolution: Essays in the History of Anthropology*. University of Chicago Press, Chicago (originally published 1968).
Stoltman, James B. (editor)
1991   *New Perspectives on Cahokia: Views from the Periphery*. Prehistory Press, Madison, Wis.

Stuiver, M., and G. W. Pearson
1986 High-Precision Calibration of the Radiocarbon Time Scale, A.D. 1950–500 B.C. *Radiocarbon* 28(2B):805–38.

Styles, Bonnie W.
1981 *Faunal Exploitation and Resource Selection: Early Late Woodland Subsistence in the Lower Illinois Valley.* Northwestern University Archeological Program, Scientific Papers 3. Evanston, Ill.

Sumner, C.
1979 *Reading Ideologies: An Investigation into the Marxist Theory of Ideology and Law.* Academic Press, London.

Tainter, Joseph
1988 *The Collapse of Complex Societies.* Cambridge University Press, Cambridge.

Tarr, John S.
1955 *The Archaeological Importance of the Cahokia Mounds and Village Sites.* Unpublished M.A. thesis, Department of Sociology and Anthropology, Washington University, St. Louis.

Taylor, Donna
1975 *Some Locational Aspects of Middle-Range Hierarchical Societies.* Unpublished Ph.D. dissertation, Department of Anthropology, City University of New York.

Terray, Emmanuel
1975 Classes and Class Consciousness in the Abron Kingdom of Gyaman. In *Marxist Analyses and Social Anthropology,* edited by M. Bloch, pp. 85–135. Malaby Press, London.
1978 Event, Structure and History: The Formation of the Abron Kingdom of Gyaman (1700-1780). In *The Evolution of Social Systems,* edited by J. Friedman and M. J. Rowlands, pp. 279–301. University of Pittsburgh Press, Pittsburgh.

Thomas, Cyrus
1985 *Report on the Mound Explorations of the Bureau of Ethnology.* Smithsonian Institution Press, Washington, D.C. (originally published 1894).

Thomson, Basil
1908 *The Fijians: A Study of the Decay of Custom.* Dawsons of Pall Mall, London.

Thornbury, William D.
1965 *Regional Geomorphology of the United States.* John Wiley and Sons, New York.

Throop, Addison J.
1928 *Mound Builders of Illinois.* Call Printing Company, East St. Louis, Ill.

Titterington, Paul F.
1938 *The Cahokia Mound Group and Its Village Site Materials.* Privately published, St. Louis.
n.d. The Razing of Powell Mound. Draft manuscript on file at the Museum of Anthropology, University of Michigan, Ann Arbor.

Valeton, Ida
1972 *Bauxites.* Elsevier Publishing Co., Amsterdam.

Vansina, J.
    1962   A Comparison of African Kingdoms. *Africa* 32:324–35.
Vincent, Joan
    1990   *Anthropology and Politics: Visions, Traditions, Trends.* University of Arizona Press, Tucson.
Vogel, Joseph O.
    1975   Trends in Cahokia Ceramics: Preliminary Study of the Collections from Tracts 15A and 15B. In *Perspectives in Cahokia Archaeology*, pp. 32–125. Illinois Archaeological Survey, Bulletin 10. Urbana (originally released as a mimeograph in 1964).
Wagner, Robert W.
    1957   *An Analysis of the Material Culture of the James Ramey Mound.* Unpublished M.A. thesis, Department of Anthropology, University of Illinois, Urbana.
Walthall, John A.
    1981   *Galena and Aboriginal Trade in Eastern North America.* Illinois State Museum, Scientific Papers 27. Springfield.
Waring, Antonio J., Jr., and Preston Holder
    1945   A Prehistoric Ceremonial Complex in the Southeastern United States. *American Anthropologist* 47:1–34.
Watts, Richard, and Brenda Watts
    1980   Trashpit, Campfire, or Kiln? *Central States Archaeological Journal* 27(2):57–58.
Weber, Max
    1958   *The Protestant Ethic and the Spirit of Capitalism.* Charles Scribner's Sons, New York.
Webster, David
    1975   Warfare and the Evolution of the State: A Reconsideration. *American Antiquity* 40:464–70.
    1976   On Theocracies. *American Anthropologist* 78:812–28.
Webster, Gary S.
    1990   Labor Control and Emergent Stratification in Prehistoric Europe. *Current Anthropology* 31:337–66.
Weiner, Annette B.
    1976   *Women of Value, Men of Renown: New Perspectives in Trobriand Exchange.* University of Texas Press, Austin.
Welch, Paul D.
    1990   Mississippian Emergence in West-central Alabama. In *The Mississippian Emergence*, edited by B. D. Smith, pp. 197–225. Smithsonian Institution Press, Washington, D.C.
    1991   *Moundville's Economy.* University of Alabama Press, Tuscaloosa.
Whalley, Lucy
    1983   Plant Remains from the Turner Site. In *The Turner and DeMange Sites*, by G. R. Milner, pp. 213–33. FAI-270 Site Reports 4. University of Illinois Press, Urbana.

1984   Plant Remains from the Stirling Phase. In *The BBB Motor Site*, by T. E. Emerson and D. K. Jackson, pp. 321–35. FAI-270 Site Reports 6. University of Illinois Press, Urbana.

White, William P., Sissel Johannessen, Paula G. Cross, and Lucretia S. Kelly
1984   Environmental Setting. In *American Bottom Archaeology*, edited by C. J. Bareis and J. W. Porter, pp. 15–33. University of Illinois Press, Urbana.

Wiegers, Robert P.
1982   The Last St. Louis Mound. *Rediscovery* 2:67–79 (journal of the Illinois Association for the Advancement of Archaeology).

Wiessner, Polly
1985   Style or Isochrestic Variation? A Reply to Sackett. *American Antiquity* 50:160–66.

Willey, Gordon R., and Philip Phillips
1958   *Method and Theory in American Archaeology*. University of Chicago Press, Chicago.

Williams, Kenneth
1975   Preliminary Summation of Excavations at the East Lobes of Monks Mound. In *Cahokia Archaeology: Field Reports*, edited by M. L. Fowler, pp. 21–24. Illinois State Museum, Papers in Anthropology 3. Springfield.

Williams, Mark, and Gary Shapiro (editors)
1990   *Lamar Archaeology: Mississippian Chiefdoms in the Deep South*. University of Alabama Press, Tuscaloosa.

Williams, Stephen, and Jeffrey P. Brain
1983   *Excavations at the Lake George Site, Yazoo County, Mississippi, 1958–1960*. Papers of the Peabody Museum of Archaeology and Ethnology, Vol. 74. Harvard University, Cambridge, Mass.

Williams, Stephen, and John M. Goggin
1956   The Long Nosed God Mask in Eastern United States. *The Missouri Archaeologist* 18(3).

Willman, H. B., Elwood Atherton, T. C. Buschbach, Charles Collinson, John C. Frye, M. E. Hopkins, Jerry A. Lineback, and Jack A. Simon
1975   *Handbook of Illinois Stratigraphy*. Illinois State Geological Survey, Bulletin 95. Urbana.

Wilson, Samuel M.
1990   *Hispaniola: Carribbean Chiefdoms in the Age of Columbus*. University of Alabama Press, Tuscaloosa.

Winters, Howard D.
1974   Some Unusual Grave Goods from a Mississippian Burial Mound. *Indian Notes* 10(2):34–46.
1981   Excavating in Museums: Notes on Mississippian Hoes and Middle Woodland Copper Gouges and Celts. In *The Research Potential of Anthropological Collections*, edited by A.-M. E. Cantwell, J. B. Griffin, and N. A. Rothschild, pp. 17–34. Annals of the New York Academy of Sciences 376. New York.

Winters, Howard D., and Stuart Streuver
  1962   The Emerald Mound Group and Village. *Living Museum* 23(11):86–87.
Witthoft, John
  1949   *Green Corn Ceremonialism in the Eastern Woodlands*. University of Michigan, Museum of Anthropology, Occasional Contributions 13. Ann Arbor.
Wittry, Warren L.
  1960a   *Report of Phase 3 Archaeological Salvage Project: FAI Route 70*. Illinois State Museum, Preliminary Reports Series 1. Springfield.
  1960b   Report of Preliminary Site Examination (Phase 2) at Cahokia: FAI Route 70, Section 60-6-1, Tracts 15A, 15B, 16, 17, 18, 19. Unpublished report. Illinois State Museum, Springfield.
  1961   Report of Phase 3 Archaeological Salvage Project, FAI 255, section 60-6-1, Tract 15A, Project I-70-1. Unpublished report, Illinois State Museum, Springfield.
  1964   An American Woodhenge. *Cranbrook Institute of Science Newsletter* 33(9):2–7.
  1977   The American Woodhenge. In *Explorations into Cahokia Archaeology*, edited by M. Fowler, pp. 43–48. Illinois Archaeological Survey, Bulletin 7. Urbana.
Wittry, Warren L., and Joseph O. Vogel
  1962   Illinois State Museum projects. In *First Annual Report: American Bottoms Archaeology, July 1, 1961–June 30, 1962*, edited by M. Fowler, pp. 15–30. Illinois Archaeological Survey, Urbana.
Wolf, Eric
  1966   Kinship, Friendship, and Patron-Client Relations in Complex Societies. In *The Social Anthropology of Complex Societies*, edited by Michael Banton, pp. 1–22. Tavistock Publications, London.
  1982   *Europe and the People Without History*. University of California Press, Berkeley.
  1990   Facing Power—Old Insights, New Questions. *American Anthropologist* 92:586–96.
Woods, William I., and George R. Holley
  1989   Current Research at the Cahokia Site (1984–1989). In *A Cahokia Atlas: A Historical Atlas of Cahokia Archaeology*, by M. L. Fowler, Appendix 5. Studies in Illinois Archaeology 6. Illinois Historic Preservation Agency, Springfield.
Wright, Henry T.
  1977   Recent Research on the Origin of the State. *Annual Review of Anthropology* 6:379–97.
  1984   Prestate Political Formations. In *On the Evolution of Complex Societies: Essays in Honor of Harry Hoijer 1982*, edited by T. K. Earle, pp. 41–77. Undena Publications, Malibu.
  1986   The Evolution of Civilizations. In *American Archaeology Past and Future*, edited by D. J. Meltzer, D. Fowler, and J. A. Sabloff, pp. 323–65. Smithsonian Institution Press, Washington, D.C.

Wright, Henry T., and Gregory Johnson
  1975   Population, Exchange, and Early State Formation in Southwestern Iran. *American Anthropologist* 77:267–89.
Yarbrough, Ronald E.
  1974   The Physiography of Metro East. *Bulletin of the Illinois Geographical Society* 16(1):12–28.
Yerkes, Richard W.
  1983   Microwear, Microdrills, and Mississippian Craft Specialization. *American Antiquity* 48:499–518.
  1986   Licks, Pans, and Chiefs: A Comment on "Mississippian Specialization and Salt." *American Antiquity* 51:402–4.
  1987   *Prehistoric Life on the Mississippian Floodplain: Stone Tool Use, Settlement Organization and Subsistence Practices at the Labras Lake Site, Illinois*. University of Chicago Press, Chicago.
  1989   Mississippian Craft Specialization on the American Bottom. *Southeastern Archaeology* 8:93–106.
  1991   Specialization in Shell Artifact Production at Cahokia. In *New Perspectives on Cahokia: Views from the Periphery*, edited by J. B. Stoltman, pp. 49–64. Prehistory Press, Madison, Wis.
  1992   Microwear Analysis of Microdrills. In *The Lohmann Site: An Early Mississippian Center in the American Bottom*, by D. Esarey and T. R. Pauketat, pp. 133–38. FAI-270 Site Reports 25. University of Illinois Press, Urbana.

Index

Abron kingdom, 30
Actor, 2–3, 13–16, 36, 188
Administration, chiefly, 9, 27
Adze blade, 79, 83, 93–94, 147–48, 173, 178–79
Agency, 13
Alienation, 15, 17, 22, 31–32, 34, 180–82, 184; Lohmann phase, 180
Alliances, 20–21, 27, 171, 183; marriage, 20, 62–63
American Bottom, 4–6, 43, 44, 46–48, 49, 50–53, 55, 57, 61–85, 92–102, 105–6, 122, 140, 152, 169, 172–78, 181, 183, 186–88; uplands, 158. *See also* Northern-Bottom Expanse
American Bottom archaeology, 5, 67, 70
Analogy-homology dilemma, 41
Appropriation, 15, 34, 187
Architecture. *See* Buildings
Aristocracy, 33, 35
Arrowheads, 83–84, 93–94, 152–53, 177; mound cache, 84, 93
Artifact density, calculation, 142
Artifacts, 37, 92–105, 141–62; density, 142, 173–74, 178; exotic, 20, 27, 59, 83, 92, 145–46, 159, 162, 163, 165; symbolic meaning, 177–78. *See also* Prestige goods
Assassination, 29, 176
Authority, 2, 5, 32, 171; chiefly, 17; regional-administrative, 3; sacral, 16, 33, 35, 38; superordinate, 30
Axeheads, 97–98, 177–78; megalithic, 80, 97–98, 178–79

Bald Cypress, 79
Bareis, Charles, 71
Beads: copper, 85, 96; shell, 83–87, 101–2, 105, 145, 153–54, 165, 179–80
Bender, Barbara, 42
Big Mound, 83
Blanton, Richard, 61
Bluffs, 68
Booker T. Washington site, 85

Bourdieu, Pierre, 16n
Brackenridge, Henry, 46, 67
Buildings, 53, 112–31; circular, 76, 88, 122; EM-2, 115; EM-3, 116; Emergent Mississippian, 51–52; L-1, 120; L-2 and L-3, 122; M-1 and M-2, 128; monumental, 87, 106, 125, 127, 185; rural, 76; S-1 and S-2, 125; single-post, 114–20, 172. *See also* Edelhardt phase; Lohmann phase; Moorehead phase; Stirling phase; Wall trenches

Cahokia, 4, 6, 66, 80–92; community remains, 109; development, 168–74; Emergent Mississippian, 53; subcommunities, 85; World-Systems Theory, 11
Cahokia Mounds State Park, 70
Cahokia-Mississippian, 7, 43
Cahokian polity, 63, 73, 172, 184, 186–88
Carneiro, Robert, 31
Cedar litters, 84
Cemetery Mound, 83
Center: Emergent Mississippian, 53, 78, 169; paramount, 27, 73; secondary, 78–80
Central Political-Administrative Complex, 5, 66, 74, 78, 80, 174
Centralization, 2–3, 8, 12, 21–38, 177. *See also* Craft production
Ceramic vessels, 53–60, 100–101; fineware, 100–101, 160–61, 173, 175. *See also* Monks Mound Red; Ramey Incised
Chief, 18, 30–31, 34, 174; manager, 40
Chiefdom, 2, 8, 10; complex, 1, 9, 24–25, 171; cycling, 21, 38; simple, 21
Chiefship, 2, 16–18, 29, 37, 172; accommodative, 37; benefits for nonelite, 18; collaborative, 35, 37, 176; divine, 6, 17, 34–35, 175–76; material manifestations, 184
Childe, V. Gordon, 2
Chronology, 47–49
Chunky stones, 84–85

About the Author

Timothy R. Pauketat is Assistant Professor in the Department of Anthropology at the University of Oklahoma.